Hiking Trails in the Southern Mountains

By Jerry Sullivan and Glenda Daniel

Sept 25, 1975
Sept 21 76

Cover design by Joseph Mistak Jr.
Cover photo by Sidney Pivecka
Cover illustration by Kent Starr
Maps and other illustrations by Kent Starr

GREATLAKES LIVING Press
Suite 2217—Tribune Tower
435 N. Michigan Avenue
Chicago, IL 60611

"If enough good people don't know about a beautiful place, chances are it won't be a beautiful place very long."

Ansel Adams

CONTENTS

Chapter 1
Scouting the South 7

Chapter 2
Problems for Backpackers 11

Chapter 3
Using Map and Compass 21

Chapter 4
The Appalachians 27

Chapter 5
The Appalachian Trail 33

Chapter 6
Virginia 36

Chapter 7
West Virginia 66

Chapter 8
North Carolina 88

Chapter 9
South Carolina 133

Chapter 10
Georgia 142

Chapter 11
Tennessee 154

Chapter 12
Kentucky 198

Chapter 13
Arkansas (and a piece of Oklahoma) 212

(See page 246 for complete trail listings)

"The soles of my feet I swear they're burning."

Bob Dylan

Scouting the South

This book was put together during a period of about six months of intensive investigation in 1974 and early 1975. We traveled a good part of that time, hiking as much as we could.

When we weren't hiking, we were bouncing around on dirt roads locating trail heads or interviewing forest rangers, hikers, and backpackers for details about the trails we couldn't cover with our own feet.

Between trips to the mountains, we spent a lot of time writing letters and making phone calls to people who had information about southern mountain trails.

What spurred this systematic research is a general interest in the area that goes back a long way. Glenda grew up in the Ozarks in northern Arkansas and southern Missouri, spending a good part of her childhood exploring the woods and creek beds near her home.

When, after the publication of our first book, *Hiking Trails in the Midwest,* our publishers asked us to pick another area for exploration, our first choice was the southern mountains.

Our longest trip to these mountains began at Cumberland Mountain State Park in Tennessee, where we took part in a two-day conference on trails in the southeast. A number of the people we met there were very helpful to us. One in particular was Bill Stalcup, who oversees trail maintenance and construction for the U.S. Forest Service in the southern region.

At his invitation, we visited the Forest Service's regional office in Atlanta. Bill was kind enough to turn the engineering office's conference room over to us for three days while we pored over maps and computer printouts detailing a complete inventory of trails on the Southern forests. (The trail numbers we use throughout this book are the Forest Service numbers assigned in these inventories and used on all Forest Service maps).

Much of our trip after those three days was spent checking out the information we got from those maps and printouts. We found that virtually all the ranger districts in the National Forests of the southern Appalachians have been without funds for trail construction or maintenance — especially maintenance — for periods of up to five years. The only exceptions were districts that had a piece of the Appalachian Trail to take care of.

With no money coming in for maintenance, many of the trails listed so plainly in the trail inventory were a good deal more obscure on the ground. Trails were blocked with brush or with downed timber. Signs at the trail heads had been torn down or shot up by vandals. Paint blazes on tree trunks and rocks had faded to obscurity.

So some of the trails on our list had to be crossed off because they simply could not be followed. Others we had to eliminate because they had undergone a change in status.

One of the legacies of the Nixon administration is an executive order requiring all agencies charged with administering federal lands to check out the feasibility of establishing motorcycle and jeep trails on government property. The executive order itself is a result of some pretty high class lobbying by bikers, and local motorcycle groups have been active in pressuring Forest Supervisors and district Rangers since the order was published.

The result, unfortunately, is that some trails have been converted from hiking trails into motorcycle trails — notably in the Cherokee National Forest. In other national forests, rangers are currently evaluating their trail systems in order to decide which trails — if any — they can set aside for the bikers.

We don't care much for off road vehicles. Ignorant backpackers can do quite a bit of damage, but the potential for destruction by bikes and jeeps is far greater. We also become angry when the peace that we head for the woods to find is not there. Dodging traffic and breathing exhaust fumes and trying to shut our ears to engine noise are things we have to do in the city, and we really resent having to do the same things in the mountains.

Once, sitting around a campfire with a group of backpackers, we fantasized about the day when recreational earth moving would be the hot new sport. It's only a matter of time before week end bull dozing becomes part of the American scene, and groups of enthusiasts — with a generous boost from the friendly folks who make the machines — will be demanding that substantial hunks of public land be set aside for them to sculpt.

The bikers have been fairly effective in pushing for motorcycle trails. The Forest Service is required to hold unit planning meetings at which the general public and the various forest users can make suggestions about forest administration. The bikers often show up at these meetings in large groups, and ringing applause for every pro-motorcycle suggestion probably has some effect.

Hikers have been somewhat less effective — except in certain localities.

However, the picture isn't all that bleak. We certainly found a lot of trails on the ground and quite hikable. This book describes enough of them to keep the most avid and active walker occupied for years.

We found that in some districts, the ranger had discovered a way to get around the lack of money for trails. If the ranger is interested in hiking, and if he is a skilled bureaucrat, some means can be found to preserve hiking areas. In some areas, hiking clubs of various kinds are active, well organized, and numerous enough to do some trail maintenance of their own.

All the rangers we talked to were quite receptive to the idea of volunteers helping out with trail blazing and maintenance. By the way, the motorcyclists have done quite a bit of this sort of thing in some areas.

To most people, hiking in the southern Appalachians means the Smokies and the Appalachian Trail. We realized before we started on this project that there was nothing of any significance that we could add to the guide books that are available for hikers on the A.T. or in Great Smoky Mountains National Park.

The Appalachian Trail Conference has published guides of extraordinary detail to every foot of the A.T. The Sierra Club Totebook on the Smokies is a really excellent piece of work. (Information on these books and where to get them is included in the appropriate sections of our guide.) At the same time, we couldn't publish a guide to trails in the southern Appalachians and leave out the most popular trails. So we decided to devote an absolute minimum of space to these trails and concentrate instead on other areas which we felt were quite attractive but not so well known.

We also had other reasons for this decision. Each year, something on the order of 300,000 persons hike on the trails of the Smokies. Traffic on the Appalachian Trail through the park has become so heavy that the park service has had to ration use of the trail. The primitive sanitary facilities near the trail shelters have been severely overtaxed. Foragers for wood have picked clean large areas around the more popular campsites. Erosion problems on the steeper grades have become quite severe.

Just a few miles south of the park in the Tellico District of the Cherokee Forest, we found trails that were practically obliterated because a maintenance crew hadn't been through in three years. In the Cohutta Mountains of north Georgia, you can hike for days without seeing another person.

Both of these places are large areas of wild country. The Eastern Wilderness Act set aside 34,000 acres of the Cohutta as a wilderness area, so it will remain as it is now — wild and roadless. So one of our purposes is to turn people on to some beautiful places that — apparently — very few people know about.

Another is to suggest that perhaps we hikers could spread ourselves out a bit. Perhaps our impact on the land would be lessened if we didn't insist on crowding into a few small places.

About the plan of this book: We open with a brief chapter on some of the problems that backpackers may encounter in the southern mountains. Following this is a discussion of basic methods of navigating with map and compass.

We provide a bit of information on the natural and human history of the Appalachians, Ozarks, and Ouachitas, but most of the book is taken up with descriptions and maps of hiking trails. We have not hiked all these trails, but we have made a considerable effort to ensure that our information on all of them is accurate.

No trail is included unless its existence and whereabouts have been verified by a person with a knowledge of the area. In most cases, this means a forest or park service ranger, or a recreation specialist with the Forest Service or with a state park system. For some trails, our sources were backpackers who had recently been over the trail themselves.

For each trail we include information on road access, length of the trail, the U.S. Geological Survey maps covering the route of the trail, and a description of the trail route itself. Information on altitudes and grades is taken from USGS maps.

Finally, we tell you where to go for more information. We believe this book is accurate. But we know that trail routes are altered for various reasons. A lack of funds is forcing the Forest Service to close roads, so directions for getting to trail heads may have to be changed. There may be timber sales in various areas that would make certain trails unattractive to hikers.

For all these reasons, we recommend that after you pick out some trails from this book, you contact people on the scene for the very latest information before you start walking.

And finally . . . enjoy yourself!

Problems for Backpackers

These days the stores are full of books on how to backpack. Two that we have found helpful are *Backpacking One Step at a Time* by Harvey Manning and *The Complete Walker* by Colin Fletcher.

Since the basics are covered so thoroughly in so many books, we are confining ourselves to a brief discussion of some of the problems which are likely to be encountered in the southern mountains. Some of these are peculiar to the area; others might be met anywhere.

A good place to begin is with the mountains themselves. There is an idea prevalent in some circles that backpacking is an activity for 20-year old athletes. This is nonsense. We have met men and women in their 70's who are avid backpackers, and we know people who take their pre-schoolers out on the trail.

However, anyone who wants to get into backpacking must develop a realistic sense of his own abilities. Even a 25-year-old who spends all his time sitting behind a desk should not expect to start clicking off 20 miles a day without some complaints from his muscles.

We have enough variety in the trails listed in this book to suit people looking for any level of physical exertion. You can stroll for two miles up a creek until you find a good camping spot. Or you can go straight up the side of a steep ridge.

If you do opt for the ridge, remember that it really is quite strenuous. And if you want to get into off-trail hiking, the level of exertion is even higher. You ought to be in good physical condition before you start out.

But even here, the activity is not something that only the young can do. We followed 69-year old Dick Murray up an Ozark mountain, and at the end, he didn't seem any more tired than we were. According to Mr. Murray, he just makes more "puffing stops" now than he used to.

Jerry, who grew up in Illinois, has a flat lander's response to a grade. When he hits a hill, he starts walking faster. This is quite a reasonable thing to do where hills are usually less than 50 feet high. You get to the top quickly, and start enjoying the level ground again.

He had to unlearn that response in the mountains. When the grade is several hundred feet, speeding up doesn't work so very well. What you have to do is slow down. Find a pace that will keep you comfortable all the way to the top. Keep your breathing at about the usual level for walking on flat ground.

At first you may find it difficult to slow down that much. But after a bit you find that the slower pace gets you up the mountains pretty fast, because you don't have to stop and rest so often. Best of all, you will not need to collapse and wheeze for a while after you get to your destination. You will also sweat less, and probably notice more about your surroundings.

If you are experienced in hiking in the western mountains, you may think that the Appalachians are just not high enough to worry about. They are not as high as the Rockies, but the differences in elevation between the high and low points can be quite significant. Mt. LeConte in the Smokies is nearly 5000 feet higher than nearby Gatlinburg, and climbs in the 2-3,000 foot range are common.

Footwear is obviously important to a hiker. You can negotiate the campground nature trail in your sneakers or sandals, but most mountain trails are rather too rough for that sort of footwear. Exposed roots and rocks are the most common problems. You need a boot with a sole and uppers thick enough to cushion the shocks of walking on rough trails.

It is easy to twist an ankle on a rough trail, so you should have boots that give you some support. We use ankle high boots ourselves. The tops of the boots are about six inches above the welt (the seam between sole and upper). Some people like a higher boot, but ten inches is probably the maximum height compatible with comfort.

The most common method of crossing a stream along the trail is hopping from rock to rock. The goal is to cross without getting your feet wet, but you don't always achieve that goal. You may also encounter all-day rains, and your boots should be able to stand up to that. Treat them thoroughly with waterproofing.

Most boots come with information on what waterproofing to use; if yours don't, check with the place where you bought them, or with a good shoe repairman.

Two other observations on equipment: if you are hiking a trail that has shelters, you can obviously dispense with a tent. Some people customarily hike without tents even where there are no shelters. In most areas of the southern mountains at most times of year, mosquitoes are not a problem. However, rain is not at all uncommon. If you go out without a tent, you are taking a chance on getting wet.

Second, you should be equipped with a poncho or similar rain repellant garment. Ideally, this should cover your legs as well as your upper body. An all-day rain on a cool day can chill you dangerously if you have no means of protecting yourself.

Food and Water

Freeze dried food has become expensive to the point of luxury. It would almost be cheaper to hire bearers to carry in a refrigerator full of steaks than to buy enough freeze dried food for a trip. Fortunately, there are some alternatives.

Check the convenience food shelves in the supermarket. Macaroni and cheese is an obvious choice, but there are many other one-dish meal packages available. Soy protein done up to imitate beef or ham is not the most succulent food in the world, but after a strenuous day on the trail, it is adequate.

Cooking time on the convenience foods tends to be somewhat longer than it is for freeze-dried meals made up especially for trail use. Freeze dried foods are slightly lighter generally, but not enough to make much difference unless you are going on a very long trip.

In most areas of the Appalachians, you can drink the water right out of the streams or springs. In the Ozarks, the springs are generally safe, but the streams may not be. The flat-topped ridges of that area are frequently used for pasture, and even a creek that looks quite wild may have a herd of cows living around its head.

Don't drink anything without treatment if the stream you are taking the water from flows past any sort of human habitation or business upstream from you. Even in the wilderness, you can have problems. If something fell into the water and died just up around the bend from you, the water will be contaminated.

Water is close at hand along the creeks, but on ridge tops, there may be none for miles. Carry a two-quart canteen and fill it before you climb up onto a ridge. Once on a ridge "top off" your canteen at every opportunity.

So, we should sum up by saying that if you want to be sure, you should boil water before drinking it (boiling is a better practice than chemical treatment).

Menaces on the Trail

Under this heading we group snakes, bears, boars, ticks, chiggers, and poison ivy.

First, the snakes. Three of North America's four types of poisonous snakes live in parts of the area covered by this book. In the east, the timber rattler and the northern copperhead are found throughout the Appalachians up to at least 5000 feet.

In Arkansas, you might see the timber rattler, the northern or southern copperhead, the western diamondback, western pygmy rattlers, and the western cottonmouth. Timber rattlers average from three to 4½ feet in length, with the record specimen just over six feet long. Copperheads are usually two to three feet long, and the record is 53 inches.

The western pygmy rattler is a tiny snake — the record is only 24 inches — with a rattle like an insect's buzz. The western cottonmouth ranges from 30 to 42 inches, with the record specimen 54 inches long. Both pygmy rattlers and cottonmouths are usually found around water; indeed, water moccasin is one of the common names for the cottonmouth. However, both snakes may wander away from water in search of food.

Statistically speaking, the western diamondback is our most dangerous snake. It inflicts more bites, and more fatalities, than any of our other poisonous snakes. It is also a large snake. The record specimen is over seven feet long. It has a reputation as a fairly aggressive snake that stands its ground when approached. The cottonmouth has a similar reputation. Conversely, the copperhead is usually regarded as a rather lethargic snake, unlikely to strike.

How concerned should you be about snakes? There are a number of variables that affect the answer to that question, but we should make a general observation. As a rule, people who are accustomed to travelling in snake country are much less concerned than those who are not. Glenda, who grew up in the Ozarks, is much less worried about snakes than Jerry, who grew up where poisonous snakes were virtually unknown.

You can wander for weeks on end through the mountains without ever seeing a poisonous snake, and if you are sensible, the snakes you do see probably will not bite you.

We decided to get some expert advice on snakes, so we went to Ed Almandarz, the curator of reptiles at Chicago's Lincoln Park Zoo.

Ed has been handling snakes for 25 years, and he frequently goes on collecting trips looking for new specimens. He gave us some points on snake behavior that can help hikers avoid unpleasant encounters.

First, snakes are cold blooded. In order to keep their body temperatures within appropriate limits, they move around, heading for cool places when it is hot and warm places when it is cool. Snakes will generally avoid a well-traveled trail, but they might lie on one on a cool night when the bare ground of the trail is somewhat warm.

Snakes don't eat as often as warm blooded animals. They tend to put away a very large meal and stay hidden for a while until they get hungry. Avoid putting your hands into places you can't see. Don't reach under rocks.

Snakes are relatively slow moving animals, so they have to rely heavily on camouflage and concealment for successful hunting. If you are picking up wood or searching for acorns on the forest floor, watch what you reach for.

Snakes in mid latitudes must hibernate during the winter months. They are most active during spring and fall. In spring, they are fresh out of their winter dens and looking for a meal. In fall, they are searching for a place to hole up for the winter.

They are generally alert enough to get out of your way in the fall, but they may not be in the spring. On warm winter days, snakes may come out of their dens to bask on rocks on south facing slopes. Roger Conant, who wrote the *Field Guide to Reptiles and Amphibians*, suggests checking with local sources to find out the location of large winter snake dens. Timber rattlers and copperheads may den up together in groups of up to 100 snakes. Running across all those snakes at once would be unpleasant.

Snakes frequently come down to streams to drink in late afternoon.

As you walk along a trail, pay attention to the ground ahead of you and to the lower branches of shrubbery or trees along the edges of the path. This is something that will become second nature after a bit; it is not something you have to think about all the time.

If you do see a snake, approach it slowly unless you are absolutely sure it is harmless. If a snake seems to be preparing to strike at you, do not follow the old Western movie strategy of freezing. The snake will strike because it thinks you are a threat. If you remain standing over it, you are just keeping up the threat. Instead of freezing, take a slow step backward. Follow this with several faster steps.

Snake bite is so uncommon in this country that the odds are that you will get struck by lightning more often than you get bit by a snake. However, this is partly the result of urbanization and the mechanization of agriculture. Most people these days are never exposed to the possibility of snake bite.

Of the people who do get bit an undetermined, but probably substantial, number get bit because they try to handle the snake, something you should not try under any circumstances, unless you have been properly trained to do it.

If you do happen to get bit, what do you do? Many guides to the outdoors just casually say use your snake bite kit. But many doctors regard the snakebite kit as a very dangerous implement.

The first aid technique used with the kit is to make shallow cuts at the point of the bite. The cuts are supposed to affect only the lymphatic system, but unskilled and frightened hands can slice into a vein or even an artery and actually be more lethal than the snake.

What is advised instead of the kit is to fasten tourniquets above and *below* the bite. The tourniquets should be tight enough to restrict lymph flow, and they should be released for a few seconds every 10 minutes or so.

Keep the victim quiet, and get him to medical help, or medical help to him, as soon as possible. Since the invention of anti-venim treatment for snake bite, the mortality rate has declined to an estimated 3% of those bitten.

This recommended treatment has certain problems for back-packers. If you get bitten a day's walk away from the nearest aid, you probably have no choice but to use the snake bite kit. But if you are close to help, it is safer to rely on the doctors than on risky first aid practices.

By the way, alcohol is a very bad treatment for snake bite. It tends to dilate capillaries and veins, thereby speeding up the flow of venom.

In order to treat you with anti-venin, a doctor must know what kind of snake bit you. So you should be familiar with the poisonous snakes in any area you hike. Any library should have books with pictures and drawings to enable you to learn about these critters.

One last point: **Do not kill snakes.** They are an important part of the ecosystem, and the animals they typically prey on — such as rodents — are a far greater threat to the environment than any reptile.

Some people apparently think snakes should be killed because they are potentially dangerous. But that argument would also justify killing off bears, bison, moose, and male deer in rutting season.

If these arguments are not convincing, we should point out that killing a snake with a stick or similar object is dangerous. People get bit while trying it.

About bears. The eastern black bear is a very shy creature by nature, made shyer by the fact that in most areas covered by this book, there is an annual hunting season on bears. However, people do encounter problems with bears in the Smokies where they are protected, and where they have become accustomed to connecting people and food.

If visitors to our parks did not litter, the problem would be much less severe. Also, if people didn't have the idea that the bear is a nice friendly fellow, they might be less eager to throw him some food. We have all been exposed to the Disney idea that animals are just people with more hair.

A bear, however, operates by a code which is distinctly non-human. He does not recognize property rights, and if you hold out some food to him, he may not be overly scrupulous about noticing where the food ends and your hand begins.

Since even a moderate sized black bear is much stronger than a human and very well armed with teeth and claws besides, you should give wide berth to any that you encounter. If a bear hears you coming, it will almost always get out of the way, but if you meet one on the trail, back up slowly and detour around the beast.

The most common sort of encounter with a park bear is in camp at night. To avoid problems, hang your food at least 200 yards from your tent. The best method is to run a rope between two trees and suspend the food bag from the rope. The food should be at least eight feet off the ground. Just hanging the bag in a tree is not enough. Bears are likely to be able to climb anywhere you can. If you can put it up, they can get it down.

Avoid getting the smell of food in your tent or sleeping bag, because bears have a very keen sense of smell. However, you should bring your pack inside your tent — after you have removed all the food from it. Bears in the Smokies have learned to associate packs with food, and they will tear a pack apart looking for goodies. If you are camping without a tent, your whole pack should be hung up out of reach.

Wild boars have become established in the Smokies and in the mountains of North Carolina and Tennessee south of the Smokies.

They tend to be nocturnal and elusive, but detour around it if you do see one.

Chiggers are beyond any doubt the most vicious animals of the southern mountains. These tiny arthropods burrow under the skin to lay their eggs. Once you get a chigger bite, it can itch furiously for weeks. Spreading insect repellent around the tops of your socks and around your waist under your belt can help keep off chiggers. We have heard that sulphur powder dusted liberally on the same areas works very well. However, the powder will also repel your friends for several days.

We have tried a number of remedies for chiggers, but we haven't carried on our investigations in a detached scientific spirit. We have applied the following remedies: clear nail polish, nail polish remover, rubbing alcohol, and various antiseptic ointments. These do work, but we don't know which is effective, because we apply all of them to all of our bites in a desperate attempt to stop the itching.

Ticks tend to be very fussy creatures. They usually crawl around on your body for a long time before they settle on a place to bite. Most of the time, you can get them off before they settle in to feed. If a tick has buried his head in your skin, a dose of alcohol splashed on him or the hot tip of a match on his backside will usually convince him to pull away.

Poison ivy can grow as an erect shrub, a climber, or a trailing vine. It has a compound leaf divided into three leaflets and white berries in season. You should learn to recognize it.

All parts of the plant contain an oil that causes skin inflammation, blisters, and swelling. Reactions to this plant can vary enormously. Some people are virtually unaffected. Others may require hospitalization after exposure.

A thorough scrubbing of the affected area with a yellow laundry soap shortly after exposure may help, and mild astringent lotions such as calamine are also commonly used. If the symptoms persist, or if the eyes are involved, see a doctor.

You can avoid most of the menaces of the woods by hiking in the winter when the snakes, poison ivy, ticks, and chiggers are not a problem. However, you must be properly prepared for winter conditions. Weather in the southern mountains can be quite severe. Heavy snowfalls and cold weather are quite common.

In the Smokies, park rangers will not issue a backcountry camping permit between November 1 and April 1 until they have inspected the equipment of the would-be camper. The list of gear which they require is a good one to follow in other areas of the mountains.

1. A sleeping bag which will keep you warm down to -20°F.

2. High top hiking shoes. They should be waterproof rubber or leather treated with waterproofing.

3. At least two sets of woolen or thermal underwear and socks.

4. Warm outer clothing, including a hood or suitable hat and gloves or mittens.

5. Waterproof matches and fire starter.

6. At least one extra day's food.

7. An adequate topographic map.

8. A sharp hunting knife.

The Sierra Club's Totebook on the Smokies adds some extra items to this list, including a foam pad to sleep on, a portable stove for cooking (we would recommend this for any time of year), a flashlight with extra batteries, snowshoes if you anticipate deep snow, crampons for crossing ice, dark glasses, and a raincoat or poncho. Also, a change of trousers, preferably wool. Wool is the only fabric that keeps a substantial part of its insulating ability when it is wet.

If you plan to hike off trail at any time of year, the extra day's food is a good idea. Also, if you want to try off trail hiking, plan a route in advance; don't just wander off in the woods.

If you are hiking in a national park, you will need to apply for backcountry camping permits. Go over your planned route with the ranger when you get the permit so he will know where you are heading and when you plan to come out.

Hiking on national forest land does not require permits. You can go anywhere you like. However, checking in with the rangers is a good idea. They, too, like to know when people are travelling through the woods. And they can advise you on places to look for and others to avoid. Much of the land within national forests is privately owned. Some land owners are indifferent to the presence of hikers on their property, but others are known to greet backpackers with a shotgun. The rangers can also steer you away from logging operations that would reduce the tranquility of your hike.

A few simple rules:

1. Do not hike alone. If there is no one to go for help, a relatively minor accident can become a disaster.

2. Stop early in the afternoon. You want to be able to get your tent up and your meal cooked and all the housekeeping done before nightfall.

3. A state license is required for fishing in national parks and

on national forest land.

4. In the fall of the year, deer, bear, and boar are all hunted in the southern mountains. Seasons vary from year to year, state to state, and county to county, so check on the dates for the specific area you want to visit. Avoid off trail hiking during hunting season. If you are hiking on a trail, wear something large in red or international orange. The type of vest worn by highway workers is cheap and lightweight. If possible, combine it with a hat and maybe a large swatch of cloth pinned to your pack. In some states, hunting is prohibited on Sunday.

We will close this chapter with a few words about place names. The mountains are full of apt, striking, and often ironic place names. Some of these are falling to the real estate developer. Near Glenda's home town of Mountain Home, Ark., is a height that used to be known as Pink Smith Knob after a man who once owned it. After a real estate man got hold of the place, it became Crystal Mountain.

Many place names are repeated over and over. The mountains are full of Caney Creeks and Crooked Creeks and Rock Creeks. Snake Den Mountains and High Knobs are almost as numerous.

At times, place names can be confusing to the outlander, so we append a brief glossary:

Creeks are creeks in the Ozarks, but in different parts of the Appalachians they may be branches, prongs, forks, drafts, or runs.

A lead is a ridge.

A bald is either an open grassy area or a treeless thicket of heath in the southern Appalachians. In West Virginia, open grassy areas are also knows as "sods," and in the Ozarks, they are "glades." Heath balds are sometimes called "slicks" or "hells."

Using Map and Compass

If you look through the trail descriptions in this book, you will notice that for every trail we have an entry headed *USGS Quad.* What that mysterious sign means is U.S. Geological Survey Quadrangle, and what that is, is a map.

The U.S. Geological Survey is a government agency that prepares and publishes maps. They print many different kinds of maps for many different purposes, but the only ones that concern us here are the large scale topographic maps of the United States called "Quadrangles."

Quadrangles come in two basic sizes. Most of the areas mentioned in this book have been surveyed and mapped onto sheets that cover 7½ minutes of latitude and 7½ minutes of longitude (a minute being 1/60th of a degree). These 7½ minute quadrangles are printed at a scale of 1:24,000. This is read "one to 24,000," and it means simply that one unit on the map equals 24,000 units on the ground. An inch on the map equals 24,000 inches, two inches equals 48,000 inches, and so on.

Put in simpler terms, an inch equals 2000 feet, and just over 2½ inches equals a mile.

Some maps listed in this book are 15 minute quads — that is, they cover 15 minutes of latitude and longitude — printed on a 1:62,500 scale. This scale is almost exactly an inch to a mile. The smaller scale maps are somewhat more difficult to use, but the principles are the same regardless of scale.

The USGS Quads attempt to show every significant feature of the landscape, whether natural or man-made. Roads, buildings, bridges, pipelines, towers — anything big enough to show at this scale — will be put on the map. Streams, lakes, swamps and forests are also shown.

Most important, the maps are topographic; that is, they show the shape of the landscape. They do this by means of contour lines. A contour line is a line on a map connecting points at the same elevation.

Contour lines are really very easy to read, and with a bit of practice, you can learn to visualize the shape of hills or canyons on the ground from symbols on a map.

USGS Quads cost 75 cents apiece. To get quads for areas east of the Mississippi, write to the U.S. Geological Survey, Distributin Center, Washington, D.C. 20242. For areas west of the Mississippi, write the Survey at Denver Federal Center, Denver, Colo., 80225. The survey also supplies free index maps for each state, showing the quadrange grid superimposed on a state map, and a booklet called "Topographic Maps" which explains the maps and the symbols used. When ordering quads, be sure to specify the state as well as the quad name; i.e., Whiteoak Flats, *Tenn.*, not just Whiteoak Flats.

The boundaries of each quadrangle are based strictly on latitude and longitude. They run, for example, from 80° to 80°7½, to 80°15', and so on. As a consequence, the maps may not be conveniently divided at political or natural boundaries.

If you look at a quad sheet, you can see first, that it has a name printed in both the upper and lower right hand corners. Quads are named after towns, mountains, lakes, or other features that are prominent features of the area shown.

At each corner of the map, the latitude and longitude coordinates are printed. Directly under the center of the map, information about scale is provided. The scale is expressed both in numerical terms (1:24,000) and in linear terms, with scales of miles, feet, and kilometers shown.

Beneath the scale information, the contour interval is stated. On most of the maps named in this book, the contour interval is 40 feet, although 20 feet is also common. This means that there are 20 or 40 vertical feet between each contour line.

If you look at a map, you will see that every fifth contour line is printed darker than the others and that the line is broken at intervals by a printed figure. This figure represents the altitude of the line. The darker lines at intervals make it more convenient to quickly ascertain altitudes on the map.

Contour lines not only tell you altitudes, they also tell you how steep the slopes are. Where the slope is steep, the lines are close together. Where the lines are far apart, the slope must be gentler. Looking at the contour lines enables you to pick out the easiest slope up a mountain you want to climb.

Two other items of information important to backpackers are printed on the bottoms of survey maps. In the lower left there will be a statement telling how and when the area was surveyed. In the lower right, under the name of the quad will be a date, the date of publication of the map.

The dates of survey and publication are important. Some geological survey maps are quite old. Some we used in the Ozarks were published in 1932. Natural features like mountains aren't likely to change in 40 years, but man made features can alter drastically. Our 1932 maps showed towns that no longer exist.

Also on the bottom of the map, you will see a representation of the angle of declination of the quad. The North Pole is true north, and the grid that the maps are laid out on is oriented toward the Pole. However, magnetic north is not at the pole. Consequently, in most areas of the country, your compass will not point to true north; it will point slightly to the right or left of true north. The difference between true north and compass north is the angle of declination. It is represented on the map by two lines, one topped with a star representing true north, and one topped by the letters "MN" representing magnetic north. The exact number of degrees in the angle is printed with the symbol.

The best way to explain the significance of the angle of declination is to go through the process of orienting a map. And in order to talk about that, we should first talk about compasses.

They are really very simple. They consist of a free swinging needle that always points toward magnetic north, and a dial usually printed with the four principal directions and with numbers. The numbers start with "0" at north, go up to 90 at East, 180 at south, 270 at west, and 360 at north again. These are degrees of the compass circle, and they are used to express "headings", that is, directions of travel.

In order to properly orient a map, you need a map, a compass, and finally, a clear idea of where you are. The procedure is to lay the map on the ground and place the compass on it. Lay your compass along the edge of the map and turn the map until the north pointing needle is parallel to the edge and pointing toward the upper end of the map.

If you get that far, you are on your way. This is where the angle of declination comes in. Suppose you look at the declination diagram and see that the angle is 7° and magnetic north is to the east of true north. To line your map up with your compass, turn the map 7° to the west.

To put that another way, if you are looking at the map right side up, turn the top of the map to the left.

A simpler way is to line up the north needle of the compass

with the magnetic north line on the angle of declination diagram. However, we are told that this angle is not always drawn precisely. However, you can check this angle with a protractor before you leave home. If it is drawn properly, you can use the arrow to align the map from then on.

When the map is aligned, the next step is to locate yourself on it. This can be a problem in the southern mountains. The thick woods may narrow your field of vision down to a few hundred yards, or even less. There may be no recognizable landmarks in that distance.

The only answer to this problem is a reasonable level of caution. If you are travelling cross country, you should keep track as closely as you can of where you are. That means you check your position and your course when you have the chance.

A great many things can be used to locate yourself. For example, roads, buildings, fire towers, and other manmade features are helpful, but once you get away from roads, you will have to orient yourself by natural features. Again, this is easier if you keep track of where you are.

You may come to a spot where two tributaries flow into a stream within yards of each other, or a bend where a stream makes a pronounced change of direction, or a sudden narrowing of a hollow. If you learn to visualize the shapes of things from the contour lines on the map — really a very easy thing to do — you can find an open spot on a ridge and orient yourself by the shapes of the mountains around you.

Once you have oriented the map and found yourself on it, the rest is easy. Bearing in mind our earlier caution about finding MN, lay your compass down on the map over your position. Find the place on the map that you want to go to and read off the number that points to it on your compass dial. That number is the expression in degrees of the compass circle of your course. For example, if you want to go northeast, you would travel on a compass heading of 45°. Going south, you would travel on a heading of 180°.

Once you have determined the proper heading to get to your destination, sight along it, and pick out some landmark you can walk to. When you get there, take another compass reading, and continue on to another landmark on the same heading.

That is strict travelling by compass, and it is probably not used as often as a more generalized direction finding. You may find yourself on a slope, and you know you want to go down that slope and hit a creek which you will follow downstream. If you keep track of where you are, your map and compass can tell you when to start down, but experience becomes very helpful when you actually begin walking down the slope.

You can learn from your compass that you want to cross a ridge between two particular peaks, but you can definitely learn about picking the best route through the gap by a lot of walking around.

One additional point should be made. If you start out from, say, a campground, and head up a mountain at a heading of 320°, it is very easy to figure the heading you should take to get back to your starting point.

If your original heading is between 180 and 360°, you subtract 180° to get your back heading. If your heading is between 0° and 180°, you add 180°. So, with an original heading of 320°, the back heading would be 140°.

And that, really, covers the basics of navigating with map and compass. Everyone can learn it quite quickly, and everyone who is planning to spend any time in the woods should learn it.

There may be a tendency to say that this is a skill only for backpackers. Somebody planning to confine himself to short strolls in the forest needn't be concerned about it. But that really is not true. People out for a Sunday promenade do get lost, and when they do, they are usually much worse off than the backpacker in similar circumstances. Usually they have no food, no extra clothing, no sleeping bags, no tents, and so on. A ranger in the Cherokee National Forest in Tennessee told us of picking up a man who had gone for a short walk in the Joyce Kilmer Memorial Forest in North Carolina. The man turned up on a forest road in Tennessee 24 hours later.

For short walks, you can usually do without the detailed map, but it is a very good idea to have a general picture of the area in your head. You should also have a compass, because it can help you get about even if you don't have a map. If you should get lost, a general knowledge of the area can tell you that there is, for example, a road to the north, and your compass can help get you there.

We know of only one book on navigating with map and compass. It is called "Be Expert With Map & Compass," and it is written by Bjorn Kjellstrom. Charles Scribner's Sons publishes a paperback for $3.50. The book is an extended commercial for the Silva compass makers, but it does have good information, and it's clearly presented.

A final word of advice: your first cross country trips should be simple. Following a creek is a good way to start. It's tough to really get lost with the stream to guide you. For a first trip, you might go up a creek, cross a divide and go back down another creek. As your experience and confidence grow, you can set off on more ambitious trips.

The Appalachians

The Blue Ridge begins to rise in Pennsylvania, slowly gaining altitude to the south through Maryland and northern Virginia. In the Shenandoah National Park, the peaks of the ridge rise above 4000 feet.

To the west of the ridge lies the Great Valley. It is the Cumberland in Pennsylvania, the Shenandoah in Virginia, and the valley of East Tennessee to the south. Early settlers used this as a highway into the mountains and beyond.

The Shenandoah Valley is divided toward its northern end by Massanutten Mountain which rises between the two forks of the Shenandoah River. Farther to the west, the mass of North Mountain forms the boundary of the ridge and valley province.

Long ridges tending northeast — southwest divided by narrow valleys are characteristic of this region. To the west, they give way to the higher ridges of the Alleghenies which rise to 4500 feet in West Virginia.

In southwestern Virginia, the Blue Ridge and the Alleghenies come together in a broad mountain belt whose greatest height is reached at Mount Rogers, 5729 feet above sea level.

To the south, the mountains split into two great chains. The Blue Ridge to the east extends in a great arc through North Carolina and into Georgia. High points of the ridge are Grandfather Mountain, 5964 feet, Pinnacle Mountain, 5964 feet, and Standing Indian Mountain just north of the Georgia border, 5399 feet.

To the west, the great chain of the Unaka Mountains follows the border between Tennessee and North Carolina south into Georgia. The northern Unakas lead to the massive bulk of the Smokies and beyond to the Unicoi Mountains. Eighteen peaks on this range rise above 5000 feet, and in the Smokies many elevations are above 6000 feet.

A number of cross ranges connect the Unaka and the Blue Ridge. The Black Mountains north of Asheville actually claim the highest peak in eastern North America, Mount Mitchell, 6684 feet high. To the south, major cross ranges include the Snowbirds and the Nantahalas.

The upheavals that created these mountains — the Appalachian Revolution — occurred at least 200 million years ago at the end of the Paleozoic Era. A great chain of mountains was created by that revolution. They were as high as the Andes and they extended from Alabama to Norway.

Since then, wind and water have been wearing away those once great peaks. The southern Appalachians escaped the ice and their generally rounded shapes are the result of gradual erosion. Only where the extremely tough rocks of the Blue Ridge resisted the waters are there cliffs and jagged areas of exposed rocks.

The slopes of these ancient mountains are covered with the most diverse temperate zone forest in the world. Europe has 85 species of native trees; the Smokies have 130. This is an ancient forest whose flora was enriched by the glaciation of the Pleistocene. As the ice sheets moved south, the plants retreated before them, retiring to warmer areas in the mountains.

When the ice retreated, many of the plants stayed behind, climbing the slopes of the mountains seeking the cooler conditions that duplicate those of more northern areas.

Anyone with experience in the woods of Minnesota or Ontario will feel right at home on the high peaks of the Smokies, the Blacks, or the Alleghenies. From about 5000 feet on up, red spruce and Fraser fir, a very close relative of the northern balsam fir, begin to appear among the hardwoods. As you move higher, the hardwoods disappear completely, and you are walking through a Canadian forest.

Flocks of juncos and chickadees feed on the ground and in the low branches around you. The most common bird noise in the high Smokies is the honking call of nuthatches. Ravens soar on the updrafts, and even such northerners as crossbills and veerys will be found nesting.

Below the spruce-fir forests of the highest summits are northern hardwood stands with abundant beech, yellow birch, various maples. Hemlocks also grow on these slopes, along with yellow poplars and American holly.

On dryer slopes, oak-hickory associations are common.

The ultimate Appalachian forest is the cove hardwood. A cove is one of the more notable features of the southern mountains. It is actually a fan delta, a common element in the western landscape. Erosion carries debris of various kinds — rocks, gravel, sand, silt — down from the mountains. As the slopes of the hills grow gentler, the flow of water slows down, and the larger particles begin to precipitate out. They eventually form a broad flat layer of rich soil sheltered by the surrounding mountains.

On the soil of the coves grows a forest like no other. Arthur Stupka, who used to be chief naturalist at the Great Smoky Mountains National Park describes the *dominant* trees of a cove hardwood forest as yellow buckeye, basswood, yellow-poplar, mountain silverbell, eastern hemlock, white ash, sugar maple, yellow birch, American beech, black cherry, northern red oak, and cucumber tree. These are just the dominant trees; many other species are also found.

One of the glories of a cove hardwood forest is the great number of flowering trees. Better than 20 species have showy blossoms.

The understory of the Appalachian forest contains a broad range of shrubs. Many of these provide beautiful flowers in their seasons. Rhododendron is doubtless the most common. It occurs in dense thickets at all elevations. Other members of the heath family include mountain laurel, flame azalea, and sand myrtle.

"Balds" are one of the mysteries of the southern mountains. Up on some of the high ridges, usually in the saddles between the peaks, are open areas of grassy meadow land. Nobody knows why these open areas are not covered with trees like the rest of the area. They are not above timberline; often higher areas nearby are thickly wooded. Some have suggested that the balds were created by human activity. Certainly they have been used as grazing areas. But many of these balds were known to the Cherokees who didn't keep any grazing animals.

Rhododendron, laurel, and azalea — members of the heath family — form another kind of bald, this one often found on the high points of ridges. Heath balds are also known locally as slicks and hells. The former term is apparently derived from the fact that heath balds do look smooth from a distance.

The latter term will be instantly comprehensible to anyone who has tried to walk through a heath bald. The plants form a nearly impenetrable tangle which Glenda dubbed "backpacker traps."

The mountains are great places for birders. Wood warblers are particularly abundant and varied. A few hours climb can take you from a woods inhabited by typical southern forms such as the worm eating or hooded warblers up to a spruce-fir forest occupied by Canada or black-throated blues.

The most common large mammals of the area are the black bear and the white tailed deer. Bobcats, raccoons, possums, beaver, mink, and a variety of other small mammals are also found.

The history of settlement begins in the late 18th century, when Pennsylvanians began to move down the great valley to the south. It increased after the Revolution when the young government offered veterans land to the west in return for their service during the war.

The first settlers moved into the coves and the bottoms where the land was rich and relatively level. These early settlers were the prototype of the American frontiersman. Living in their isolated cabins, they were largely self-sufficient, gaining their living through their skill at farming and hunting. Many of the attitudes that developed out of their experience survive today.

The pioneers found a land of such abundance it seemed it could never be exhausted. When the good land in the coves was taken, farmers began to move up onto the slopes. Disastrous erosion followed, but if a man's land wore out, he could easily move on.

Game was treated in a similarly cavalier fashion. Dr. Thomas Walker, the man who discovered the Cumberland Gap, led a small surveying party into southwestern Virginia in 1750. His journal records that "We killed in the Journey 13 Buffaloes, 8 Elks, 53 Bears, 20 Deers, 4 Wild Geese, about 150 Turkeys, besides small game."

When the activities of the lumber companies were added to those of the hunters, disaster resulted. The timber companies moved in late in 19th and early in the 20th century. Their philosophy was the same as that they had followed earlier in New England and the Great Lakes States. They went in and cut every stick of timber that was worth hauling out, and then they packed up and went elsewhere.

Animal populations can survive heavy hunting pressure, but when you combine hunting with wholesale destruction of habitat, the game is over. Those buffalo and elk that Dr. Walker found so plentiful are completely gone from the Appalachians, except for a tiny elk population recently reintroduced into the Thomas Jefferson National Forest. The eastern mountain lion and the wolf are also no more.

Even the wild turkey and the white tailed deer disappeared from many areas and had to be reintroduced — at considerable expense.

With the timber gone from the slopes, catastrophic floods became a common occurrence in the mountains and adjacent low

lands. Fires raged through the slash left behind by the lumbermen. In some areas, the peaty soil of the forest floor, stripped of
its shade, dried out, caught fire and burned down to bed rock.

Things have improved since then. Vast areas of land in the
mountains have been incorporated into the national forest system.
Environmentalists find a number of forest service practices ques-
tionable, but no one would seriously question their desire to preserve the forests.

The mountains are still threatened by a number of enemies.
The land can recover from poor farming and lumbering practices,
but strip mining is another matter. Substantial chunks of the
mountains, primarily in West Virginia, Virginia, and Kentucky
have simply been shoveled away. What is left behind is a pile of
tailings that may never grow anything, and a polluted water
supply.

Real estate types are also moving in to create vacation home
developments and resorts of various kinds, often with as little regard for environmental values as the old time lumbermen who
preceded them.

There are a number of organizations fighting to preserve the
mountains. In West Virginia, the Highlands Conservancy has
been very active. Their address is in our chapter on West Virginia.
The Sierra Club has several chapters in the Appalachians. They
are:

Sierra Unit Chapters
POTOMAC CHAPTER
Monongahela Group
William R. Powell, Acting Chairman
388 Stewart Street
Morgantown, West Virginia 26505
Phone: 304/396-4938

POTOMAC CHAPTER
Old Dominion Group
Stuart H. Maule, Chairman
Route 14, Box 334
Richmond, Virginia 23231
Phone: 804/795-2477

CUMBERLAND CHAPTER (Kentucky)
Oscar H. Geralds, Jr., Chairman
320 Mariemont Drive
Lexington, Kentucky 40505
Phone: 606/299-6851

CUMBERLAND CHAPTER (Tennessee)
P.O. Box 2721
Nashville, Tennessee 37219

CHATTAHOOCHEE CHAPTER
Metro Atlanta Group
Alastair Black, Chairman
455 Brentwood Drive NE
Atlanta, Georgia 30305
Phone: 404/266-8899

JOSEPH LECONTE CHAPTER
Edward Easton, Chairman
818 Henley Place
Charlotte, North Carolina 28207
Phone: 704/376-2881

Other local organizations are listed where appropriate throughout the book.

The Appalachian Trail

The Appalachian Trail is, to quote the guidebooks of the Appalachian Trail Conference. "a continuous, marked footpath along the crest of the ranges generally referred to as Appalachian." It extends from Mt. Katahdin in Maine more than 2,000 miles south to Springer Mountain in northern Georgia.

It passes through 14 states on its way. The part of the Appalachian Trail that is in the southern mountains traverses Virginia, West Virginia, Tennessee, North Carolina and Georgia. Much of the land along its route in these states lies within five national forests — the George Washington and Thomas Jefferson in Virginia; the Cherokee in Tennessee; the Nantahala in North Carolina; and the Chattahoochee in Georgia.

The idea for such a long trail came from a New England forester named Benton McKay. He suggested it in an article written in 1921 for the *Journal of the American Institute of Architects*. By the following year, a segment was already completed in the Bear Mountain section of the Palisades Interstate Park by clubs affiliated in the New York-New Jersey Trail Conference.

An official Appalachian Trails Conference was established in the late 1920s to arouse interest and coordinate efforts of various local hiking clubs throughout the Appalachians. Maintenance of trail sections is still the responsibility of these local clubs. To their efforts we now also owe the existence and maintenance of many other trails in national forests.

We have included in this book those sections of the A.T. which pass through the southern mountains, but we have been deliberately terse in our descriptions.

There are two reasons for this. (1) The Appalachian Trail Conference (address: P.O. Box 236, Harpers Ferry, W. Va. 25425) has already published a series of guidebooks that describe the trail route in minute detail. (You may join this worthwhile organization, by the way, by paying $7 in annual dues). (2) We feel the

Appalachian Trail is already well-known and heavily used. It is so heavily used in some areas, as a matter of fact, that erosion has caused severe damage to the landscape. Huge trees have fallen alongside the trail's path in the Smokies, partly because foot travel wore topsoil away and exposed the trees' roots. When storms came, those trees were much more vulnerable and many toppled over.

The Appalachian Trail is beautiful; we hope you get a chance to sample it while you're in the southern mountains. We thought it was a good idea to use most of our allotted space, however, to tell you about the hundreds of miles of southern mountain trails that are also beautiful but are hardly ever used.

Four separate Guidebooks published by the Appalachian Trail Conference cover the area included in this book. From south to north, they are:

Guide to the Appalachian Trail in the Great Smokies, the Nantahalas, and Georgia. $6

Guide to the Appalachian Trail in Tennessee and North Carolina, Cherokee, Pisgah. and Great Smokies. $6

Guide to the Appalachian Trail in Central and Southwestern Virginia. $5.50

Guide to the Appalachian Trail and side trails in the Shenandoah National Park. $4.25

THE APPALACHIAN TRAIL IN GEORGIA

The southern terminus of the entire Appalachian Trail is at Springer Mountain (elevation 3782 feet) in northern Georgia. A six-mile approach trail from Amicalola Falls provides access to the trail at this end.

The A.T. follows the Blue Ridge for 78 miles northeast through the Chattahoochee National Forest to Bly Gap at the North Carolina border.

THE APPALACHIAN TRAIL IN THE NANTAHALA NATIONAL FOREST, NORTH CAROLINA

The Appalachian Trail enters North Carolina at Bly Gap and Continues north along the crest of the Nantahala Mountains, a "cross-range" between the two forks of the oval of the southern Appalachian Mountains. Most of the trail lies within boundaries of the Nantahala National Forest. Exceptional views may be seen from many of the peaks, particularly Standing Indian Mountain, Wayah Bald, and Wesser Bald. The trail crosses into Tennessee at Fontana Dam and enters the Great Smoky Mountains National Park.

APPALACHIAN TRAIL IN TENNESSEE AND ALONG THE TENNES-SEE-NORTH CAROLINA BORDER

The A.T. follows the high ridgeline of the Smokies on the Tennessee—North Carolina border northeast from Fontana Dam through the national park to the Pigeon River. It continues, then, to follow the state border northeast of the Smokies. It also follows the border between Tennessee's Cherokee National Forest and North Carolina's Pisgah National Forest. The mountain ranges here — the Bald, the Iron, and the Unaka — are, according to the Appalachian Trail Guidebook, "the distinctive remains of long erosion in some of the oldest rock formations in the country."

The A.T. leaves the state border near Roan Mountain State Park and heads north through Tennessee's Cherokee National Forest, past Watauga Lake near Elizabethton and into Virginia at Damascus.

THE APPALACHIAN TRAIL IN VIRGINIA AND ALONG THE VIR-GINIA—WEST VIRGINIA BORDER

The Appalachian Trail follows the Blue Ridge through Virginia from Damascus in the south to the northern boundaries of Shenandoah National Park. (The trail continues on through Virginia to that state's border with Maryland, but we have set Shenandoah as an arbitrary boundary for our definition of "Southern Mountains.") There are more miles of Appalachian Trail in Virginia (just over 500) than in any other single state.

The highest mountains along the trail in Virginia are in the southern part of the state, although peaks in Shenandoah National Park rise to more than 4,000 feet.

Most of the trail in Virginia lies in the Jefferson and Washington National Forests and in Shenandoah National Park.

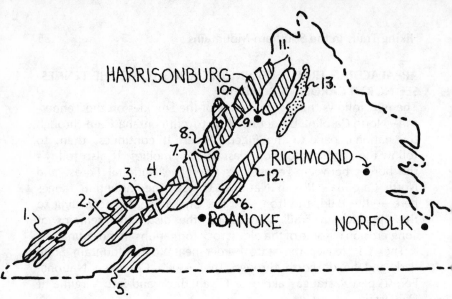

JEFFERSON NATIONAL FOREST
1. Clinch Ranger District
2. Wythe Ranger District
3. Blacksburg Ranger District
4. New Castle Ranger District
5. Marion Ranger District
6. Natural Bridge Ranger District

GEORGE WASHINGTON NATIONAL FOREST
7. James River Ranger District
8. Warm Spring Ranger District
9. Deerfield Ranger District
10. Dry River Ranger District
11. Lee Ranger District
12. Pedlar Ranger District

13. SHENANDOAH NATIONAL PARK

TRAILS IN VIRGINIA

The southern Appalachians begin in Virginia. To the north, the peaks of the Appalachian chain are comparatively low in elevation. The mountain country is somewhat less rugged and more open to settlement.

In northern Virginia, the long ridges begin to rise more steeply above the broad river valleys. These valleys are populous today. They have been settled since the 18th century, when they served as highways south and west into the mountains and over them into Kentucky.

As you travel south in Virginia, the mountains get higher and the valleys get narrower. The highest peak in the state is Mount Rogers, just a few miles from the North Carolina border.

To the west, the ridges get steeper, higher, and closer together as you approach the rugged mountains of West Virginia.

The long, northeast-southwest ridges of the mountains give Virginia an enormous amount of land that is attractive to hikers. The state has more miles of the Appalachian Trail than any other, and numerous shorter trails follow the ridge lines.

With its long history of settlement, Virginia has little land that has not been affected by human activity. The timber that covers the mountainsides is second growth, and in many areas the trees are growing up in a clearing that was once a mountain farm. The grassy balds are often kept open by grazing of cattle and sheep. A hiker on the ridge tops looking off into the distance will usually see a populated area somewhere on his horizon.

Virginia is a great place for exploration, especially for hikers without long experience in wilderness travel. Roads flank the ridges and cross the mountains at frequent enough intervals to make most areas accessible even to weekend travellers. If you do get lost, civilization is generally nearer at hand than in the less settled areas to the south.

This is not a call for novices to march off into the woods without preparation or forethought. But if you have a bit of experience and you are eager to extend your capabilities, this area is a good one for it.

The Appalachian Trail in this state is maintained by nine separate organizations which are each responsible for a section of the path. If you are interested in meeting other hikers, these clubs are good places for it. The Appalachian Trail Conference, Inc., P. O. Box 236, Harpers Ferry, W.Va. 25425 can give you information on the local clubs.

Our account of Virginia Trails begins with the Shenandoah National Park in the northeast and goes south through the George Washington and Thomas Jefferson National Forests.

Shenandoah National Park

This is one of our more popular national parks. Its location, an easy weekend drive from Washington and Baltimore, and its great natural beauty bring visitors by the hundreds of thousands every year.

The park is basically a long, relatively narrow strip that follows the crest of the Blue Ridge from Front Royal in the northeast to Waynesboro in the southwest, a distance of about 80 miles. Within the park are 193,000 acres of land.

Shenandoah National Park was officially dedicated in 1936, but the process of creating it began a decade earlier. The western national parks were simply created out of the vast lands of the public domain. But in the east, much land had to be acquired from private land owners. Financing for this acquisition came in part from the state of Virginia and in part from private sources. In the early stages, very little federal money was involved.

Creating the park also meant moving people. The mountaineers who lived on the small farms within the boundaries of the park had to be relocated to new homes in the valley.

When the park was dedicated, it bore little resemblance to the wilderness the early settlers had found. The land had been farmed since the 18th century, and extensive logging of the cut-and-get-out type had left the slopes devoid of timber in many areas. With the destruction of their habitat, the animal populations of the area had declined seriously.

Today, after almost 40 years as a park, the Shenandoah is returned to at least an approximation of its aboriginal state. The wonderfully diverse hardwood forest of the southern mountains — with a considerable admixture of pines — covers much of the land. On the higher peaks, balsam fir and red spruce, Canadian zone trees, are dominant. The fall color in the park is a spectacular sight.

Bears and white tailed deer, among the larger mammals, have come back, and many smaller mammals are now common.

The major trail in the Shenandoah is the Appalachian Trail. It runs the length of the park, covering more than 100 miles in all. For nearly all of this distance, the trail parallels the Skyline Drive, the scenic highway in the park. The trail and highway cross each other many times, and short access trails provide a means of getting to the trail when it strays from the road.

About 230 miles of short side trails of various kinds are available for hikers. Many of them can be combined with the A.T. into loops of various lengths. About 85 miles of these side trails are maintained by the Potomac Appalachian Trail Club, which also takes care of the A.T. in this area. These trails are well kept and marked with blue paint blazes.

The Park Service maintains about 65 miles of graded trails. The remaining miles of side trails are fire roads and Park Service maintenance trails, many somewhat difficult to follow.

In addition to maintaining trails, the Potomac Appalachian Trail Club maintains five cabins (another is under construction) in the park along the A.T. route. The cabins are provided with enough equipment to make it possible for hikers using them to get by with carrying a sleeping bag or other bedding, food, and clothing and other personal articles. Kerosene lanterns are even provided.

The cabins are kept locked and must be reserved in advance through the Potomac Appalachian Trail Club, 1718 N St., N.W., Washington, D.C. 20036. The telephone is 202-638-5306.

Twenty-one trail shelters are also available for hikers. These are open and usable on a first-come first-served basis. They are all either on or very near the Appalachian Trail. Those near the trail are reachable by short access trails from the A.T.

If you are using a car as a base for short hikes, the Park Service operates four campgrounds and a group camp in the park. A park concessionaire, ARA-Virginia Sky-Line Co., Inc., Box 727, Luray, Va. 22835, operates a lodge and cottages that can accommodate over 900 guests.

The fantastic growth in backpacking in the last decade has had a considerable impact on our more popular parks. Shenandoah, located as it is near some of America's largest cities, has really been hit. In 1967, there were 34,000 back country packing nights; that is, the number of times the camps were used by various persons over the course of a year. In 1973, the figure had leaped to 120,000.

The park had been using a system of designated campsites, 39 in all. But with so many people using them, these sites began to look like used battlefields. In 1973, the park adopted a new policy for back country use.

Under the new policy, back country users can camp anywhere they like with the following restrictions:

1. camping within 250 yards — or in sight of — any paved park

road or the park boundary is prohibited.

2. Campers must be more than ½ mile from, and out of sight of, any auto campground, lodge, restaurant, visitor center, picnic area, ranger station, administrative or maintenance area, or other park development or facility except a trail, an unpaved road, or a trail shelter.

3. While you can camp near a shelter, trail, or unpaved road, you must not be in sight from any of these things. You must also be out of sight of any sign posted by park authorities to designate a no-camping area.

4. Campers must be out of sight of other camping parties. Under normal circumstances, you have to stay away from trail shelters, but "backcountry campers may seek shelter and sleep within or adjacent to a trail shelter with other camping groups, during periods of severely unseasonable weather when the protection and amenities of such shelter are deemed essential." If you are about to freeze to death, you can get inside.

5. Camping is prohibited within 25 feet of any stream.

6. You can't camp in any one place for more than two nights. The letter of the law says that you have to move at least 250 yards to a new campsite after two nights.

7. No wood or charcoal fires are allowed except in fireplaces at trail shelters. Fires are very destructive in heavily used camping areas. The dry wood scattered on the ground gets used up, and when that happens a few idiots will pull down saplings or tear low branches off living trees. The wood is green and won't burn, but that doesn't seem to be much of a deterrent. In the Shenandoah, the park service recommends portable stoves for backpackers.

8. Campers are not allowed to carry food or drink in discardable glass containers in the backcountry. All other discardable material must be packed out. Nothing is to be buried.

9. Except in established privies, do not urinate or defecate within 10 yards of any stream, trail, unpaved road, or park facility. Fecal material must be placed in a hole and covered with not less than three inches of dirt.

This rule should be followed routinely by backpackers everywhere. Also, use at least three inches of soil to cover fecal material, but don't use much more than that. The bacteria that will decompose this material are concentrated in the upper layers of soil, so going too deep is not a good idea.

10. Dogs are prohibited on certain trails which are posted by appropriate signs. Dogs must be on a leash at all times. This rule

should be followed everywhere. Dogs just don't belong on back-packing trips.

11. No group of more than 10 persons is allowed to camp together.

12. Finally, you can't camp without a permit. The permits can be picked up at the park headquarters, all entrance stations, visitors' centers, or from any park ranger. You can get them by mail, but be sure to include in your request your name, address, the number in your party, and the location and date of each planned overnight camp. Permits may be denied "when such action is necessary to protect park resources or park visitors, or to regulate levels of visitor use in legislatively designated wilderness areas," according to the Park Service.

In addition to these rules, the Park Service requests off-season hikers to let a ranger know where they are planning to go.

Finally, it costs $2.00 for a carload of people to enter the park. If you come in on foot, the cost is 50 cents.

Since the major trail in the Shenandoah is the Appalachian Trail, we will follow the same practice we are using for other sections of this trail. The map of the park shows the trail, the shelters, and the cabins maintained by the Potomac Appalachian Trail Club. In addition, it shows distances between points on the trail as well as various park facilities such as developed campgrounds.

We will also include brief general descriptions to some of the more interesting side trails in the park. If you want an exhaustively detailed account of both the A.T. and the side trails, we recommend the 260-page book put together by the Potomac Appalachian Trail Club. The book is available from the Appalachian Trail Conference, P.O. Box 236, Harpers Ferry, W.Va. 25425. The cost is $4.25.

In addition to the book, the club has produced a series of three maps of the park. These cost $3.00 for the set. The maps are based on USGS Quads and are printed in a 1:62:500 scale. The contour interval is rather confusing. The map legend says "Contour interval 20 and 100 feet." When you actually count the lines, they come out to an 80 foot interval.

The USGS also publishes a set of three maps of the park on the 1:62:500 scale. The Potomac maps were revised and reprinted in 1973, and since they are done specifically with hikers in mind, they are probably the best ones to get.

The Park Service has provided concrete posts as trail signs. The posts have metal bands around them with the trail information imprinted on the bands.

In the northern section of the park, the Matthews Arm Campground makes a good base of operations. Forty miles of side trails are accessible directly or via connecting trails from this point. You can connect with the same trails from the Range View Cabin maintained by the Potomac Appalachian Trail Club, or from the Elkwallow Shelter on the A.T. The Piney River and Little Devils Stairs are two trails that follow streams through rugged gorges.

The Big Blue Trail in this area is planned as the southern end of a 220-mile trail that will provide an alternate to the A.T. When completed, this alternate trail will extend north into Pennsylvania.

If you are arriving at Front Royal by public transportation and you want to get into the park, the Dickey Ridge Trail takes off from the junction of the Skyline Drive and U.S. Route 340 about ½ mile south of Front Royal. The nine-mile trail links up with the A.T. near Compton Gap.

A number of trails to the east of the A.T. and the Skyline Drive can be reached from either of their major routes about two miles south of U.S. Route 211. About 20 miles of trails form a network accessible from that point or from the parking area at the Pinnacles on the Skyline Drive.

From the Skyline Drive near Skyline, a parking area provides access to the White Oak Canyon Trail, which is just over five miles. White Oak is a deep, narrow, heavily forested canyon whose stream drops over 1500 feet in a mile. Six waterfalls with drops of over 50 feet lie along the trail route. It is possible to connect this trail with others in the Old Rag Mountain Area.

Toward the southern end of the park, the Loft Mountain campground makes a good base of operations. The Appalachian Trail loops around the campground, providing access to about 27 miles of interconnecting trails in the Big Run area. Big Run is another of the park's beautiful gorges. You can also get to these trails from the Big Run Overlook on Skyline Drive, which is just south of the Loft Mountain campground.

The Potomac Appalachian Trail Club's Doyles River cabin and the Big Run trail shelter are just south of the Loft Mountain campground and also provide access to the trails in the area.

A fire road provides a trail that follows Big Run itself, and connections are possible from that trail to trails that follow the ridges on either side of the gorge.

On the other side of the Skyline Drive, the Falls Trail, 4½ miles long, provides a look at falls on both Doyle River and Jones Run — or Jones Falls Run. This trail can be made into a loop of eight miles with a piece of the A.T. Be prepared for some climbing. The trail drops 1300 feet from the Skyline Drive and then climbs back up almost the same distance.

The A.T. used to follow Moormans River, and a gated fire road allows hikers to use this route today. It begins at Black Rock Gap and heads down into the valley to the east. It follows the river south to rejoin the A.T. and Skyline Drive at Jarman Gap, the southern boundary of the park.

If you are continuing on the A.T., it is just under eight miles from the park boundary to Rockfish Gap and the James River.

TRAILS IN THE GEORGE WASHINGTON NATIONAL FOREST

The George Washington comprises well over 1,000,000 acres of land. It extends from the northern edge of the Jefferson Forest in the south to Strasburg, Va., only 100 miles from Washington, D.C., in the north.

It is divided into sections that follow the ridges northeast, extending into West Virginia in many areas. We have selected trails in four of the forest's six districts for description. Maps and information on the forest are available from the Forest Supervisor, George Washington National Forest, 210 Federal Blvd., Harrisonburg, Va. 22801. The telephone is 703-433-2491.

Trails in the Lee Ranger District

The Lee is the northernmost and easternmost district of the George Washington National Forest. It is made up of two separate sections. The southern section lies between the North and South Forks of the Shenandoah River, while the northern section straddles the Virginia-West Virginia line.

All of the trails described below are in the southern section between New Market and Strasburg. The area to the south of New Market is a wildlife management area that is the district's principal bear management area. If you are looking for wild country, go where the bears are.

The trails in the wildlife management area are in rather uncertain condition, but if you are equipped to do some exploring, check in at the Massanutten visitors' center on U.S. Route 211 between New Market and Luray. The folks at the center have current information on the state of trails in all sections of the Lee District.

You can write for information to the District Ranger, Professional Bldg., Edinburg, Va. 22824. The phone is 703-984-4101.

404 — Massanutten Mountain Trail — From Elizabeth Furnace to
Camp Roosevelt.
Length: 23 miles
USGS Quads: Strasburg, Va.; Bentonville, Va.; Rileyville, Va.;
Luray, Va.; Hamburg, Va.
Description: The trail follows the ridge line of Massanutten
Mountain. To reach it, take a jeep trail southeast from the Eliza-
beth Furnace Recreation Area. The trail climbs from about 700
feet up to over 1500 on the ridge top.

The trail follows the ridge southwest. Just over a mile south, a
rough trail crosses the Massanutten Mountain Trail, and four
miles farther, a trail heads off to the south. This trail leads ½
mile to Milford Gap at 1600 feet. It then turns northeast for ½
mile before splitting into two forks. The north fork leads downhill
to the Hazard Mill Recreation Area at 560 feet.

The main trail continues southwest, crossing another side trail
4½ miles farther on. About four miles beyond that junction, a
side trail heads to Kennedy Peak.

About two miles farther, the trail hits a road which it follows
south for ½ mile before doubling back on the road just under a
mile to Camp Roosevelt Recreation Area.

Duncan Hollow Trail — From Camp Roosevelt to U.S. Route 211
at Big Run.
Length: 8 miles
USGS Quad: Hamburg, Va.
Description: From Camp Roosevelt, the trail follows the road a
short distance north before doubling back south along a dirt road
up Duncan Hollow. After a mile, the road gives way to a trail that
climbs gradually along the creek from 1300 feet to 2500 feet four
miles farther south. There the trail turns west, climbing up over a
low divide and dropping down again to Big Run at 2300 feet.

The trail follows Big Run south, dividing ½ mile north of U.S.
211. Both forks hit the highway about one mile apart.

402 — Signal Knob — From Virginia Route 678, ½ mile north of
Elizabeth Furnace Recreation Area to Signal Knob and the Massanutten Mountain North Trail.
Length: 4.5 miles
USGS Quad: Strasburg, Va.
Description: Heads west at a dirt road off Virginia 678 from 770
feet. Turns north after a short distance, climbing up to reach Buzzard Rock Overlook at 1500 feet after 1½ miles. It turns southwest ½ mile to the Fort Valley Overlook at 1800 feet, and then
north ½ mile to the Shenandoah Valley Overlook at 1900 feet.

From there it is west and then north to Signal Knob at 2106 feet.

403 — Bear Wallow Trail — From the Elizabeth Furnace Recreation Area to the Massanutten Mountain North Trail.

Length: 3 miles

USGS Quad: Strasburg, Va.

Description: Heads west from the campground, climbing steadily up to 2100 feet on Green Mountain. From there it drops to 1850 feet at its junction with the Massanutten Mountain North Trail.

408 — Massanutten Mountain North Trail — From Signal Knob to Forest Road 66.

Length: 2 miles

USGS Quad: Strasburg, Va.

Description: From Signal Knob at 2106, the trail heads southwest, dropping down to 1850 at just over one mile where it meets the Bear Wallow Trail. Continuing southwest, the trail follows Little Passage Creek past the Strasburg Reservoir at 1700 feet 1½ miles from Signal Knob.

A half mile beyond the reservoir, the trail meets the road. It is possible to continue along this road, but it soon passes through a patch of private land that is being "developed" in a fashion that is likely to displease hikers.

The Signal Knob, Massanutten Mountain North, and Bear Wallow Trails can be combined into a loop of about nine miles beginning and ending at Elizabeth Furnace.

Trails on the Pedlar District

The best hiking in this area is in the Big Levels Wildlife Management Unit at the north end of the district. Big Levels is a broad, flat area up about 3400 feet. It is wooded, mainly with scrubby black gum, pitch pine, and bear oak. One interesting feature of the place is Green Pond, a sink hole pond of some ecological significance.

Several trails climb up to Big Levels from the valley below, some following creeks, others the spines of spur ridges. Another trail just east of Big Levels connects the Sherando Lake Recreation Area with Bald Mountain.

For current information on trails in this district, contact the District Ranger, Post Office Building, Buena Vista, Va. 24416. The phone is 703-261-6105.

Cold Springs Trail — Take Virginia Route 608 to Forest Road 41 and go east past the Mount Joy Church to Forest Road 42 (Coal Road). Turn north (left) for 2½ to 3 miles to the trail at Cold Springs Branch.

Length: 4.5 miles
USGS Quad: Big Levels, Va.
Description: The trail heads up the creek from 2083 feet. At ¾ mile, the Cold Springs are off to the south. At 1½ miles, a steep, short spur trail leads north to the top of a knob. From this junction, at 3400 feet, the ground becomes flat. You are on top of Big Levels.

At 3½ miles, the Stony Run Trail comes in from the north, and at 4½ miles, you reach Green Pond at 3208 feet. A trail from this point leads north out Kennedy Ridge (see following), while another trail goes south to Flint Mountain. From there a gated road — Forest Road 162 — leads south past Bald Mountain to the Blue Ridge Parkway.

500 — St. Mary's River Trail — Take Virginia Route 608 to Forest Road 41. Follow 41 up the river to the gate.
Length: 6 miles
USGS Quad: Vesuvius, Va., and Big Levels, Va.
Description: The trail follows the river, a stocked trout stream, for two miles before Sugartree Branch comes in from the south. A side trail follows this creek briefly and then turns east to parallel the river past some mines on private property.

If you continue to follow the river, you will pass four tributaries coming in from the south. Where the river itself curves south, continue east on up the hill onto Big Levels and an eventual meeting with the Cold Springs Branch Trail.

478 — Stony Run Trail — For Stony Run and Forest Road 42, seven miles north of Forest Road 42.
Length: 3 miles
USGS Quad: Big Levels, Va.
Description: The easiest way to describe this trail is with a picture. The trail starts at 1819 feet at the road, climbs to 3000 feet in the first 1½ miles and then climbs more slowly to 3219 at the junction with Cold Springs Branch Trail. Check the map for details on the twists, forks, and junctions along the trail route.

479 — Kennedy Ridge Trail — From Forest Road 42 between Kennedy Fields campground and Coles Run to Green Pond on Big Levels. There is a parking area at the trail head.
Length: 3.5 miles
USGS Quad: Big Levels, Va.
Description: From 1800 feet on the road, the trail climbs up onto Kennedy Ridge, rising to over 3000 feet. For the last mile of the trail, the ground is level.

507 — Sherando Lake to Bald Mountain — From the Sherando

Lake Recreation Area on Forest Road 9 to the Blue Ridge Parkway at the Bald Mountain Overlook.

Length: 4 miles

USGS Quad: Big Levels, Va.

Description: The trail heads northwest past the campground water tank, climbing up onto Torry Ridge, gaining 800 feet in altitude in the first mile. A trail comes in from the northeast on the ridge, and the two trails join and head southwest up the ridge, rising to 3000 feet.

The trail turns northwest on the ridge, climbing up onto Bald Mountain, reaching 3587 feet at the lookout tower.

A dirt road goes northeast down Bald Mountain and then doubles around to the left to head southwest to the Blue Ridge Parkway at the Bald Mountain Overlook.

Trails in the Dry River District

The district offers a number of trails scattered over its length. For current information contact the District Ranger, 510 N. Main, Bridgewater, Va. 22812. The phone is 703-828-2591.

1020 — Shenandoah Mountain — Take U.S. 33 to the Virginia-West Virginia border and turn south on Forest Road 85. A short distance from the highway, the road forks. The left fork climbs to the High Knob Fire Tower while the right fork continues south briefly before deadending at the trail head. South end of the trail is at Bother Knob.

USGS Quad: Brandywine, Va.

Description: The trail follows the ridge line south from High Knob, with elevations varying from about 3600 to 3800 feet. On the southern half of the trail, two side trails come in, almost together, from the west. One leads to a dirt road that parallels the trail. The other crosses that road and heads down Miller Run to end on private property.

To the south, the trail climbs to 4344 on Bother Knob, then goes briefly downhill to a dirt road (Forest Road 85). You can take this road south about two miles to Virginia 924. Or you can take it east to Flagpole Knob and the Slate Springs Mountain Trail about two miles away.

428 — Slate Springs Mountain Trail — From Flagpole Knob about five miles north out a dirt road (Forest Road 85) from Virginia 924 to U.S. 33 at Rawley Springs, Va.

Length: 8 miles

USGS Quads: Brandywine, Va., Rawley Springs, Va.

Description: Forest Road 85 continues east from Flagpole Knob for a few hundred yards. Trail 428AA branches off to the south, and 428 continues east where the road turns sharply north.

The trail follows the ridge east, dropping from over 4000 feet to 3900 feet about one mile out. There, the trail forks with 428 heading north and 428A heading south.

Trail 428 heads north along a narrow ridge that flattens out at the hamlet of Maple Springs about two miles away. The trail follows the dirt road north through the community. Where the road ends on Chestnut Ridge, the trail turns east, beginning a slow descent along the ridge. It continues to drop until it reaches Bum Run, which it parallels on a dirt road into Rawley Springs.

428A — Slate Springs Trail — From Trail 428 east of Flagpole Knob to Virginia 257 near the forest boundary about 11 miles west of Dayton.

Length: 4 miles

USGS Quad: Brandywine, Va., Reddish Knob, Va., and Briery Branch, Va.

Description: From the fork where it splits from Trail 428, this trail heads southeast down a ridge. At Pond Knob, trail divides in three take the middle tine. It crosses Oak Knob at 3500 feet and goes east from there to a fork. Take the south fork, continuing out the ridge. At another fork about ½ mile farther, take the left — east — tine. The trail ends at the road near Rocky Run.

428AA — Slate Springs Trail — From Forest Road 85 at Flagpole Knob to Hone Quarry Run. Trail down Hone Quarry Run continues as far as Hone Quarry Dam. Dirt Road leads to Hone Quarry Recreation Area.

Length: 4 miles

USGS Quads: Brandywine, Va., and Reddish Knob, Va.

Description: The trail heads south from the road, dropping from 4200 feet to 3400 feet in the first mile. Altitude is 2300 feet where the trail meets Hone Quarry Run. From there, follow the jeep trail southeast to the campground.

435 — Hone Quarry Mountain — Take Virginia 257 west from Dayton. Inside the forest boundary, road turns south, becomes Virginia 924. Trailhead is ½ mile south of Forest Road 62 on 924. To get to the other end, take 924 west to Forest Road 85 and north one mile to Forest Road 539, which heads back east.

Length: 8 miles

USGS Quads: Reddish Knob, Va., and Briery Branch, Va.

Description: Forest Road 259 is a gated road, open only during hunting season. The trail follows it east for two miles, dropping steadily from 3900 feet to 3400. One mile beyond the end of the road, the trail forks, with the south fork being a side trail down the side of Hone Quarry Ridge to Mines Run and the Mines Run Trail.

One mile beyond this fork is another. The Big Hollow Trail goes off to the left. In another mile, a trail branches to the right — south — to Virginia 924 just below Briery Branch Dam. The main trail continues on down the ridge to the road, elevation 1700 feet.

430 — Big Hollow Trail — From the Hone Quarry Mountain Trail to the Hone Quarry Recreation Area.

Length: 2 miles

USGS Quad: Reddish Knob, Va.

Description: Heading east from the Hone Quarry Mountain trail at 3220, the trail drops steadily to 1950 where it hits Hone Quarry Run just above the campground.

Mines Run Trail — From Virginia 924 just above Briery Branch Dam to a dead end up Mines Run.

Length: 3 miles

USGS Quad: Reddish Knob, Va.

Description: The Trail follows the creek from the road at 2050 feet, climbing to 2600 feet at the dead end. About half way along, a trail to the north climbs up the ridge to the Hone Quarry Mountain Trail.

431 — Timber Ridge Trail — Begins at the Reddish Knob fire tower. Take Virginia 924 10 miles from the forest boundary to Forest Road 85. Turn left — south — and go two miles to the Reddish Knob tower. At the eastern end, take Forest Road 101 four miles south from 924. The trail head is just north of Hearthstone Lake.

Length: 8 miles

USGS Quad: Reddish Knob, Va.

Description: The Reddish Knob tower is at 4397. The trail heads east from there, dropping downhill for about ½ mile to a fork at 4100 feet. Take the south (right) fork down Timber Ridge.

Four miles from the trailhead, the Sand Spring Mountain Trail branches off to the left at 3700 feet. The Timber Ridge Trail goes southeast down Hearthstone Ridge, dropping steadily to 1781 feet at the road.

Sand Spring Mountain Trail — From the Timber Ridge Trail to Forest Road 101 two miles north of Hearthstone Lake.

Length: 3 miles

USGS Quad: Reddish Knob, Va.

Description: Leaving the Timber Ridge trail at 3700 feet, the trail heads east down to 2000 feet at the road.

425 — Chestnut Ridge — From Bridgewater, Va., take Virginia Route 42 east to Virginia 727, just outside of town, and follow the latter road southeast to Virginia 730. Take 730 into the forest to the Stokesville community. Take Virginia 718 west past Stokesville. Just past the bridge over the Little River, turn north on Forest Road 101 for about 500 feet. Then go west on Forest Road 95. After another 500 feet a short, dead end road turns north to the trail head. Western end of the trail is at Little Bald Knob.
Length: 7 miles
USGS Quads: Stokesville, Va., Reddish Knob, Va., Palo Alto, Va.
Description: From the eastern end, the trail begins at 1600 feet and goes north briefly upslope to 1800. It then turns west along the ridge, climbing steadily to 2700 feet and 1½-2 miles. A half mile farther west, the Little Skidmore gated jeep road comes in from the south.

The trail continues up Chestnut Ridge, climbing to 3000 feet. It turns north briefly to meet the Grooms Ridge Trail, doubles back to the south, and then turns west again; from 3200 feet at the junction, it climbs to 4300 on Little Bald Knob.

A trail goes north from Little Bald Knob, following a ridge line for about five miles, angling east to meet Forest Road 85 about a mile north of the Shenandoah Recreation Area.

To the south, a trail goes from Little Bald Knob down to Forest Road 95 at Camp Todd.

424 — Grooms Ridge Trail — From the Chestnut Ridge Trail to Forest Road 101 about 1½ miles south of Hearthstone Lake.
Length: 4 miles
USGS Quad: Reddish Knob, Va.
Description: The trail follows Big Ridge, dropping steadily but never steeply, eastward, from 3200 feet at the junction to 1700 feet at the road.

North River Trail — Follows the river upstream (north) from Forest Road 95 to the Shenandoah Recreation Area.
Length: 4 miles
USGS Quad: Palo Alto, Va
Description: Starting about 2½ miles north of Camp Todd at 2700 feet, the trail heads up river to 3000 feet before making a sharp climb to the west up to the campground at 3600 feet.

422 — Dull Hunt Trail — Take Virginia 763 from Harrisonburg. About a mile past the forest boundary Forest Road 72 goes off to the left. This very curvy road goes six to seven miles to White Oak Flats and the gated jeep road of Dull Hunt Trail. A branch of the trail meets Forest Road 72 about five miles beyond this point.

The trail ends at Forest Road 240 which winds 2½ miles over Leading Ridge down to the Little Dry River and Forest Road 87.
Length: 8 miles
USGS Quads: Cow Knob, Va., and Rawley Springs, Va.
Description: From the gated road at about 3300 feet, the trail heads northeast down Trail Ridge, turning north and then dropping with a series of switchbacks down to 1800 feet at Slate Lick Run, two miles from the trailhead. Crossing the creek, it climbs up on Gauley Ridge to 2200 feet, turns northeast for ½ mile and then doubles back west going steeply downhill into Dull Hunt Hollow, meeting Bible Creek and following it northeast at 1930 feet.

A branch of the trail continues across the creek, rather than turning down it, and turns northwest up Middle Mountain, climbing to 2800 feet quickly and then more slowly to 3200 feet where it meets Forest Road 72.

The main trail continues down to the confluence of Bible Run and Spruce Lick Run, which comes in from the west. Here the trail forks. Follow the fork up Spruce Lick Run less than ½ mile to Forest Road 240. The other branch continues down Bible Run onto private property.

447 — Shenandoah Mountain — This trail has the same name as trail number 1020, but it is actually the northern end of a long trail in the Deerfield Ranger District. From Forest Road 95 just west of Forest Road 85 to Tearjacket Knob and the sections of this trail in the Deerfield District.
Length: 3.5 miles
USGS Quad: Palo Alto, Va.
Description: This trail was described to us as "good but steep." From 3000 feet at the road, it climbs quickly up the ridge to 4000 in about one mile. It follows the ridge south to Tearjacket Knob — 4200 feet — and connects with the trails coming north past Hardscrabble Knob.

Trails in the Deerfield District
This district has a number of trails of various lengths. Most of the details in this section came from District Ranger Leonard McNeal who apparently carries a very precise map of the district around in his head. For current information on the Deerfield Trails, contact the District Ranger, 2304 W. Beverly, Staunton, Va. 24401. The phone is 703-885-1911.

447 — Shenandoah Mountain Trail — From Virginia Route 627 north to Tearjacket Knob.
Length: 31 miles

USGS Quad: (south to north) Williamsville, Va., Deerfield, Va., McDowell, Va., West Augusta, Va.

Description: According to the district ranger, this trail has not been maintained in several years. However, it gets enough use to stay open and followable. Maps show it extending south to Virginia 678 near Fort Lewis, but the ranger recommends starting at Scotchtown Draft Road — Va. 627.

From the road, the trail climbs steeply from 2000 feet to 3088 on South Sister Knob. From there, it continues north along the ridge in a series of ups and downs, skirting North Sister Knob on its east side at 3000 feet.

Five miles from 627, the trail meets the Jerkemtight Trail, which comes in from the right (east) at 3600 feet on the slopes of Northeast Peak. Eight miles from the start Jerkemtight branches off to the left (west).

At the first intersection with Jerkemtight, another trail comes in from the west, and a short trail heads south up to Wallace Peak at 3795 feet. There are some grassy balds in the Wallace Peak area.

The trail stays on the ridge at elevations in the 3000-3200 foot range, passing to the west of "The Bump" six miles beyond the point where the Jerkemtight Trail branches to the west. Three miles past "The Bump," the trail crosses Forest Road 173.

Four and a half miles to the north, the trail begins to follow a dirt road, passing Tim's Knob at 3400 feet. The trail passes a spur trail which comes in from the west and follows another dirt road north, climbing as high as 3800 feet.

After two miles, the road forks, and the trail follows the left fork, going downhill to intersect U.S. 250 at 2831 feet.

Continuing north, the trail drops slightly, then rises, staying on the ridge at 3200 to 3600 feet. Three miles north of 250, it reaches a three-pronged fork. The middle tine continues the Shenandoah Trail, while the right goes down Jerrys Run. There is a shelter on this creek one-half mile from the Shenandoah Trail. This section of the Shenandoah Trail is maintained by the Potomac Appalachian Trail Club. It is in good shape and marked by blue blazes. Watch in this area for a grove of chestnut oaks of great size, many of which will be lying on the ground.

According to Ranger McNeal, when the Forest Service bought this land about 1913, the lumber company that owned it had not yet got around to logging off this area. Since then, the rangers in the district have also avoided cutting. The area never carried any official designation to protect it from logging, but each ranger passed the word to his successor to stay away from it.

Now many of the old trees are dying off. You are not likely to get many chances to see a piece of eastern hardwood forest dying of old age.

The trail continues north from Jerrys Run to Tearjacket Knob which is located in a 1700-acre Natural Area. A trail there winds around the knob to the east, while another continues north to Forest Road 95. See the Dry River District for a description.

Jerkemtight Trail — Virginia Route 629 four miles south of Deerfield, Va., to the Shenandoah Trail.

Length: 4.5 miles

USGS Quads: Deerfield, Va., Williamsville, Va.

Description: Back in the days when logging operations depended on oxen, the ox drivers had to "jerk-'em-tight" on this steep slope. A dirt road off Va. 629 to the west forms the lower end of the trail. The creek here is a stocked trout stream. Things get steep soon, as the trail climbs from 2074 at the road to 3600 at the junction with the Shenandoah Trail.

We were told that the section of this trail that lies west of the Shenandoah Trail is not in good shape. Also, its lower end is on private land.

Jerrys Run Trail — From Forest Road 68 2½ miles north of U.S. 250 to the Shenandoah Trail. Forest Road 68 is gated about one miles north of 250.

Length: 2.5 miles

USGS Quad: West Augusta, Va.

Description: The trail follows the creek for almost all of its length, climbing from 1800 feet to just over 3000. A shelter is located at the upper end of the trail, about ½ mile from the Shenandoah Trail.

Ramseys Draft Trail — Forest Road 68 heads north from U.S. 250. About one mile north of the highway, the road is gated, and there the trail begins. It climbs up to the Hardscrabble Knob area and a junction with the Dividing Ridge Trail.

Length: 4.5 miles

USGS Quad: West Augusta, Va.

Description: Ramseys Draft is a stocked trout stream. The trail follows it north along the remains of Forest Road 68 until the road gives way to a trail. The trail climbs up beyond the head of the creek and turns northwest, climbing to nearly 4000 feet at its junction with the Dividing Ridge Trail. Hiner Spring is to the left of the trail just beyond the junction.

Dividing Ridge Trail — Take Forest Road 96 north from U.S. 250

about 4½ miles. The road follows a creek and then climbs a low divide where the trail heads off to the east on a jeep road. The trail ends between Tearjacket and Hardscrabble Knobs at a junction with the trail leading north to Forest Road 95. Connections can also be made with the Shenandoah Mountain Trail. A short branch of this trail leads to Camp Todd on Forest Road 95 in the Dry River Ranger District.

Length: 5 miles

USGS Quad: West Augusta, Va.

Description: From 2312 feet at the road, the trail follows a jeep track for about a mile, climbing up to 2600 feet. From there it is a foot trail climbing up the narrow crest of Dividing Ridge between Mitchell Branch and the Calfpasture River.

At 3700 feet, 2½ miles from the road, the trail passes a small pond. It then turns northeast and back to the northwest over Big Bald Knob at 4100 feet, 3½ miles from the trailhead.

From there, the trail goes north about a mile to where the trail to Camp Todd branches off to the northeast. If you follow that trail, you will go downhill for a mile and a half, dropping from 3700 feet to 2357 at Camp Todd.

The Dividing Ridge Trail continues west. The Trail up Ramseys Draft comes in from the south and a few hundred yards farther, the trail forks. The south fork is a short path to the top of Hardscrabble Knob, 4282 feet high. The north fork leads past Tearjacket Knob to join with the Shenandoah Mountain Trail.

Walker Mountain Trail — From Forest Road 61 two miles north of Yost, Va., to Virginia Routes 600 and 629 a mile south of deerfield.

Length: 8 miles

USGS Quads: Green Valley, Va., Craigsville, Va., Deerfield, Va.

Description: The south end of the trail is a gated road heading off to the west from Forest Road 61. This jeep track climbs to 2000 feet heading north. It then doubles back to head southwest from about ½ mile before doubling back again to the northeast to climb up Walker Mountain to 2800 feet. A second gate is located just beyond this second sharp turn. These gates are opened during hunting season.

The trail follows the ridge top for nearly its whole length, climbing as high as 3000 feet, but staying nearly level, without any severe grades. Two trails branch off to the southeast down to Little Mill Creek.

As the trail nears its northern terminus, it begins to lose altitude, dropping to 2100 feet where it intersects a dirt road. The road goes west to Virginia Route 629 and east to Virginia Route

600 about one mile south of Deerfield.

A series of trails runs north and south along Great North Mountain from Virginia Route 687 in the south to U.S. 250 in the north.
443 — North Mountain Trail — From Virginia Route 687 to Elliott Knob. Note: Virginia 687 is also known as Ramsey Draft Road, named for the creek it follows up the mountain. Do not confuse this with Ramseys Draft Road (and trail) previously described.
Length: 10 miles
USGS Quads: Craigsville, Va., Deerfield, Va., Elliott Knob, Va.
Description: Maps show this trail continuing south of Virginia 687, but the district ranger advises that it is in bad shape and difficult to follow.

North of the road, the trail climbs up the ridge of Great North Mountain from 2184 feet to around 3000. Five miles north of the road, the trail reaches 3259 feet. Seven miles along, it crosses Hite Hollow Road (Forest Road 82) at 3182 feet.

Beyond Hite Hollow Road, the trail winds through open stands of black oak. It has been recently maintained in this area and is marked with yellow blazes.

Two miles north of the road, at 3581 feet, a short trail leads off to the left. It dead ends ¼ mile away at Chestnut Flat Springs. A split rail fence made of chestnut can be seen near the spring.

From the side trail, the main trail climbs over Hogback (4447 feet) to Elliott Knob, at 4463, the highest point in the George Washington National Forest.

The trail hits a dirt road as it approaches Elliott Knob. To the left the road leads up to the fire tower. Straight ahead is a TV antenna. To get to the Elliott Knob Trail that heads north from here, go right a short distance to where the trail goes left from the road. Downhill, a few steps farther on the road, are a spring and a pond off to the left. A cleared area by the pond makes a good camping spot. It may take some searching here, because both spring and pond may be blocked by laurel thickets and thus hard to see from the road.

A caution about the North Mountain Trail. It is easy to get off the trail onto a finger ridge. Keep in a northeasterly direction. Don't head due east, and don't follow any old roads off the ridge top.
Elliott Knob Trail — From Elliott Knob to Virginia Route 688.
Length: 4.5 miles
USGS Quad: Elliott Knob, Va.
Description: This section of trail has also been marked with yellow blazes. It follows the ridge northward, slowly losing alti-

tude. About 2½ miles from the start, a trail leads off to the east about 200 yards to Buffalo Spring. The trail continues north downslope to 2581 feet at the road.

Crawford Mountain Trail — A jeep trail, gated except during hunting season. The south end is on Virginia Route 688 opposite the north end of the Elliott Knob Trail. The north end is at U.S. 250 three miles west of the forest boundary. Yellow blazes and a sign identify the north end of the trail.

Length: 6 miles

USGS Quads: Elliott Knob, Va., West Augusta, Va., Stokesville, Va.

Description: A ridge line trail through open stands of northern hardwoods: maples, beech, and birch. It climbs quickly from 2581 at Va. 688 up to 3000 on Crawford Mountain.

Two miles from 688, at 3600 feet, the trail intersects the Chimney Hollow Trail. The intersection has no signs to mark it, and it could be easily missed. Watch for a trail coming in from the left on a heading almost parallel to the Crawford Mountain Trail. If you take the Chimney Hollow Trail, you will be going back southwest, almost the direction you came from. About 200 yards farther north, the Crawford Knob Trail comes in from the east (right). The Crawford Mountain Trail continues northeast, gradually losing altitude, dropping to under 2500 feet at U.S. 250.

Chimney Hollow Trail — From the Crawford Mountain Trail to U.S. 250 just east of Forest Road 96, and ¾ mile east of West Augusta, Va.

Length: 3 miles

USGS Quads: Elliott Knob, Va., and West Augusta, Va.

Description: Heading southeast from the Crawford Mountain Trail, the trail drops steeply down off the ridge to 2800 feet and then turns northwest along the slope of Chair Draft Hollow. It then skirts the west slope of Coal Pit Knob at 2600 feet before turning into Chimney Hollow. It follows the hollow northwest down to 1900 feet at the road.

Crawford Knob Trail — From Crawford Mountain Trail to Virginia Route 720 at Jerusalem Church.

Length: 4 miles

USGS Quads: Elliott Knob, Va., Churchville, Va.

Description: From Crawford Mountain, the trail goes southwest over Crawford Knob at 3728 feet and on out the ridge. It drops steeply from 3000 feet to 2100 feet in ½ mile. It then hits a dirt road (Forest Road 289) which it follows to Va. 720 at 1684 feet. The lower portion of the trail is open to vehicles, but the upper portion is gated except during hunting season.

THE JEFFERSON NATIONAL FOREST

Over 1,500,000 acres of land are within the boundaries of the Jefferson National Forest; 546,000 acres are actually owned by the United States. The land extends in long strips from the Tennessee and Kentucky lines in the southwest to beyond Roanoke to the north.

The trails described here are located in four of the forest's ranger districts, from Mount Rogers in the south to the Glenwood district around Natural Bridge in the north. General information and maps of the forest can be obtained from the Forest Supervisor, 3517 Brandon Ave., Roanoke, Va. 24018. The phone is 703-343-1581.

Note: The elk that used to roam the mountains are long gone, but in the Jefferson, these magnificent animals have been reintroduced. The population is estimated to be 65 individuals, so your chances of seeing one are slim, but you can always hope.

Mount Rogers, at 5729 feet, is the highest point in Virginia. The peak and some 150,000 acres around it have been set aside as a National Recreation Area. The area is a long, narrow strip running generally east-west from near Damascus, Va., to the New River north of Galax.

The Appalachian Trail enters Virginia just south of Damascus and goes east past Mount Rogers before turning northeast over Glade Mountain into the valley of the Holston River. Other than the A.T., the major trail in the Mount Rogers area is the Iron Mountain Trail, which follows an old route of the A.T. It exists in two sections. The western section branches off from the A.T. about two miles north of Damascus and then rejoins it west of Virginia Route 16.

The eastern section runs from U.S. 21 south of Speedwell, Va., via connecting trails to Virginia Route 602.

Between these two sections, the old A.T. Route still exists. It is a ridge top trail, at times following old logging roads. However, it has not been maintained in some time, and parts of it run across private land, so we cannot really recommend it.

If you are looking for a long trip, the A.T. and the western section of the Iron Mountain Trail can be combined into a loop over 50 miles long. If you want a good hike on a slighly less heavily traveled path, head for the eastern section of the Iron Mountain Trail.

A long horse trail called the Virginia Highlands Trail winds from Mount Rogers northeast. Hikers can use this trail if they wish, but since it is mainly used by equestrians, we have not included a description.

For up-to-date information on trails in this area, contact the U.S. Forest Service, District Ranger Office, 1102 N. Main St., Marion, Va. 24354. The phone is 703-783-5196.

301 — Iron Mountain Trail — From the intersection of Virginia Route 16 and Virginia Route 650 west to the Appalachian Trail 2½ miles east of Damascus, Va.
Length: 24 miles
USGS Quads: Trout Dale, Va., (east to west) Whitetop Mountain, Va., Knooarock, Va., and Damascus, Va.
Description: When the A.T. was rerouted in 1972, this trail was re-marked with yellow blazes. Watch for these, since a number of other trails and logging roads intersect the Iron Mountain Trail. Three trail shelters, all near water, lie along the route, remains of the time when this was the A.T.

From the road at 3400 feet, the trail heads west, descending to cross Comers Creek at about 1½ miles. The trail follows the creek briefly to Comers Creek Falls and then starts uphill, rising about 4000 feet as it heads west. Just under seven miles from the start, the Iron Mountain Trail crosses the new A.T. From here, you could take the A.T. south to Mount Rogers or north to loop back around to where the A.T. crosses Va. 16 near your starting point.

The trail climbs to the top of Flat Top at 4451 feet, and about one mile beyond, it reaches the Cherry Tree shelter. To the west, the trail stays on the ridge, reaching the trail down Little Laurel Creek at about 10 miles.

Thirteen miles from your beginning, the trail hits Virginia Route 600 which it follows briefly to the north before heading west again. The Forest Service Skulls Gap Picnic Area is located off Va. 600 on the trail route.

About two miles west of Va. 600 is the Straight Branch Shelter. West of here, the trail follows the ridge top of Iron Mountain. Parts of this area are open fields.

The trail crosses Forest Road 90 19 miles from the beginning, and a half mile farther along it reaches the Sandy Flats Shelter. The junction with the A.T. is about four miles west of the shelter.
Little Laurel Creek Trail — From the Iron Mountain Trail to Virginia Route 600.
Length: 3.5 miles
USGS Quad: Whitetop Mountain, Va.

Description: A short spur trail from the Iron Mountain Trail. It leaves that trail at about 4400 feet on an old dirt road, and heads almost due east down the creek to meet the road at 3300 feet.

166 — Mount Rogers Trail — From Va. Route 603 at the Grindstone Recreation Area to the Appalachian Trail at Deep Gap.

Length: 6.9 miles

USGS Quad: Whitetop Mountain, Va. (quad does not show trail)

Description: From the campground, the trail climbs along Grindstone Branch and then up onto ridge at 3600 feet. It continues up rather quickly to 4400 feet and heads southwest along the west slope of Mount Rogers reaching 5000 feet before descending slightly to meet the A..T at Deep Gap (4800 feet).

The Deep Gap shelter is just to the west of the trail junction. You can follow the A.T. west a short distance to get a look at the high meadows on the slopes of Whitetop, the second highest mountain in Virginia.

To the east it leads 1½ miles to the top of Mount Rogers. Unlike Whitetop, Mount Rogers is heavily wooded with Fraser fir and red spruce. This is Canadian zone forest like the crests of the higher Smokies and Black Mountains farther south. Mount Rogers is the northernmost station for Fraser fir. North of here, the equivalent species is balsam fir.

301 — Iron Mountain Trail — The eastern section of the trail begins at U.S. 21 at the intersection with Forest Road 57 east of the Comers Rock campground. It ends at the beginning of the Bournes Branch Trail.

Length: 10.5 miles

USGS Quads: Speedwell, Va., Cripple Creek, Va., Austinville, Va.

Description: Another ridge top trail. About four miles along, the Horse Heaven Trail comes in from the north. The trail ends at Jones Knob, where the Bournes Branch Trail continues east.

An Outward Bound group maintained this trail in 1973, so it should be easy to follow. They cleared out brush and painted yellow blazes along the route.

306 — Henley Hollow Trail — From U.S. Route 21 two miles south of Speedwell, Va., to the Horse Heaven Trail.

Length: 1.4 miles

USGS Quad: Speedwell, Va.

Description: Heads southeast from the road, up Henley Hollow, climbing from 2485 at the road to 3100 feet where it meets the Horse Heaven Trail.

307 — Horse Heaven Trail — From the Henley Hollow Trail to the Iron Mountain Trail.

Length: 3.1 miles
USGS Quad: Speedwell, Va.
Description: The trail follows Horse Heaven ridge east from the Henley Hollow Trail at 3500 to 3800 feet. It turns south on a dirt road that carries it downhill to Forest Road 14 along the East Fork of Dry Creek. It then climbs up to the south and the Iron Mountain Trail at 3744 feet.

308 — Rocky Hollow — From Virginia Route 619 east of Speedwell to the Horse Heaven Trail. Take 619 from Speedwell to the bridge over Cripple Creek. A dirt road goes off to the south here, follows the creek from a short distance, and then crosses it at a ford. The trail begins south of the ford.
Length: 2.5 miles
USGS Quad: Speedwell, Va.
Description: The trail heads up Laurel Hollow from the ford and then climbs up onto a ridge at 3400 feet. It passes a spring just before joining the Horse Heaven Trail.

317 — Bournes Branch Trail — From Iron Mountain Trail at Jones Knob to Virginia Route 602 just north of the Sheperds Corner campground. Jones Knob is just east of the intersection of the Iron Mountain Trail and Virginia Route 653.
Length: 6 miles
USGS Quads: Cripple Creek, Va., Austinville, Va.
Description: Heads east from the Iron Mountain Trail, dropping off Jones Knob at 3400 feet down to Bournes Branch. Bournes Branch runs into Brush Creek which the trail follows to Va. 602.

310 — Yellow Branch Trail — From the Bournes Branch Trail to Va. 602.
Length: 3.5 miles
USGS Quad: Cripple Creek, Va.
Description: This trail branches off to the north from the Bournes Branch Trail two miles from the Iron Mountain Trail. It quickly hits Yellow Branch which it follows north. The trail hits a dirt road along the way. When that road forks, follow the left fork to Va. 602.

Blacksburg Ranger District

The Blacksburg District lies north of the New River along the Virginia-West Virginia line. The Appalachian Trail runs through a part of the district.

For current information on trails in the district, contact the District Ranger, 104 Hubbard, Blacksburg, Va. 24060. The telephone is 703-552-4641.

55-1 — Potts Mountain Trail — From the Appalachian Trail 1¾ miles east of Virginia Route 613 to Va. 636 at the state line.
Length: 7.5 miles
USGS Quads: Waiteville, Va., Interior, Va.
Description: The A.T. crosses Va. 613 just south of the White Rocks Recreation Area. Follow the A.T. past Stony Creek Lookout tower, climbing from 3972 feet at the road to 4128 feet at the tower. Beyond the tower, the A.T. turns south and the Potts Mountain trail continues east at 4100 feet.

After another 1⅔ miles at White Rocks, the trail turns north, dropping from 3900 to 3700 feet and then turning northeast for ½ mile. The trail then forks. Take the right fork back to the state line ridge, which is Potts Mountain, and follow it northeast to Va. 636.

New Castle Ranger District
This district lies immediately north of the Blacksburg District.

For current information on trails, contact the District Ranger, New Castle, Va., 24127. The telephone is 703-864-5195.
55-2 — Potts Mountain Trail — From Virginia 636 (the district boundary) at the state line about three miles south of Waiteville to Va. Route 311 10 miles west of New Castle at Forest Road 177.
Length: 12 miles
USGS Quads: Waiteville, Va., Craig Springs, Paint Bank, Va., Potts Creek, Va.
Description: This is a continuation of the trail described on the Blacksburg District. From 2900 feet at 636, the trail heads northeast on the ridge of Potts Mountain, climbing slightly to 3300 feet in about two miles. The trail forks north of the highway; follow the left fork.

Arnolds Knob at 3932 feet is the highest point on the ridge that the trail follows. Six miles from 636, the trail begins to follow a dirt road on which it continues for 3½ miles. Then two trails head north within a few yards of each other. They cross just off the road, and from the cross, the trail to the left goes to a spring and the Potts Mountain trail heads to the right, winding around to the east.

The trail ends at 311 at 3454 feet at a picnic area along the road.
184 — Potts Arm Trail — From Forest Road 177 3½ miles northeast of Va. 311 to Forest Road 176 about one mile north of Forest Road 604.
Length: 6 miles

USGS Quad: Potts Creek, Va.

Description: From the road at 3500 feet, the trail follows a long spur ridge east, staying fairly level for a good part of its length and then dropping steeply downhill to 2200 feet at the road.

334 — Price Broad Mountain Trail — From Forest Road 184 (Patterson Creek Road) six miles northeast of Va. Route 606 to Forest Road 183 or Va. Route 748.

Length: 10 miles

USGS Quads: Oriskany, Va., New Castle, Va.

Description: The trail heads south up a hollow from 1133 feet, climbing up onto Price Mountain at 1900 feet. Once on the ridge, it turns southwest, gradually climbing to 2710 feet. It then begins a slow decline in altitude until it reaches Va. 606 at 1964 feet. The Sulphur Ridge Trail comes in from the northwest about a mile to a mile and a half north of 606.

From 606 south, the trail follows the ridge of Broad Mountain along the Craig-Botetourt County line. It climbs as high as 2964 feet before dropping to 1900 at Forest Road 183.

149 — Sulphur Ridge Trail — From Sulphur Springs alongside Va. Route 606 one mile south of the junction between 606 and Virginia Route 612. Ends at Price Broad Mountain Trail 1½ miles north of Va. 606.

Length: 4.8 miles

USGS Quad: New Castle, Va.

Description: From the springs at 1400 feet, the trail heads north up the ridge and the curves around to the southeast to hit the Price Broad Mountain Trail at 2600 feet.

262 — Lick Branch Trail — From Forest Road 183 ½ mile east of the Craig-Botetourt County Line (the terminus of the Price Broad Mountain Trail) to Virginia Route 311 ½ mile south of New Castle. A dirt road heads east from 311 for 1½ mile to a ford over Craig Creek at the mouth of Lick Branch.

Length: 6.7 miles

USGS Quads: Catawba, Va., and New Castle, Va.

Description: From the lower end, the trail follows Lick Branch southeast from 1300 feet. Near its head, the creek makes a sharp turn to the northeast. Passing the head of the creek at 1800 feet, the trail turns southeast to climb up quickly to Broad Run Mountain at 2600 feet.

The trail turns northwest and then forks with the right fork angling downslope to Forest Road 183. Take 183 ½ mile north to the county line and the meeting with the Price Broad Run Mountain Trail and the North Mountain Trail.

263 — North Mountain Trail — From Forest Road 183 at the Price — Botetourt County Line to Va. Route 311 at McAfee Gap.
Length: 13.2 miles
USGS Quads: New Castle, Va., Catawba, Va., Looney, Va.
Description: This trail follows the ridge line of North Mountain for its entire length. Average elevation is about 2400 feet. It drops to 1700 feet at McAfee Gap.

Glenwood Ranger District

The Appalachian Trail runs through this district. It also offers a number of short trails which connect with the A.T. or with each other. For current information, contact the District Ranger, Natural Bridge Station, Va., 24579. The telephone is 703-291-2188.

326 — Wildcat Trail — From the Cave Mountain Recreation Area to the top of Wildcat Mountain.
Length: 4 miles
USGS Quad: Arnold Valley, Va.
Description: A pretty fair climb. The trail heads south from the campground on a dirt road from 1200 feet following a creek bed. After about a mile, it leaves the road and makes a steep climb up to the top of the mountain at 2695 feet.

15 — Pine Mountain Trail — From Virginia Route 622 to Forest Road 768. From Arcadia, Va., and Va. 614, the trailhead is one mile north on the east side of the road.
Length: 4.9 miles
USGS Quad: Arnold Valley, Va.
Description: The trail follows an old jeep road from 820 feet at Va. 622. It climbs up to the west briefly and then doubles back east, climbing with switchbacks up to 1986 feet. It then makes a slower climb to 2198 on Pine Ridge 2½ miles from the start.

After heading northeast on the ridge, it doubles back southeast along Thomas Mountain, hitting a dirt road at 2052 feet. This road is Forest Road 768. Go left briefly to Forest Road 780 which leads north to the Cave Mountain campground four miles away.

18 — Cornelius Creek Trail — From Forest Road 59 two miles east of the North Creek campground to the Appalachian Trail.
Length: 3.1 miles
USGS Quad: Arnold Valley, Va.
Description: The trail follows the creek up stream from North Creek which parallels the forest road, climbing from 1500 feet at the road to 2300 feet. Two trails climb from the creek to Backbone Ridge to the east. Both reach a dirt road on the ridge about ½ mile apart.

Take the dirt road south and it becomes a trail to the A.T. Take it north and it winds along the slope of the Blue Ridge to Apple Orchard Falls.

17 — Apple Orchard Falls — Forest Road 59 2½ miles east of the North Creek campground to the Appalachian Trail at Forest Road 812.

Length: 2.7 miles

USGS Quad: Arnold Valley, Va.

Description: This blue-blazed trail heads south from Forest Road 59 at 1600 feet, proceeding up the creek toward Apple Orchard Falls a bit over a mile upstream. The falls are at 2400 feet. In the area of the falls, the trail is quite steep. It continues to climb, hitting the Appalachian Trail at 3200 feet. Take the A.T. a short distance east to Forest Road 812. The road heads south a short distance to the Blue Ridge Parkway at the Sunset Field Overlook.

2 — Piney Ridge Trail — From Forest Road 54 to the Appalachian Trail. Forest Road 54 looks like a driveway that branches off to the west of U.S. Route 501 1½ miles south of the Snowden Bridge over the James River. From 501, 54 goes ½ mile to the forest boundary. About 100 yards beyond the boundary, the trail takes off on a logging road to the right. The junction with the A.T. is just north of the Marble Spring Shelter.

Length: 3.5 miles

USGS Quad: Snowden Va.

Descritpion: The trail leaves the road at about 900 feet and starts climbing up the ridge. It reaches the ridge crest at about 1800 feet and then.climbs slowly on the ridge to 2400 feet at the A.T.

3 — Hunting Creek — From Forest Road 45 to the Appalachian Trail. To reach the trail head, take Va. 602 north from Va. 122 to Forest Road 45 which parallels Hunting Creek. The Trail takes off from the end of the road. At the other end, the trail meets the A.T. and the Blue Ridge Parkway just south of the Thunder Ridge Overlook.

Length: 3 miles

USGS Quad: Snowden, Va.

Description: The trail takes off from the end of the road at about 1900 feet, following the creek up to about 2390 feet. From there, it climbs steeply up the side of Thunder Ridge with many switchbacks to reach the Parkway and the A.T. at 3500 feet.

7 — Balcony Falls — From Va. 782 to the Appalachian Trail. Va. 759 crosses the James River south of Natural Bridge Station. Va. 782 branches off to the east. Follow it to a dead end where Forest Road 602, which is gated, branches off to the right. The trail

meets the A.T. on the north slope of Hickory Stand at 2588 feet.
Length: 3 miles
USGS Quad: Snowden, Va.
Description: From 800 feet at the road, the trail skirts the foot of
the ridge, heading northeast roughly parallel to the James River.
It turns southeast after about one mile to begin a steep ascent of
the Blue Ridge, climbing quickly to 1800 feet. On the ridge, it
turns southwest and then almost straight south on a gentler up
slope to its junction with the A.T. Much of the trail on the ridge
top follows an old road. It meets the A.T. about ½ mile north of
the trails up Gunter Ridge and Belfast Creek.

8 — Gunter Ridge — From Virginia Route 759 to the Appalachian
Trail. Follow 759 south from the James River for about a mile to a
sign identifying the trail. At the upper end, the trail joins with the
Big Belfast Trail to meet the A.T. on the west slope of Hickory
Stand.
Length: 4.5 miles
USGS Quad: Snowden, Va
Description: From the highway, the trail goes east on a gradual
ascent from about 750 feet to 1000 feet where the trail crosses
Little Hellgate Creek. From the crossing, the trail climbs steeply
with many switchbacks up Gunter Ridge, reaching 2000 feet
quickly and then climbing more slowly to the junction with the
Big Belfast Trail at 2517 feet. The two trails proceed east together
a few hundred yards to the A.T. The junction is about two miles
north of the Marble Spring Shelter.

9 — Big Belfast Trail — From Virginia Route 781 to the Appalachian Trail. Va. 781 goes south from the James River to Va. 759
which angles southeast along to East Fork of Elk Creek to Belfast
Creek and a sign identifying the trail. The trail meets the A.T.
along with the Gunter Ridge Trail described above.
Length: 3 miles
USGS Quad: Snowden, Va
Description: The trail follows Belfast Creek to its head at 2200
feet, up from 1000 feet at the road. From the head of the creek it
is just over ½ mile to the junction with the Gunter Ridge Trail at
2517 feet.

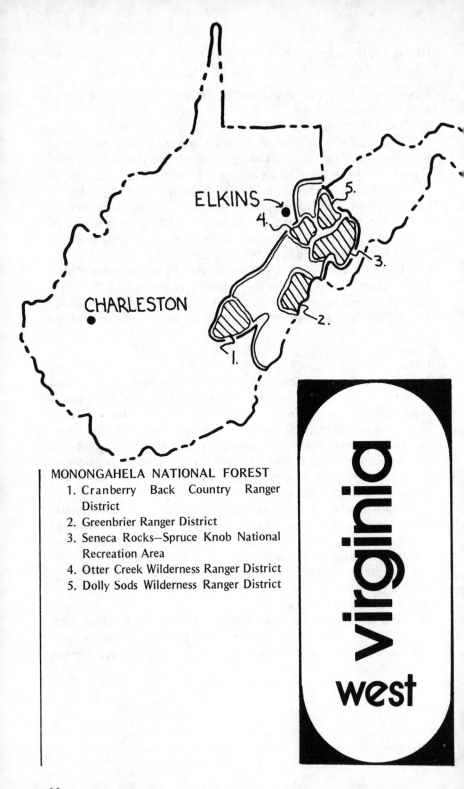

ELKINS

CHARLESTON

MONONGAHELA NATIONAL FOREST
1. Cranberry Back Country Ranger District
2. Greenbrier Ranger District
3. Seneca Rocks–Spruce Knob National Recreation Area
4. Otter Creek Wilderness Ranger District
5. Dolly Sods Wilderness Ranger District

west virginia

The best hiking in this state, and from a naturalist's point of view some of the most interesting hiking in the entire southern mountains, is in the Monongahela National Forest.

It stretches over 820,000 acres of the Allegheny Mountain Range of the Appalachian System, extending from near Eglon in Preston County southwest for about 100 miles to within six miles of White Sulphur Springs in Greenbrier County. From east to west it extends from near Petersburg in Grant County to the junction of the Cherry River with the Gauley River in Nicholas County, or about 80 miles.

The forest is divided into two geologic provinces, the Ridge and Valley Province and the Allegheny Plateau Province.

The eastern part is within the Ridge and Valley Province. The western boundaries of this province are Allegheny Front Mountain in the north, Timber Ridge and Back Allegheny Mountain farther south. The topography, like that of the national forest lands in Virginia, consists of long narrow valleys interspersed with mostly longitudinal ridges. The difference in elevation between the ridges and valleys often is close to a thousand feet.

Trails in this section of the forest generally follow along the ridgetops or on the banks of streams. Short side paths connect the long trails by wide switchbacks or steep, straight climbs.

The forest lying west of the Allegheny Front is included in the Allegheny Plateau. This portion is characterized by high altitude plateaus interspersed with scores of rugged peaks that rise to elevations of more than 4000 feet.

Rainfall is much greater in the Plateau than in the Ridge and Valley Province, because weather fronts come generally from the west and most of the moisture is dissipated before it gets over the mountains to the state's eastern border.

The broad expanses of level land in the Plateau Province provide little protection from wind. The huge numbers of treeless areas can partly be explained by the effects of widespread fires and the low temperatures and frequent winter ice storms that keep vegetation stunted.

The soil in many areas is highly acidic, which also discourages growth of trees. The heath meadows in West Virginia's highlands are comparable to the heath balds on the Appalachian peaks farther south.

There is reason to believe there were once many more trees than there are today, however. Lumbering interests clear-cut huge areas of red spruce, and early settlers set fires to convert the fields to pasture or to encourage blueberry growth. This practice had worked where soil was underlain by limestone, but in the fragile ecosystem of the high plateaus, where peat moss was often the major ground cover, the fires simply burned down to bedrock. The landscape is still recovering. Today, coal companies and proponents of more expressways and other kinds of heavy development offer different threats.

The fact that so many interesting and beautiful wilderness areas are still preserved in the state is due to the diligent efforts of a number of conservation organizations.

One of the most active of these is the West Virginia Highlands Conservancy. The efforts of the Conservancy's membership have been largely responsible for saving places like Dolly Sods, the Otter Creek Drainage System, and Cranberry Back Country from complete destruction by various commercial interests. Dolly Sods and Otter Creek have now been declared wilderness areas, and Cranberry Glades is a wilderness study area. Their status does not completely protect them. Mining claims can still be pressed. But they are much safer than they were.

If you plan a trip to West Virginia, we heartily recommend that you order from this group the booklets they have put together on these areas. Their publications provide thorough descriptions of the natural and human history of these wilderness areas and also detail the threats to these places and the lobbying efforts to save them.

This organization has also published a *Hiking Guide to the Monongahela National Forest and Vicinity* ($2.00) which is one of the best local efforts we've ever seen. It was compiled by a committee of 20 people who, over a period of several years, personally hiked all the trails they describe.

We believe part of the purpose of our book is to act as a kind of catalog to acquaint you with such local guides in specific regions where they exist. The address for the West Virginia Highlands Conservancy is c/o Carolyn Killoran, 6202 Division Road, Huntington, West Virginia. The publications can also be purchased from Mrs. Mary Rieffenberger, Rte. 1, Box 253, Elkins, West Virginia 26241. Membership in the Conservancy is $5. Cost of the *Dolly Sods* book is $1.25; the *Otter Creek* book is 75 cents; and the *Cranberry Back Country* book is 50 cents.

The Potomac Appalachian Trail Club has also done much work on trail maintenance in the Monongahela National Forest, and a new organization, the West Virginia Scenic Trails Association, is currently planning an Allegheny Trail which will run the entire length of the forest. Address of this group is P.O. Box 4042, Charleston, West Virginia 25304.

Trails in the Dolly Sods Scenic Area

Location: Red Creek Campground, which makes a good base camp for exploration in this area, can be reached by driving east from Laneville on Forest Road 19 about five miles, then north on Forest Road 75 for five more miles. The official Scenic Area comprises 10,500 acres located north of Highway 19 and east of Highway 75.

Length: The 10 trails within the Scenic Area total 27 miles

USGS Quads: Laneville, Blackbird Knob, Hopeville, Blackwater Falls, W. Va.

Description: The Dolly Sods Scenic Area is located in the highlands of the Allegheny Plateau. It is bordered on the east by Allegheny Front Mountain and on the west by Cabin Mountain. The area is drained by Red Creek and its tributaries.

The region that can be identified geographically as Dolly Sods actually includes more than 32,000 acres, much of it in private land. In 1975, a portion of this that overlaps but does not duplicate the Scenic Area was named one of 16 new National Wilderness Areas by the U.S.Congress.

Dolly Sods contains a number of wooded areas, especially along stream banks. But it is particularly known and revered by botanists for the unusual vegetation found on its treeless upland bogs and windswept plains. The terrain and vegetation is normally found much closer to the Arctic Circle. Peat and spaghnum moss are found in the bogs; so is sundew, a tiny insectivorous plant.

The plains are filled with huckleberries (blueberries to you non-West Virginians); these plants draw local visitors in late summer. During the middle of September, hawk migration takes place in Dolly Sods and naturalists gather to identify and band the various species.

Dolly Sods was not always so bare of trees, according to the Forest Service. Prior to extensive logging and extensive burning to create pastureland in the last century, the plains were covered with trees — virgin stands of red spruce and hemlock, along with excellent stands of northern hardwood in the cove areas. These forested sections were interspersed with heath barrens (similar to the heath balds of the Appalachians farther south) and small open bogs.

Erosion increased when the tree cover was gone, and many local settlers (possibly including descendants of the original Dahle or "Dolly" family) were driven from their homes by flash floods. (The last major floods occurred in the 1950s).

Tree and ground cover are growing over the area again today. You can find patches of land in all stages of ecologic succession.

Current threats to the plains come from strip coal mining concerns, proponents of an expressway across the Sods, and an electric power project.

Before we describe the trails in the Scenic Area, we should note that the spring thaw can't be counted on in this high plateau country until May. If you go then or earlier, plan on coping with lots of melting snow. Be sure to carry your compass and extra food supplies. The trails are not always well marked, landmarks are sometimes hard to come by in this kind of terrain, and fog shrouds the plains, particularly in spring and late fall.

Early summer is a good time to see wildflowers, but until you've seen a bog in the fantastic fiery colors of autumn you've never seen a real fall display.

511 — Blackbird Knob Trail — 2 miles. This trail runs west from Red Creek Campground on Forest Road 75 to Blackbird Knob (elevation 3950 feet). The area is mainly open country, with occasional clumps of red spruce. There are beaver ponds near the point where you cross Alder Creek, about half a mile from the campground. At the trail crossing of Red Creek, a jeep trail cuts off to the right.

The east side of Blackbird Knob is partially wooded. The trail does not actually climb to the top of this mountain but skirts its southern slopes to join the northern end of Red Creek Trail.

The U.S. Geological Survey map shows Blackbird Knob Trail continuing west across the left fork of Red Creek and on to Cabin Mountain, but Forest Service maps show it stopping at the Knob. The West Virginia Highlands Conservancy people say the portion of the trail west of the Knob is "essentially nonexistent."

514 — Red Creek Trail — 6¾ miles. Runs south from Blackbird Knob gently downhill to Red Creek at the point where it forks. (Another trail goes west here — #553, Breathed Mountain Trail).

Red Creek Trail follows the stream for which it was named its entire length. The water in Red Creek is an unusual color, a mixture of brown, red, and yellow that results, according to the Highlands Conservancy booklet, "from tannic acid derived from spruce needles, and from the numerous spaghnum bogs."

From the fork in the creek, the trail continues south down the west banks on steep slopes above the creek at elevations between 3500 and 3600 feet. The area along the creek is wooded.

Soon after you pass a junction with Rocky Point Trail (#554), the Red Creek Trail will cross the creek — just south of the mouth of Fisher Springs. Another trail goes east up Fisher Springs Run.

Red Creek Trail continues south along an old railroad grade above the creek past the official Scenic Area Boundary at the mouth of Big Stonecoal Run. (Stonecoal Trail, #513, branches northwest here across Red Creek on a footbridge.)

Red Creek Trail angles west, still along the creek at an elevation of about 3100 feet, and comes to another trail (#552) at the mouth of Little Stonecoal Run. The trail ends at Laneville Cabin on Forest Road 19 — four miles east of Route 32 and 2½ miles west of Dolly Sods Picnic Area.

553 — Breathed Mountain Trail — 2½ miles, heads west uphill quickly about 300 feet to an elevation of 3800. It turns southwest then across a wide flat treeless area before turning northwest through a forested section, past a stream blocked by beaver dams, and uphill gently west to a junction with Big Stonecoal Trail and Forest Road 80. There's a designated backcountry campsite at this junction.

513 — Big Stonecoal Trail — 4 miles, starts at the headwaters (near highway 80) and follows the streamcourse of Big Stonecoal Run south 3½ miles to a junction with Red Creek Trail. Much of the northern part of the trail is on an old railroad bed; the southern part follows a logging road. Some of the area is forested but there are also treeless areas. You will pass a number of waterfalls and rapids.

There are four designated camping areas along the way. You will be able to see the signs of previous occupancy; camp there anyway to avoid despoiling new areas.

The first campsite is at the north end of the trail, just off highway 80. The second is just past the mouth of a small intermittent stream in an open area. The third is past a second small stream; and the fourth is at a junction with Dunkenbarger Trail.

Shortly after this junction and about a mile north of Red Creek you will see Rocky Point Trail coming in from the east.

554 — Rocky Point Trail — 2 miles, connects Red Creek Trail north of Fisher Springs with Big Stonecoal Trail. It heads uphill from Red Creek, then south around the southern end of Breathed Mountain (elevation 3820) and north again to meet Big Stonecoal Trail.

510 — Fisher Springs Trail — 2 miles, runs northeast from the mouth of Fisher Springs Run at Red Creek along an embankment above the creek for a mile, then northeast across a high plateau another mile east to Forest Road 75. Elevation ranges from 3500 feet at the creek to 3900 feet at Forest Road 75.

552 — Little Stonecoal Trail — 1¾ miles, runs north and west from the mouth of Little Stonecoal Run to a junction with Cabin Mountain and Dunkenbarger Trails. It follows the creek for the first mile in a climb of 800 feet from 2800 feet to 3600 feet. Waterfalls are plentiful. We are told that parts of this trail may become overgrown from time to time by fast-growing rhododendron.

Cabin Mountain Trail — 2½ miles, continues northwest from the north end of Little Stonecoal Trail through wooded land and a couple of treeless areas 2½ miles to Forest Road 80. Then it proceeds along the road to a junction with Stonecoal and Breathed Mountain Trails and on north outside the Scenic Area along the slopes of Cabin Mountain.

552 — Dunkenbarger Run Trail — 1¼ miles, connects Little Stonecoal and Cabin Mountain Trails with Big Stonecoal Trail. It passes through mature forest on a railroad grade.

Rohrbaugh Plains Trail — 3 miles. This trail, opened by the Forest Service and the Potomac Appalachian Trail Club in the fall of 1973, is one of very few in the scenic area that gives you a look at the open plains of the Sods away from a creek bank. It runs north from the Dolly Sods Picnic Area to Fisher Springs Run just west of Red Creek. The trail is blazed with blue paint.

Trails in the Otter Creek Area

Location: Take U.S. Route 33 and West Virginia Highway 4 east 12 miles from Elkins to the Alpena Gap Recreation Area. Turn north on a gravel road, past several strip mines, to the road's end at the headwaters of Otter Creek. (Forest Road 91, the Stuart Memorial Drive, heads west from this road just before its end to nearby Bear Heaven Campground and on into Elkins).

Length: There are 56 miles of interconnecting trails in the Otter Creek drainage.

USGS Quads: Parsons, Mozark Mountain, Bowden, and Harman, W.Va.

Description: Otter Creek basin is a high, wild plateau of some 18,000 acres that towers over the hills and valleys that surround it in northeastern West Virginia. It is completely uninhabited and seems much more remote than its size would indicate because it incorporates an entire watershed system. The mountains that rise to the east and west of Otter Creek cut off even the sounds of civilization.

Timber in the area was last cut over about 60 years ago and

since there are many fast-growing species of trees in the region, the forest is so well-grown today that ferns and grasses, rhododendron and laurel are the main understory. Most of the terrain is wooded, but there are three notable bogs with Canadian-zone vegetation. Trails that we describe touch two of those bogs.

This area shelters a stable breeding population of black bear. There are also wild turkey, deer and grouse, and trout fishing is allowed on Otter Creek between its mouth at Dry Fork and Big Springs Gap.

Otter Creek and the trail which runs alongside it form the heart of this wilderness. The stream flows north from a swampy area just north of Dry Fork mountain (at the end of the Alpena Gap road) some 11 miles to empty into Dry Fork Creek. A hike along this trail will give you the best look at the entire area. There's an Adirondack shelter located near the trail's midpoint at the mouth of Devil's Gulch Creek at the junction with the Moore Run Trail. Here's a detailed description:

Otter Creek Trail, 11 miles. The entire route follows an old railroad bed and offers fairly easy walking. The trail crosses the creek five times and in wet weather may require some knee deep wading.

After the first mile, Yellow Creek Trail branches off to the left (west).

At mile three, you will reach a junction with Mylius Trail, which runs east about half a mile to connect with the area's other major trail running along the top of Shavers Mountain (Shavers Mountain Trail, 11 miles).

At mile four, just past Devil's Gulch, you will pass Moore Run Trail heading left (west) up to and along Moore Run Creek. Elevation on the creek at this point is 2750 feet. The shelter here has accommodations for six people, and the area around it is flat and ideal for setting up tents. There is also a picnic table.

Possession Camp Run is the small stream coming down a draw from the east just south of Moore Run.

At mile 5.5 you will cross from Randolph into Tucker County. The creek elevation is a little lower now — about 2300 feet. Hills slope up on both sides to more than 3300 feet. The creek and trail curve east just past mile 8 at Big Springs Gap. Big Springs Gap Trail runs west from this point to connect with a road that leads north four miles to the town of Parsons.

From Big Springs Gap to the trail's end at Dry Fork Creek is a distance of just over 2¾ miles. There is a steep drop down to Dry Fork and a bridge across it to connect with West Virginia Route

72 some 2½ miles south of the town of Hendricks.

Spur trails east and west from Otter Creek Trail:

Yellow Creek Trail, 3 miles, leads west from an elevation of 2990 feet at Otter Creek along the banks of Yellow Creek for 1¼ miles to a swampy area and a junction with McGowan Mountain Road and the Little Black Fork Trail. (*Little Black Fork Trail* heads west on Little Black Fork Creek one mile, then cuts south across a peak of Dry Fork Mountain — elevation 3850 feet — and down to Stuart Memorial Drive just east of Stuart Knob).

The Yellow Creek Trail follows McGowan Mountain Road west and north for half a mile before branching left and north to parallel the road for 1¼ miles. This part is within sight and sound of traffic on the road and for that reason is not highly recommended. Yellow Creek Trail deadends at a back country designated campsite and becomes McGowan Mountain Trail just south of the road crossing.

McGowan Mountain Trail, 2⅔ miles, continues north parallel to and on the east side of McGowan Mountain Road. It follows bluffs above the road downhill from 3870 feet to 3350 feet at another designated campsite and a junction with Moore Run Trail.

Moore Run Trail, 4 miles, heads west from Otter Creek (at elevation 2750) at the shelter just north of Devils Gulch. It runs north to join Moore Run, then west to a swampy area (elevation 3200 feet) and junction with Turkey Run Trail at mile 2.5. This spot is one of the three bogs we mentioned earlier. The trail continues west another 1½ miles to the designated campsite (elevation 3350 feet) at a junction with McGowan Mountain Trail just east of McGowan Mountain Road. This trail is uphill all the way, a climb of some 600 feet through mature forest. There are occasional good views of Otter Creek.

Turkey Run Trail, 2 miles, runs north to connect Moore Run Trail with Turkey Run Road (which connects with McGowan Mountain Road and leads north four miles to the town of Parsons). Most of it follows gentle slopes up to, along and down from the wide flat top of a spur of McGowan Mountain. Elevation on top is about 3600 feet. The trail ends at the road near the headwaters of Turkey Run Creek. Much of the timber is spruce and hemlock.

Green Mountain Trail, 5 miles, runs east from Otter Creek at a designated campsite (elevation 2250 feet) just south of Turkey Run Creek. It connects with Shavers Mountain Trail at an elevation of 3700 feet. Most of the climbing is in the first mile, a very steep grade up from 2250 to 3400 feet. The trail on top of Green

Mountain after the first mile curves south and then west to reach Shavers Lick Run at mile four. At the headwaters of this creek is another of the Canadian-zone bogs.

Go north downstream half a mile to a fork, then turn south to reach the ridgetop of Shavers Mountain and the junction with Shavers Mountain Trail in another half mile.

Big Spring Gap Trail, one mile, goes west from the Otter Creek Trail at the big bend three miles from the junction with Route 72 at Dry Fork. There's a designated campsite at the junction of Otter Creek and Big Spring Gap Trails. You will climb in the mile's walk from 2050 feet at Otter Creek to 2550 feet at the wilderness boundary and road that leads north to Parsons.

Shavers Mountain Trail, 13 miles. This trail follows the ridge top of the mountain that forms the eastern boundary of the Otter Creek Wilderness. Portions of this trail can be found farther south in the Greenbrier District of the forest, but there are gaps between that part of the trail and this.

Shavers Mountain Trail actually begins at the Alpena Gap Recreation Area on U.S. 33, but some maps label the first two miles as Middle Mountain Trail. You can also reach it from the headwaters of Otter Creek and beginning of the Otter Creek Trail by taking the Hedrick Camp Cutoff Trail one mile east to the top of Shavers Mountain.

About 3¾ miles north of the Hedrick Camp Cutoff, you will come to another link with the Otter Creek Trail. The *Mylius Trail* runs downhill and west about a mile to Otter Creek Trail. It also runs downhill off the east slopes of Shavers Mountain to connect with West Virginia Route 12 at its junction with state route 162 on Glady Creek.

Elevation on the Shavers Mountain Trail varies between 3600 and 3815 feet. The last 2½ miles follow a dirt road that leads east across Dry Fork to West Virginia Route 72 five miles south of Hendricks.

Loop trips can be made using a variety of the side trails connecting the long Shavers Mountain and Otter Creek Trails.

Cranberry Back Country
Location: In the southwestern part of Pocahontas County, Gauley Ranger District of the Monongahela National Forest, about two miles by Forest Service Road from West Virginia Route 39 between Mill Point and Richwood.
Length: There are 75 miles of hiking trails in the Cranberry Back Country. There are also 75 miles of roads closed to unauthorized

motor vehicles; most of the roads are located along streams and combine nicely with the trails to make loop hikes. One should limit a day's hike to six or eight miles because of the rough topography.

USGS Quads: Western Springs SW, W. Va.; Western Springs, SE, W. Va.; and Camden on Gauley, W. Va. These are the only 7½' maps available for this area. The Mingo, Lobelia and Richwood 15' maps are quite old but will give you a general idea of contour and drainage systems.

Description: The most interesting aspect of the Cranberry Back Country is its bogs or muskegs, known in West Virginia as glades. These are treeless, poorly drained areas found high in the mountain valleys. There are numerous bogs in all stages of development and of various sizes scattered throughout this state. Cranberry Glades is by far the largest area in the Monongahela National Forest.

It covers a level area three miles long and one-fourth to one mile wide, lying at an elevation of 3400 feet and surrounded by mountains ranging from 4000 to 4600 feet. It includes "about 400 acres covered with a dense thicket of shrubs, chiefly speckled alder, about 200 acres of bog forest, and 120 acres of open glade covered with spaghnum lichens and mosses," according to a booklet by Roy B. Clarkson called *The Vascular Flora of the Monongahela National Forest, West Virginia.*

The officially designated Back Country which includes the Glades consists of about 53,000 acres. It was acquired by the Forest Service in 1934. No motorized traffic except Forest Service maintenance vehicles is allowed.

The recently designated Cranberry Wilderness Study Area includes 36,300 acres.

West Virginia's bogs, like the high peaks of the Great Smoky Mountains farther south, are refuges for life normally found in Canada. The ancestors to these Canadian plants and animals were presumably forced south by the glaciers of the Ice Age nearly 10,000 years ago. For this reason, places like Cranberry Glades are a delight to both amateur and professional botanists.

Muskeg is an Algonquin Indian word meaning "trembling earth," and Cranberry Glades certainly fits that description. If you stand on one side of the spaghnum moss bed at Big Glade and jump up and down, you can see trees shake on the far side of the glade. The large hummocks you will see in the big wet open areas are probably pigeon-wheat moss.

Cranberry Glades contains the southernmost communities of

quite a few plants and animals. Maurice Brooks, professor of wild-life management at West Virginia University and author of an excellent layman's natural history book called *The Appalachians*, describes a fascinating incident in which he and his father (botanist Fred E. Brooks) discovered a yellownose vole in Cranberry Glades. It had not previously been known south of New York's Catskills, and its closest relative, the yellow-cheeked vole, is abundant in the Arctic prairie.

The area is the southernmost known breeding spot for six bird species — Swainson's and hermit thrushes, Nashville and mourning warblers, northern waterthrushes, and purple finches.

The presence of carnivorous plants like sundew and horned bladderwort is particularly interesting; and bog rosemary is found in Cranberry Glades hundreds of miles south of the next most southern station in the Pocono Mountains of Pennsylvania.

Other major bogs in the Monongahela National Forest can be found at: Canaan Valley, Backbone Mountain, and the head of Fisher Spring Run (Otter Creek Wilderness) in Tucker County; Sinks of Gandy and Blister Run, Randolph County; and Blister Swamp in Pocahontas County.

Rainfall is more than 60 inches during the year and annual snowfall is 90 inches in the Cranberry Back Country. The temperature is lower and the humidity higher than in most regions of the Southern Mountains, points which backpackers should keep in mind when collecting their gear. Water tables are just below the surface, and soaked spaghnum moss is a good insulator.

There are eight trail shelters in the area, each accommodating six people and all of them located along the Cranberry River drainage. They are equipped with fireplaces, wooden picnic tables, and garbage cans.

If you are tent camping, there are no restrictions on where you seek shelter for the night. Nor are permits required for campfires. Obviously, you are expected to clean up your camp before moving on and to pack out everything you brought in. Otherwise, specific restrictions will soon be necessary.

The Kennison Mountain Trail and the Forks of Cranberry Trail are probably the most scenic of those we shall describe. If you want real solitude, however, the Middle Fork of the Williams is a good spot.

When you first look at a trail map of the Cranberry Back Country, it seems hopelessly confusing. There is a sort of method to the madness, however. There are three major east-west routes, and all the other trails are spurs branching off north and south from them. This arrangement allows you to put together a huge variety of loop trips.

The northernmost east-west route is Forest Service Road 108, which parallels the Middle Fork of the Williams River. The Forest Service has deliberately kept this area as primitive as possible. There are no campgrounds and no trail shelters.

The middle east-west route is called, ironically, the North-South Trail. It was given this name because the Forest Service eventually plans to extend it all the way from Blackwater Falls near Dolly Sods south to end at Summit Lake at the southern boundary of the Cranberry Back Country.

The southernmost east-west route is Forest Service Road 76, which parallels the Cranberry River. All the Adirondack shelters are either on or very near this road.

Trails Near the Middle Fork of Williams River

242 — Little Fork Trail — 3½ miles. Follows the Little Fork Creek north from the North-South Trail to reach Forest Road 108 and the Middle Fork of the Williams River directly across that river from the County Line Trail (#206). In wet weather there may be difficulty in fording. The Middle Fork can be rather swift.

Laurelly Branch, 2⅔ miles. This trail is not listed on the U.S. Forest Service map of the area, but the West Virginia Highland Conservancy's *Hiking Guide to Monongahela National Forest* says it does exist on the ground and provides a good link between F.R. 108 and the North-South Trail. It begins on 108 about halfway between Laurelly Branch and Hell-for-Certain Branch and runs southwest to join the North-South Trail between Birchlog Run and Tumbling Rock Run.

206 — County Line Trail, 11½ miles. It begins at Forest Road 108 directly north across the road from the Little Fork Trail (#242). To get on this trail requires fording the Middle Fork of the Williams River, which may be difficult after periods of prolonged rainfall.

The trail follows a ridgetop between the Middle Fork and north (main) fork of the Williams River to a peak at 3541 feet. It runs south then along northern and eastern slopes of a hill at elevation 3400, crossing from Webster into Pocahontas County, then northeast along level ground to cross District Line Trail (#248) and Lick Branch. It continues north across Forest Road 108 and the Middle Fork of Williams River and up Bannock Shoals Run to connect with Turkey Mountain Trail (#209).

209 — Turkey Mountain Trail — 16 miles. This trail is not marked and may be difficult to see at its eastern end on F.R. 135 just north of Tea Creek Campground. It runs west to reach Forest Road 133 at the headwaters of White Oak Fork. The terrain is mainly wooded but there are occasional views of the Williams River and its tributaries to the south. At the headwaters of Twin Branch Run about 10 miles west of the trail's eastern end a short spur trail, *Twin Branch Trail* [#205) leads south 2½ miles to F.R. 86.

248 — District Line Trail — 3 miles. Its northern terminus is at County Line Trail where Lick Branch crosses it. The south end is at Big Beechy Trail just east of the headwaters of Beechy Run. It follows a wide, flat ridgetop at elevations of 3800 to 4100 feet.

207 — Big Beechy Trail — 4½ miles. The western end of this trail is at F.R. 108 at the mouth of Beechy Run. It follows the creek a short distance north, then curves south and gently uphill from an elevation of 2800 to 4000 feet in the first two miles, following a ridge line east and then downhill in a southeasterly direction to cross North Branch Creek, then F.R. 76. The trail ends at West Virginia Route 150, the Highland Scenic Highway, about five miles south of the Tea Creek Campground.

688 — North-South Trail — 19½ miles. This trail is called the Red and Black Trail on USGS maps. It begins at Forest Road 76 east of the gate by Cranberry Campground, heads north uphill to a point just south of the headwaters of Johnson's Run, then east and slightly south along a ridgetop at about 3700 feet. At mile 3½, it reaches a junction with *Lick Branch Trail* (#212). This short side trail leads south two miles along the creek to a shelter on F.R.76.

A mile east of that junction, the North-South Trail intersects Little Fork Trail (#242), heading north. In another ¼ mile you will intersect *Big Rough Run Trail* (#213), which follows that stream south 3½ miles to F.R. 76 about half a mile west of a trail shelter.

The next side trail east from Big Rough Run is *Birch Log Trail* (#250). This one heads south three miles along Birch Log Run to route 76 just west of the Tumbling Rock Shelter. If you want to rejoin the North-South Trail by a different route, you can take a *Tumbling Rock Trail* #214 northeast along Tumbling Rock Run three miles to a junction with the North-South about ¾ miles east of where you left it.

The last four miles of this long trail continue along the top of a wide plateau (except for one brief dip down to the headwaters of Cashcamp Run) across F.R. 76 and onto the Highland Scenic Highway about six miles south of Tea Creek Campground.

Trails in the Cranberry River Area

245 — Forks of Cranberry Trail — 5¾ miles. This trail begins on the Cranberry River about a mile south of the trail shelter located at the junction of Forest Roads 76 and 102. It heads east and sharply uphill to follow a ridgetop over to the Highland Scenic Highway on Black Mountain east of the Glades and just north of Bartow Top. It offers excellent views of Cranberry Glades to the south.

The last two miles traverse an area burned down to bedrock in the Black Mountain Fire of 1937. Scars are still eloquently visible. The West Virginia Highlands Conservancy Guide says that in June this section of the trail is "a symphony of hermit thrushes."

244 — Kennison Mountain Trail — 8½ miles. It runs southeast from the Cranberry River and F.R. 76 from the mouth of Houselog Run about a mile east of a trail shelter. It follows a long spruce-covered ridge of Kennison Mountain at elevations of 4200 and 4300 feet. It joins with Frosty Mountain Trail (heading west) just north of Forest Road 39 about 2½ miles east of the Cranberry Visitor Center. South of the Road, this trail climbs to the top of Blue Knob (elevation 4426 feet) at the junction with the Pocahontas Trail.

253 — Cow Pasture Trail — 7 miles. This trail is one of the most interesting in the entire area. It circles the big open spaghnum bogs of Cranberry Glades. Visitors are not allowed off the trails or boardwalk in the Glades without special permission, however, because of the fragile ecosystem.

235 — Frosty Gap Trail — 5¾ miles. Runs west from the Kennison Mountain Trail just north of that trail's junction with route 39. It crosses F.R. 232 in about ¼ mile, then heads uphill to Frosty Gap at elevation 4250 feet 'and follows along a ridgetop to a lookout tower at the southern end of a Forest Road on Miles Knob.

263 — Pocahontas Trail — 18 miles. This trail runs west from the Cranberry Visitor Center on the Highland Scenic Highway up to Blue Knob (elevation 4426 feet) in one mile where it intersects the Kennison Mountain Trail. It continues west through a wooded area three miles to cross Forest Road 39 about a mile east of the Falls of Hills Creek Scenic Area.

The trail heads northwest to meet *Eagle Camp Trail* (#239) in another 1½ miles. (*Eagle Camp Trail* leads south 1½ miles to the Cherry River at Forest Road 39).

The Pocahontas Trail continues northwest along a ridge at about 4000 feet, 3½ miles to the Summit Shelter at F.R. 99 and the junction with the *Fisherman Trail* (#231). *Fisherman Trail* leads north 1½ miles to the Cranberry River. Another trail shelter is located on the north side of the river at that point, but high water in wet weather may make it inaccessible.

From the Summit Shelter the trail continues west three miles more to end at F.R. 99. The West Virginia Highlands Conservancy says the Pocahontas Trail was used by pioneer settlers before the Civil War and was also a branch of the Seneca Indian Trail (now U.S. Route 219).

If you walk north on F.R. 99 about half a mile from the western end of the Pocahontas Trail, you can connect with the *Barrenshe Trail* (#256), 4½ miles. This trail leads west up to the south slopes of Briery Knob (elevation 3765 feet) then down to the headwaters of and along Barrenshe Run to F.R. 76, about a mile south of the Woodbine Picnic Area.

Spruce Knob — Seneca Rocks National Recreation Area

Location: This recreation area, established in 1965 by Act of Congress, is comprised of 100,000 acres of lush back country divided into two units and separated by West Virginia Route 28 running north and south between Jordan Run and Circleville.

Length: The Seneca Rocks Unit contains one major 23-mile trail and a number of short spur trails providing access from the main trail to roads. The Spruce Knob Unit contains a network of trails that totals about 56 miles.

USGS Quads: Whitmer, W. Va.; Spruce Knob, W.Va.; and Onego, W.Va. for the Spruce Knob Unit. Circleville NW, Onego SW, Upper Tract, Hopeville, and Petersburg NW for the Seneca Rocks Unit.

Description: The *Seneca Rocks Unit* is named for a 1,000 foot quartzite formation which rises above the North Fork Valley at the mouth of Seneca Creek. Besides its interest to sightseers, Seneca Rocks is considered by climbers to be the best rock climb in the east.

The unit also contains a number of other massive and interesting rock formations. North Fork Mountain is the dominant range and runs north to south almost the entire length of the unit. It is capped with erosion-resistant White Medina Sandstone and forms a habitat for a number of unusual wildflowers, lichens, mosses, and ferns.

Champe Rock, Blue Rock, and Chimney Rock are frequented by rock climbers almost as much as Seneca Rock.

The Smoke Hole, a canyon through which the South Branch of the Potomac flows for 20 miles, is located at the far northern end of this unit. There are a number of caves in the region, including the commercially-developed Smoke Hole Cave. Its name was allegedly derived from the Indians who used it as a smoke curing chamber for preserving meat. Another explanation suggests that the name came from the mist which forms when moist air rising from the cave meets the cool air outside and gives the appearance of smoke.

Smoke Hole is one of two areas in the unit designated as a Pioneer Zone and managed as a Wilderness. The other Pioneer Zone is in Hopeville Gorge.

The main hiking trail in the Seneca Rocks Unit is the *North Mountain Trail* (#501), 23 miles. Several short spur trails provide access to roads.

This trail follows the ridgetop of North Fork Mountain from U.S. 33 about five miles east of Judy Gap north almost the whole length of the Seneca Rocks Unit to Chimney Top about ¼ mile north of the spot where a spur path called the Landis Trail goes east off the mountain to Forest Road 74.

The trail is well-marked, easy to follow, and offers frequent views of the valley along the South Branch of the Potomac River to the west and of the Spruce Knob and Dolly Sods areas on the high plateau beyond that river.

There are no water sources on the mountain, so be sure to carry enough.

Elevations vary between 3000 feet and 3795 feet along the trail, but there are never any sudden, sharp climbs or descent.

The first access trail off the mountain to the east is about four miles north of route 33 at the southern boundary of the Recreation Area. This trail, actually an abandoned road, leads two miles to join West Virginia Route 8. The area around this southern section of the trail is referred to on the 1924 Circleville 15 minute map of the Geological Survey as "German Settlement." The Dolly School, possibly named for the Dahle family that also settled Dolly Sods, was located on Route 33 just west of the trail.

The second access is five miles farther north at the lookout tower just past High Knob where Forest Road 79 climbs up to the ridge top. The main trail follows this road for about a mile north of the tower, then leaves it where the road turns sharply east downhill to connect with route 74 near the Smoke Hole Campground.

The third access is three miles farther north. *The Kimble Trail* goes downhill east to Forest Road 74 directly across from the point on the main trail which offers a view of Champe Rocks. From here to the north end of the trail is about 11 miles.

The fourth access is some three miles north and is called the

Redman Trail. It proceeds northeast to the headwaters of Redman Creek and then follows that stream about two miles down to Forest Road 74.

The last access is ¾ mile south of the trail's northern terminus at Chimney Top. It is called the *Landis Trail* and also connects with Forest Road 74 about three miles south of that road's junction with West Virginia 28 leading east to Petersburg.

The *Spruce Knob Unit* of the Recreation Area is named for the high point of Spruce Mountain, highest point in West Virginia. Its elevation is 4860 feet, and its vegetation is mainly wind-stunted red spruce. Wildflowers include beautiful colonies of wild bleeding heart, dwarf dogwood, fireweed, painted trillium, and pink lady's slipper.

The main trails on this unit are the *Spruce Mountain* and *Lumberjack Trails,* which combine for a ridgetop hike of 13½ miles; the *Seneca Creek Trail*, which follows that stream for 11½ miles; and the *Allegheny Trail,* which follows the western boundary of the Recreation Area on the west side of the mountain top for 8½ miles. Smaller spur trails connect these longer trails to each other and provide access to roads.

533 — Spruce Mountain Trail — 3½ miles. This trail starts from the observation tower on Spruce Knob and runs north through wooded areas and across open heath fields to intersect with the Lumberjack and Horton-Horserock Trails uphill from the Judy Springs Campground on Seneca Creek. To reach the campground, turn left on the Horton-Horserock Trail for two miles, then south on the *Judy Springs Trail* (#512) two miles.

534 — Lumberjack Trail — 10 miles, is intersected by the other two trails near its midpoint. South of the junction with Trails #530 and #533, it runs south about 3½ miles along a west slope of the mountain to Forest Road 103. North of the junction it follows the ridge crest 6½ miles to the Strader Run Road about six miles south of Onego.

515 — Seneca Creek Trail — 11½ miles, follows the east bank of Seneca Creek along an old logging road 3½ miles north from F.R. 103 to the Judy Springs Campground, then north, still along the creek, 8 miles to the end of another old logging road at the Falls of Seneca. The road leads north about four miles to reach West Virginia Route 7 a couple of miles west of the Seneca Campground. Seneca Creek is a stream of spectacular waterfalls and wild beauty, and has the reputation of being one of the best trout streams in West Virginia.

532 — The Allegheny Trail — 8½ miles, runs north from a gate on Forest Road 103 just north of the Gatewood Lookout Tower. It follows an old road for the first 3½ miles or so along the western boundary line of the Recreation Area. When the road turns west and goes downhill to join West Virginia Route 29 at Little Italy, the trail continues north to hook up with another road at the headwaters of Gulf Run. It continues northwest on that road to state highway 31 about 1½ miles north of Whitmer.

527 — Big Run of Gandy Trail — 3 miles, goes west from Forest Road 103 at the same spot where the Allegheny Trail originates (elevation 3950 feet). It drops down to the headwaters of the South Fork of Big Run at elevation 3780 feet, then follows that creek west to state road 29 just south of Taylor Knob (elevation 3350 feet). About halfway, you will reach a junction with the North Fork of Big Run. A side trail with the cumbersome name, *North Fork of Big Run of Gandy Trail*, goes north along that stream 1½ miles to a junction with a primitive road that heads east up the mountain to intersect the Allegheny Trail and then goes on to Seneca Creek.

529 — Swallow Rock Run Trail — 2½ miles. This trail runs west from the Seneca Creek Trail about one mile south of Judy Creek Campground. It begins south of the creek named Swallow Rock Run but soon joins it and follows it west to West Virginia Route 29 and Gandy Creek about four miles south of Whitmer. About half a mile west of Seneca Creek you will cross an old road that is now the Allegheny Trail (#532).

535 — Little Allegheny Trail — 5 miles. This trail forks right (northeast) off the Allegheny Trail just before the Allegheny Trail joins a primitive road at Gulf Run. It leads north about ¼ mile, west of and parallel to Trail 515, joining Trail 515 at Highway 7 about a mile west of Seneca Campground. Elevation about 2700.

530 — Horton-Horserock Trail — 8 miles. This trail begins at the junction of Trails 533 and 534 on top of Spruce Mountain. It heads west down to the Seneca Creek Trail and follows it for ¼ mile before crossing the creek. It heads west uphill then to cross the Allegheny Trail, descends to join Lower Two Spring Run, and follows it west to highway 29 about half a mile south of Whitmer.

Trails in the Greenbrier District
Location: The part of this district that concerns us is mainly the watershed area of the Greenbrier River, with Cheat Mountain, Shavers Mountain and Back Allegheny Mountain rising above the river on the west, Little Mountain on the east. U.S. Route 33 running east from Elkins forms the area's northern border and Seneca

State Forest is at its southern end.

Length: The recently-maintained trails that we shall describe in this district total 75 miles.

USGS Quads: Glady, W.Va.; Spruce Knob, W.Va.; Thornwood, W.Va.; Durbin, W.Va.; and Beverly East, W.Va.

Description: A number of trails listed on the Forest Service Recreation Map were not in good condition or recently maintained when we visited the district in November 1974. The numbers of those trails were: 305, 307, 316, 320, 336, 337, 338, 340, 346, 347, 348, 350, 351, 361, 370, 371, 372, 374, 375, 376, 380, 381, 382, and 383.

A number of trails had been recently maintained, however, and marked with blue blazes. Much of the work had been done by men employed through the Older Americans Act (called Green Thumb in some regions of the southern mountains).

One of the most beautiful, accessible, and characteristic scenic spots in this area is found in the vicinity of Cheat Bridge. According to Roy B. Clarkson in a book called *The Vascular Flora of the Monongahela National Forest,* "here within a radius of a few miles can be seen one of the few remaining original stands of red spruce, excellent pure stands of second-growth spruce, the southernmost known colony in eastern North America of balsam fir, typical stands of northern hardwoods, and some of the rarest herbaceous plants in the state. The entire area has a Canadian aspect both in its flora and fauna. Most of the area lies at an elevation above 3700 feet and many surrounding knobs rise about 4200 feet."

One of the district's best and longest trails, *Shavers Mountain Trail* (#332), 16 miles, begins near Cheat Bridge at the Gaudineer Scenic Area on U.S. Route 250.

This trail follows the ridgetop of Shavers Mountain at elevations varying between 3600 and 4500. The eastern slopes are steep, dropping quickly down to the Greenbrier River Valley. The west slopes descend more gently to the banks of Shavers Fork.

There are two Adirondack-type shelters along the trail, one about four miles north of the Gaudineer Scenic Area, the other about 11 miles north of the Scenic Area.

Just south of the first shelter, the trail intersects a short spur, *Johns Camp Trail,* which runs west downhill ¾ mile to Forest Road 27.

About three miles farther north, it crosses Trail 338, said by rangers in the district not to be in good condition. It leads east down across the railroad tracks and the Greenbrier River to Forest

Road 44.

Two more side trails (#338 and #351) intersect the Shavers Mountain Trail south of the second shelter. Both are said not to be currently well-maintained.

The northern terminus of this trail is at West Virginia Route 22 in the town of Glady.

The second major trail in this area is the *Laurel Fork Trail* (#306), 15½ miles. This trail begins at Forest Road 97 just east of Forest Road 14 about four miles south of Laurel Fork Campground and runs north along an old jeep trail through the valley of Laurel Fork along the east side of the creek. The northern terminus is on Forest Road 14 where Beaverdam Creek crosses that road about a mile south of the McCray Creek Trail.

The Laurel Fork Trail intersects *Camp Five Run Trail* (#315) about a mile north of its beginning point. This short trail runs west 1½ miles to F.R. 14 along the banks of Camp Five Run creek. If you walk south a few hundred yards on the highway you will come to the *Lynn Knob Trail* (#317).

That trail runs west 4¼ miles up to Lynn Knob, then along an old logging road to Forest Road 44 and the Greenbrier River.

310 — Beulah Trail — 3¾ miles, crosses the Laurel Fork Trail just south of the Laurel Fork Campground and runs west across Forest Road 14 and Forest Road 183 at a creek, then uphill to Forest Road 44 about 3½ miles south of Glady.

Laurel Fork Trail continues north past some beautiful small waterfalls and cascades along the creek past the campground to intersect with two more short spur trails leading west to F.R. 14. It then leaves Laurel Fork to head west along Beaverdam Creek to F.R. 14 and trail's end. The swampy area on the west side of the road at this point was created by beavers.

The two short intersecting trails are *Middle Mountain Trail* (#307), 1.5 miles, and Trail #305.

302 — McCray Run Trail — 4½ miles, runs west from F.R. 14 about a mile north of Beaverdam Creek down to Glady Fork and across it to reach West Virginia Route 27 about three miles south of Alpena.

311 — County Line Trail — 5 miles, follows a side ridge off Middle Mountain west from F.R. 14 about a mile south of Laurel Fork Campground, down into a gap and then up again to a fork. The right hand fork heads north to connect with the Beulah Trail (#310) and the south fork continues west to F.R. 44. This trail is blue-blazed and was last maintained in April 1974.

322 — Burner Mountain Trail — 6 miles, follows the ridge of Burner Mountain from F.R. 15 east to F.R. 14. The river downhill to the east is the East Fork of the Greenbrier.

There are several trails in the Greenbrier District that are on Cheat Mountain, just east of the Tygart Valley and West Virginia Route 92.

A good loop trip can be made using parts of the *Chestnut Ridge Trail* (#327), 5½ miles; *McGee Run Trail* (#328), 2½ miles; and *Laurel Run Trail* (#331), 3 miles.

The last trail in this area that is currently well-maintained is the *Little Mountain Trail* (#349), 5½ miles. It runs west along a road that crosses West Vriginia Route 28 about two miles south of the ranger station at Bartow. The trail splits off to follow the south banks of a stream, and then curves south and climbs up to the top of the ridge, continuing south to Trail #347, which goes down to the Greenbrier River on the mountain's western slopes. The peak you can see directly west across the river is Bald Knob, second highest point in West Virginia (elevation 4842 feet). This trail is not marked at the access road, so look carefully to find it.

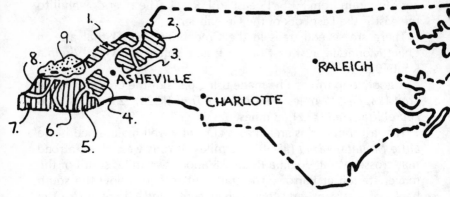

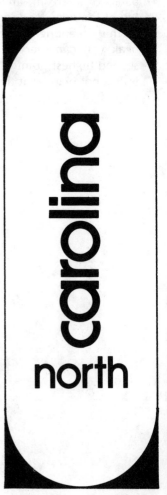

PISGAH NATIONAL FOREST
1. French Broad Ranger District
2. Grandfather Ranger District
3. Toecane Ranger District
3. Pisgah Ranger District

NANTAHALA NATIONAL FOREST
5. Highlands Ranger District
6. Wayah Ranger District
7. Tusquitee Ranger District
8. Cheoh Ranger District

9. **GREAT SMOKY MTNS. NATIONAL PARK**

NANTAHALA NATIONAL FOREST

Nantahala is a Cherokee Indian word meaning "land of the noon-day sun." It was given to this steep mountain area of north-western North Carolina because its valleys are said to be so narrow and deep they receive the direct rays of the sun only at midday. Veteran hikers of the Appalachian Trail tell us there is more up-and-down climbing through the Nantahalas than anywhere else on the A.T. route from Mt. Katahdin in Maine to the trail's southern end in Georgia.

There aren't numerous hiking trails in the 420,000-acre Nanta-hala National Forest, but those that do exist are invariably loca-ted in beautiful and interesting country.

Trails in the Cheoh District

The Cheoh District is located directly south of the Great Smoky Mountains National Park and east of the Cherokee National For-est's Tellico District in Tennessee. It is the most popular part of this forest for hikers and therefore gets more use than some other sections.

We were unable to hike in the Cheoh, ourselves, but studied the U.S.Geological Survey maps and also got some excellent first-hand information from Wayne Shepherd, a backpacker and a landscape architect for the Forest Service who used to be sta-tioned in this district. He now works in the Forest Supervisor's office in Asheville.

For a good mile-by-mile description of some of this district's trails, we recommend that you read the Sierra Club Totebook entitled *Hiker's Guide to the Smokies* by Dick Murless and Con-stance Stallings. It includes a section on the Joyce Kilmer Mem-orial Forest and on trails in the Slickrock Creek area.

The Cheoh District ranger office address is Route 1, Box 16-A, Robbinsville, N.C. 28771.

Trails Around Snowbird Creek

Location: East of Santeetlah Lake and accessible via Forest Road 75 which runs west from F.R.1127 and deadends at Snowbird Creek.
Length: The network of trails in this area totals 31 miles.
USGS Quads: Santeetlah Creek, N.C.; Big Junction, Tenn.; Mar-ble, N.C.
Description:
Hooper Bald Trail — (#60 on U.S.Forest Service inventories), 11½ miles. This trail provides the main access into the Snowbird Creek area from the north and Joyce Kilmer Memorial Forest. It

begins at Forest Road 81 about six miles west of County Road 1127 and Santeetlah Gap. It follows an old logging road that parallels Santeetlah Creek for about 2½ miles to the Bemis Logging Camp.

The road continues south from the logging camp, but the trail turns east uphill to about 5000 feet, then turns south past Huckleberry Knob to Hooper Bald (elevation 5429 feet). King Meadows Junction Trail (#63), heads southeast from Hooper Bald; Laurel Top Trail (#154) heads southwest. Hooper Bald Trail turns straight west along a ridge to the border with Tennessee at Laurel Top (elevation 5317 feet). It continues south along the border to Big Junction and connection with Trails #154 and #64.

154 — Laurel Top Trail — 2½ miles, heads southwest from Hooper Bald, as we noted, along an old wagon road built in 1910 to haul wild boar up to a game preserve at Cherokee Lodge (see Tennessee chapter for details of Cherokee Lodge and the introduction of European boar to the Appalachians). It reaches the border at Big Junction to connect with trails #60 and #64.

63 — King Meadows Junction Trail — 7½ miles. This trail begins on Snowbird Creek near the west end of Forest Road 75 and just west of Junction. Big Snowbird Trail (#64) begins at this point, too, but Big Snowbird Trail continues south along F.R.75 (just a jeep trail by now) and Snowbird Creek, while King Meadows Junction Trail heads north up to and along Firescald Ridge, past Deep Gap and across King Meadows)4600 feet) to reach Hooper Bald and links with trails #60 and #154.

64 — Big Snowbird Trail — 6 miles. This trail starts on Snowbird Creek just west of the hamlet of Junction on Forest Road 75 where the King Meadows Junction Trail also begins. Big Snowbird heads south along F.R.75 to Sassafras Creek (a short side trail, *Sassafras Creek* #65, 2½ miles, leads to Sassafras Falls), then west and still along Snowbird Creek to another side trail (*Middle Falls Trail,* #64-A, 1 mile) that leads to a second scenic waterfall. Several streams flow into the swift-running Snowbird Creek (Meadow Branch, Rockbar Branch, and Bearpen Branch) from the north before you reach the border with Tennessee at Big Junction, just south of Laurel Top.

A good loop hike using Trail #63, 154, and 65 would give you a weekend of spectacular scenery and a trip of some 16 miles.

Trails Around Slickrock Creek
Location: West of U.S.129 south of Tapoco on the Little Tennessee River and east of the Unicoi Mountains on the Tennessee-North Carolina border.

Length: The network of trails in this area totals about 24 miles.

USGS Quads: Tapoco, N.C.; Santeetlah Creek, N.C.

Description: **45 — Ike Branch Trail —** 2¾ miles. This trail provides as good an entrance as any to the network of trails around Slickrock Creek. It begins at the U.S.129 bridge over Lake Calderwood in Tapoco and runs south on a logging road to Yellowhammer Branch. From there it runs west to connect with Hangover Lead Trail (#43) heading south and then with Slickrock Creek Trail (#42) and Nichols Cove Branch Trail (#44) at the state border.

42 — Slickrock Creek Trail — 8¼ miles. This trail begins at the mouth of Slickrock Creek where it flows into the Little Tennessee River and runs south, following the creek, along the border between North Carolina and Tennessee. After about 2½ miles it meets the Stiff Knee Trail (#106), a Tennessee trail that follows Little Slickrock Creek east to its mouth at Slickrock Creek and the state border (See Cherokee National Forest section in Tennessee chapter for details of Trail #106. In North Carolina that trail dead-ends into the Ike Branch Trail).

Slickrock Creek Trail continues south on the creek along the border, passing Nichols Cove Branch Trail just south of Little Slickrock Creek.

This stream is famous for its excellent trout fishing, but since it follows a state border it poses potential problems about fishing licenses. The states have made an attempt to deal with this problem by painting yellow blazes on large rocks in the stream at the actual state line.

When the trail reaches Big Fat Branch, it leaves the state border and curves east to meet Big Fat Branch Trail (#41) at a back country campsite. Slickrock Creek Trail continues south about three more miles to end at a point just east of Glen Gap. The mountains that rise so spectacularly to your west on this trail are the Unicoi Mountains. A trail in the Cherokee National Forest (Fodderstack Trail) follows the ridge of the Unicois parallel to Slickrock Creek.

43 — Hangover Lead Trail — 5½ miles. This trail can be reached at its northern end via the Ike Branch Trail from Tapoco. It runs south from an elevation of 1900 feet at Yellowhammer Gap, up to 2800 feet on a mountain peak, along Caney Ridge and then up to 3400 feet at Cold Spring Knob. It descends to Big Fat Gap (2500 feet) and then south another two miles to Hangover Mountain (5249 feet).

44 — Nichols Cove Branch Trail — 2 miles. This trail branches east and south from Slickrock Creek Trail just south of the mouth of Little Slickrock Creek. It runs south along Nichols Cove Branch to a back country campsite at a junction with Big Fat Branch Trail.

41 — Big Fat Branch Trail — 1.5 miles. Runs west from Trail #43 at Big Fat Gap along Big Fat Branch to its mouth at Slickrock Creek. There's a back country campsite here at the junction of Big Fat Branch Trail with Nichols Cove Branch Trail and Slickrock Creek Trail.

Deep Creek Trail — 3 miles. Runs northeast from Saddle Tree Gap just south of Hangover Mountain along Deep Creek to the south end of a forest road. The road leads north to Indian Grave campground and junction with U.S.129.

Trails in the Joyce Kilmer Memorial Forest

Location: East of Santeetlah Lake. Accessible via F.R. 1127 west of U.S.129 south of Tapoco.

Length: The trails total 19 miles

USGS Quad: Santeetlah Creek, N.C.

Description: This forest consists of 3800 acres of virgin timber, most of it yellow poplar, hemlock, beech, sycamore, basswood, and oak. The trees have been preserved for us to enjoy because the Belton Lumber Co., which made preparations to log the area in 1890, went bankrupt before it could accomplish that purpose. The government bought the land and, in 1936, set it aside as a memorial to Joyce Kilmer, author of the poem "Trees." Kilmer died in action during World War I in France, and the request for the memorial was made by the Bosemain Bulges Post No. 1995 of the Veterans of Foreign Wars.

No camping is allowed within the boundaries of the Memorial Forest, but there is a developed campground just east of it at Horse Cove. Camping is also allowed on the ridge tops just off the trails that follow the perimeters. There are several short loop trails near the picnic area, but there are only three long trails in Joyce Kilmer.

Naked Ground Trail — (#55 on U.S. Forest Service inventories) runs west 4½ miles along Santeetlah Creek and through the center of the forest to the ridgetop on Naked Ground at the far western boundary.

Naked Ground Trail and Haoe Trail leave the picnic area together from the wooden sign on which Mr. Kilmer's poem is carved. Within a few hundred yards, however, they split. The Haoe Trail goes right to circle the northern boundary line and the Naked Ground Trail goes left.

The climb is continual but very gradual for the first 3½ miles; there are particularly large hemlocks on this part of the trail. The path leaves the creek for the last mile, however, and climbs steeply up the ridge to Naked Ground. Elevation range is 2400 feet at the picnic area and 4845 feet on the ridge top. Camping is allowed at Naked Ground. (Naked Ground no longer fits its name, by the way. It was apparently once one of those mountain meadows the Indians and early white settlers used for grazing cattle; now it is grown over in young second growth forest).

53 — Haoe Trail — 5¾ miles, also begins at the picnic area. It climbs steeply to the ridge and northern boundary line of the park (2400 feet to 3000 feet) in the first mile or so, then continues to climb, but more gently, using occasional switchbacks to reach Jenkins Meadow at an elevation of 4800 feet at mile three. There are views along this ridge in winter, but in summertime the heavy canopy of leaves blocks distant vistas. The trail reaches Haoe Overlook after about four miles. A short spur trail leads north to Hangover Mountain and a link with the trails in the Slickrock Creek area.

Camping is allowed on both Haoe and Hangover Mountains. The trail winds southwest from the overlook, still following the Memorial Forest boundary, to Naked Ground and a junction with Naked Ground Trail and Stratton Bald Trail in 1¾ miles.

54 — Stratton Bald Trail — 8½ miles. This trail also begins in the picnic area. It goes left (south) and crosses Santeetlah Creek almost immediately on a log footbridge. (If you've done a lot of wading and precarious rock hopping on other Appalachian mountain trails, you'll appreciate these little touches of civilization in Joyce Kilmer).

The trail climbs up to the ridge on the southern bundary of the Memorial Forest in the first 1½ miles and follows the south side of that ridge a mile to Obadiah Gap (elevation 3600 feet). It continues along the ridge, climbing at first gently then more steeply to reach Stratton Bald (elevation 5341 feet) at approximately mile 6½. This bald is visited much less often than those in the Smokies and has a fantastic display of flame azalea in early summer.

A short spur trail (*Bob Bald Trail*) runs west 1½ miles from Stratton Bald to Bob Bald and a connection with the Fodderstack Trail (#95) that runs north and south on the ridge top of the Unicoi Mountains in Tennessee's Cherokee National Forest.

The Stratton Bald Trail turns north, meanwhile, to connect in another two miles with the Naked Ground Trail and Haoe Trails at Naked Ground.

There is one more long trail in the Cheoh District near its far
northern border just south of the Smokies. This is the **Yellow
Creek Mountain Trail,** #48, 8 miles.
Location: This trail used to be part of the Appalachian Trail and is
still used by A.T. travelers as an alternate route. Its eastern end is
at the current A.T. just south of Fontana Lake at Black Gum Gap.
Its western end is at Forest Road 362 about a mile east of U.S.
129 at Tapoco.
USGS Quads: Fontana Dam, N.C.; Tapoco, N.C.
Description: It follows the ridgetop of the Yellow Creek Mountains for its entire length and offers a number of excellent views.
Elevation ranges from 2800 feet to 3400 feet. A cross trail about
three miles from the main trail's eastern end goes north one mile
to Fontana Village, south two miles to Yellow Creek and F.R.363.

Trails in the Tusquitee District
USGS Quads: Topton, N.C.; Andrews, N.C.; and Hayesville, N.C.
Description: **67 — Snowbird Mountain Trail —** 6½ miles. This
trail runs west from the town of Topton on U.S. Route 19 and 129
along a ridgetop of the Snowbird Mountains to the Joanna Bald
Lookout Tower. A forest road (#325) runs north from the lookout
tower to connect with U.S.129 west of Tulula.

To reach the eastern beginning point of the trail, turn north
from U.S.129 at the "Prevent Forest Fires" sign. Take a driveway
up the ridge until you see the trail going off to the west. This trail
is a "dug" trail, constructed to minimize erosion, by the Civilian
Conservation Corps in the 1930s. It is still in excellent condition
and maintained regularly. Elevation varies between 4200 and
4500 feet for much of the trail, although it dips down to 3700 at
several gaps. The elevation of Joanna Bald at the western end is
4616 feet. There are good views in all directions from the lookout
tower.

70 — Rim Trail — 27 miles. This trail supposedly follows a ridge
line of the Tusquitee Mountains west from Tusquitee Bald about
15 miles, then turns north four miles on a lead (down Leatherwood Branch and up to Big Peachtree Bald) that connects with
the Valley River Mountains on the north. The trail turns back east
then on a ridge of these mountains to rejoin the Tusquitee Bald
Trail (see the section on trails in the Wayah District).

We were unable to locate this trail in attempts at several supposed access points, but the district ranger in Murphy told us that
the Forest Service plans to do some maintenance on it during the
spring and summer of 1975 and that they will put up signs on access roads at that time. For that reason we include a short men-

tion of it.

In looking for the Rim Trail, we did find another interesting trail, however, (*Big Stamp Trail*, 7 miles), and we also found a beautiful, rustic, 100-year-old cabin which the Forest Service rents for $6.50 a night. (The place is furnished and has about a dozen beds — in two bedrooms — so if you're camping with a group, the price is an even better bargain). The Bristol Cabin has running water and indoor plumbing, but all lighting is by kerosene lamps.

To reach it (and the *Big Stamp Trail*) from Murphy, take U.S.64 south about nine miles to a blacktop road that leads left at an old Exxon service station. Take that road about four miles to a gravel road heading left. (If you cross a creek, you've gone about 200 feet too far). Proceed six miles on the gravel road; you will see the cabin in an open meadow below you on your right. If you decide to rent it, arrangements must first be made with the Tusquitee Ranger office in Murphy.

A short trail leads up onto the Tusquitee Mountain Range across the creek (on a wooden bridge) from the Bristol Cabin to connect with the Rim Trail. We found the short little spur trail all right; but at the top of the mountain we found nothing but an impenetrable tangle of rhododendron.

Across the road from the cabin, however, is the *Big Stamp Trail*. This path is well-marked and maintained. Be sure to turn right and sharply uphill almost immediately from the sign at the road, however; a jeep trail goes off to the left and looks more promising at first. Big Stamp Trail leads north along a ridgetop about seven miles (the last two on a road the Forest Service no longer maintains) to Big Stamp Mountain.

We were particularly fond of this trail because the rhododendron was so neatly trimmed it felt like walking inside a hedge. A bare phone line that also follows the trail (and once provided communication with the ranger on the Big Stamp fire tower) may trip you up occasionally if you make this trip in autumn when dry leaves hide it from view.

The ranger office for this district is in Murphy. The address is P.O.Box 577, Murphy, N.C. 28906.

Trails in the Wayah District

26 — Trimont Trail — *Location:* The eastern end of this trail is in the town of Franklin; the western end is on Wayah Bald at a junction with the Appalachian Trail. To get on it from the Franklin end, take the Baird Cove Road north from U.S.64 west of town to the end of pavement. Cross a creek and follow a dirt road west through a housing development to the end of road at the trail. (Because this part of town is being inundated with new construction, the trail may be rerouted at this end via Wallace Branch Road. For up-to-date information, we suggest you write the Nantahala Hiking Club, c/o the Rev. William Hazelden, Route 3, Box 131, Sylva, N.C.).

Length: 10½ miles

USGS Quads: Wayah Bald, N.C.; Franklin, N.C.

Description: The trail heads north from Franklin and uphill about 200 feet in elevation to the crest of Trimont Ridge. It turns west then and follows the crest about two miles to Trimont Mountain (elevation 3314 feet). Just west of Trimont Mountain is Brassy Knob. Another half mile brings you to Wolfpen Gap (elevation 2900 feet). Continue west along the ridge two miles to the south slopes of Bruce Knob (elevation 3200 feet), then a mile to Locust Tree Gap and up to a peak at 3443 feet. Continue west to Wilkes Knob, southwest 2½ miles to Wildcat Knob (elevation 3588 feet), and down to Poplar Cove Gap at elevation 3300 feet.

(Two jeep roads lead south from Poplar Cove Gap about five miles to North Carolina Route 106). Continue west on the ridge-top at elevations of 3600 to 3800 feet about three miles to Locust Tree Gap. Another mile west is Wayah Bald, elevation 5342 feet, the end of the Trimont Trail and junction with the Appalachian Trail.

There are excellent views in all directions from this bald, a wide variety of wildflowers in spring and summer and, according to the scientists at the Biological Research Station in Highlands, a number of rare plants, including a kind of narrow-leaf grape fern.

The Appalachian Trail follows a road south from Wayah Bald five miles to Highway 106 at the Wayah Crest Campground. If you follow this road south from the bald about a mile you will reach an intersection with the *Holloway Branch Trail,* #18, which leads west 1½ miles up to Wine Springs Bald at elevation 5400 feet. The trail continues northwest of this peak along Rocky Bald Ridge to Rocky Bald (elevation 5280 feet).

The ranger office is in Franklin. Address is District Ranger, U.S. Forest Service, Franklin, N.C. 28734.

Trails in the Upper Nantahala River Country

Location: To reach this area, take old U.S. Route 64 west from Franklin to Wallace Gap where the Appalachian Trail crosses the road. There will be a forest service sign directing you south to Standing Indian Campground.

USGS Quads: Rainbow Springs, N.C.; Prentiss, N.C.

Description: The Nantahala Mountains form a huge horseshoe in this area to make a beautiful, unpolluted watershed for the Upper Nantahala River which runs north and south through the center of the basin. The Appalachian Trail follows the ridgeline around the horseshoe and a number of newly-blazed, well-maintained side trails lead down the creeks and side ridges to the Nantahala River and the forest road that parallels it. At the north end of the basin is Standing Indian Campground. There are enough good trails in this region to occupy your attention for an entire two-week vacation using the campground as a base for exploration.

The river is famous in North Carolina for its supply of trophy rainbow and brown trout; it also contains smaller but still tasty native brook trout. The forest is carefully managed for grouse, deer, and wild turkey.

Just south of the highway on the forest road, you will note a short spur trail leading half a mile east to the John Wasilik Memorial Poplar. This yellow poplar or tulip tree is the second largest of its species on record in the United States. It was the largest on record until 1972 when a bigger one was discovered in Virginia. The tree is named for Ranger John Wasilik, an early ranger on the Wayah District.

The campground is about a mile south. Four trails originate from its southern boundary in Whiteoak Bottoms. We investigated two of them, the *Kimsey Creek Trail* (3.7 miles) and the *Lower Trail Ridge Trail* (3.5 miles) in one leisurely overnight hike that also took us along a short stretch of the A.T. to Standing Indian Mountain, noted for its spectacular views.

The forest along these trails was made up of fairly young second-growth timber, but the appearance of the woods was still rather park-like because the Forest Service has spaced the trees for maximum growth and the understory is not dense.

The government bought the land in 1920, but the owners of the Ritter Lumber Co. reserved timber cutting rights for 20 years. They managed to denude almost the whole basin during the 1930s and it is just now beginning to recover. Standing Indian Campground was their main logging camp.

The *Kimsey Creek Trail* is not as steep as the *Lower Trail Ridge Trail,* so we chose it for our ascent to Standing Indian Mountain. A sign at the southeast end of the campground (across the river) identifies it, and the route is marked with bright and frequent blue blazes. Two blazes signal changes in direction.

The trail follows an old road along the creek. Crossings are bridged. About two miles (1 hour's hiking time) from the beginning, two creeks join. There's a clearing that would make a good campsite. A couple of fire rings show previous use. Apple trees, planted by the forest service as part of the game habitat improvement program, border this meadow. The fruit was ripe, tart and juicy when we visited.

The trail south of the creek heads up over a low ridge and then back down to the stream. The second time it climbs, it leaves the creek for good (about 1½ hours from the campground). In another 15 minutes, it hits a forest road and follows it uphill to a junction with the A.T. at Deep Gap.

We turned left (east) on the A.T. It follows a jeep road for a few hundred feet, then branches right to head uphill on another road. Numerous switchbacks ease the climb. After about 15 minutes, you will reach a sign pointing to a shelter visible from the trail on the left. The wooden-floored shelter is very pleasant, watertight, and contains a rock fireplace. There's a picnic table in front and a small creek flowing by.

The trail continues uphill with many more switchbacks to Standing Indian. The trail follows the west edge of the ridge. A wooden sign on a blue-blazed side trail points .01 miles (right) to the summit. This side trail passes through a stand of rhododendron, a few fir trees (planted), a grassy bald with remains of old campsites to the summit at 5399 feet. This is a good spot for spreading a picnic lunch or just sitting for several hours to watch the clouds drift by.

Back on the A.T. another side trail goes steeply downhill (left) to a spring. There's a sign. Within 50 yards of the spring-summit intersection, a blue-blazed trail (no sign) leads steeply down to the left. This is the *Trail Ridge Trail* and follows that ridge back to the campground. It stays on the crest of the ridge to within a couple of miles of the campground, above White Oak Bottoms. Then switchbacks take you down a very steep hillside. The forest cover on the ridge crest was almost entirely hardwoods. We managed to gather several backpack pockets full of hickory nuts. When you reach Whiteoak Bottoms, however, the timber changes to hemlock mixed with rhododendron, yellow birch and poplar. The trail crosses a game meadow where an old road goes right and the trail goes left across two bridges into the campground. The sign at this end of the trail doesn't give its name but merely says "Foot Trail."

Whiteoak Bottoms, by the way, is reputed to shelter a number of rare and unusual wildflowers and other plants in its boggy areas. Among them are cotton grass and grass of parnassus.

The other trails that originate at Standing Indian Campground are the *Park Gap Trail,* 4 miles, and the Long Branch Trail, 2.3 miles.

To reach *Park Gap Trail,* walk north from the campground on the west side of the Nantahala River along an old railroad bed about ¼ mile to the trailhead. It, too, is well marked with blue blazes. Proceed west, uphill to Bee Tree Knob (a climb of one mile and about 500 feet in elevation), then turn south along Middle Ridge. The trail follows the crest of that ridge south and then west to Pentland Gap and a forest road that heads west and north to U.S. Route 64 at Chunky Gal Mountain.

Long Branch Trail — 2.3 miles, heads east across the road from the campground up that creek just north of Blackwell Ridge to the Appalachian Trail just south of Glassmine Gap. (Elevation change is from 3500 to 4200 feet).

To reach the other trails in the Nantahala River basin, drive — or walk — south on the old logging road, now a forest road, from Standing Indian Campground. The first one you will come to is *Hurricane Creek Trail* (#36 on Forest Service inventories), 2 miles. It also leads east uphill to the Appalachian Trail along Hurricane Creek. It reaches the A.T. south of Sassafras Ridge and just north of the trail shelter at Bigspring Gap.

At this point another trail (we don't know its name) leads west from the A.T. three miles past Pinnacle Mountain and Little Pinnacle Mountain into the Coweeta Experimental Forest. Several trails are marked on Forest Service inventories in the Coweeta Forest, but they had not been recently maintained when we visited so we excluded them from this guide. If you're planning a trip to the area, you may wish to inquire about them at the ranger station in Franklin.

Just over a mile south of the Hurricane Creek Trail on the Nantahala River road, you will reach *Big Indian Trail* (#34), 3.7 miles, on your right (west of the river). It climbs in classic serpentine fashion, up the mountain, past Nichols Branch in the first mile and onto Upper Trail Ridge. It crosses Big Shoal Branch at its headwaters, then turns south to follow the slopes of the mountain range parallel with the A.T. about two miles to Kilby Gap. A spur heads left here about 1½ miles back down the road just north of Big Laurel Falls. The right fork joins the Appalachian Trail at Beech Gap.

22 — Bearpen Gap Trail — 2.7 miles, runs east from the road just south of the eastern terminus of Big Indian Trail. It follows Bearpen Creek for the first ¾ mile, then leaves it and turns north for a mile-long climb to Yellow Bald at elevation of 4040 feet. It turns west here to reach a road on Albert Mountain (excellent views) that heads both east and west to join the Appalachian Trail south of Bigspring Gap Shelter and north of Bearpen Gap.

Back on the main road, if you continue south on it, past the spur from Big Indian Trail to a sharp curve in the road, you will see signs directing you south to Big Laurel Falls. The falls is just half a mile from the road and is accessible by a circular trail. You can continue south from the falls, however, along *Laurel Branch Trail* 1½ miles, along Timber Ridge to the Appalachian Trail just east of Carter Gap shelter.

If you stayed on the main road around the big curve past the trail to Big Laurel Falls, you would soon reach the end of the road's auto-navigable part. You can continue walking along the road about ¼ mile to Mooney Falls, and then, still along the road, parallel Hemp Patch Branch and Mooney Branch to junctions with the Appalachian Trail at Betty Creek Gap, Mooney Gap and Bearpen Gap.

You will be able to see from the map accompanying this section that trails in the Upper Nantahala River Country lend themself to a variety of loop hikes.

Trails Around Apple Tree Group Camp

Location: Apple Tree Group Camp is located 24 miles west of Franklin, N.C. From Franklin take U.S. 64 west to the Wayah Bald Road. Follow this paved road north over Wayah Gap and past Nantahala Lake to the Junaluska Road. Turn left on the Junaluska Road; the Group Camp is about three miles.

Length: There are eight signed trails in this area with a total length of 32 miles.

USGS Quad: Topton, N.C.

Description: The use of Apple Tree Group Camp is limited to organized groups and on a reservation basis. However, individuals may use the trails, but you should first contact the District Ranger, U.S.Forest Service, P.O.Box 469, Franklin, N.C. 28734.

Appletree Trail — 2 miles. This trail is a well-worn one. Early pioneers used it because it was already there when they arrived; it was used by the Cherokees who preceded them in this fertile terrain on the banks of the Nantahala River. Obviously, it used to be much longer. It begins today at the group camp where Appletree Branch flows into the Nantahala River. It heads west up the creek and after 1½ miles it crosses Piercy Creek and a junction with the *Laurel Creek Trail* and *Diamond Valley Trail*. It continues west uphill (gaining about 600 feet in elevation) for half a mile to end

on the slopes of London Bald and intersect the *London Bald Trail*.
Nantahala Trail — 6 miles, runs north from the campground
along the Nantahala River for two miles, then turns west at
Poplar Cove just north of a small stream and proceeds past Turkey Pen Cove to join Piercy Creek near its headwaters. It follows
the creek about half a mile to a junction with *Laurel Creek Trail*,
where Piercy Creek turns south. The Nantahala Trail continues
west another mile to end at the northern terminus of the London
Bald Trail. (Nantahala, London Bald, and Junaluska Trails combine to make a 19-mile loop that circles the entire area and connects with all the other trails).

London Bald Trail — 9 miles, begins at Southerland Gap, at the
eastern end of the Nantahala Trail. It runs south along a low
ridge, passing Piercy Bald and London Bald on their western
slopes. Apple Tree Trail heads east from the London Bald Trail
about two miles south of Southerland Gap.

The trail continues south along the ridge, passing Hickory Knob
in another mile, then a junction with the *Hickory Branch Trail*,
1½ miles. (This short spur trail leads southeast along Hickory
Branch to Dicks Creek and a junction with the Junaluska Trail).

About two miles southwest from Hickory Branch, the London
Bald Trail turns southeast to cross Pine Branch and end at Juna-
luska Gap. The Junaluska Trail goes north from this gap and the
Choga Trail goes south.

Junaluska Trail — 4 miles. This trail follows Dicks Creek north
from Junaluska Gap to the campground. It crosses three small
streams along the way; all are bridged. (They are, from south to
north, Matherson Branch, Hickory Branch — where the Hickory
Branch Trail comes in — and Youngs Camp Branch). After the
third creek crossing, you will reach a junction with the Diamond
Valley Trail. Continue northeast another mile to the campground.

Diamond Valley Trail, 1 mile. This trail, combined with the Laurel
Creek Trail, makes a north-south axis through the center of this
recreation area. It runs north along a stream from Dicks Creek
through a valley to dead-end at a crossing with the Appletree
Trail.

Laurel Creek Trail — 2 miles, continues north from the end of
Diamond Valley Trail along the banks of Piercy Creek (nobody
seems to know why this trail is called Laurel Creek Trail) to a junction with the Nantahala Trail.

Choga Trail — 6 miles, makes a wide circle around Rich Knob
and ends where it began, at Junaluska Gap. Southeast from the
gap it touches the headwaters of two forks of Laurel Branch, then

continues downhill gently to join Ingram Branch and follow it to Nantahala Lake.

It follows the borders of the lake around to the mouth of Wolf Creek where it turns northwest along the bed of an old dismantled railroad and follows that to Wolf Creek Gap. A short spur trail (about half a mile long) leads south to Forest Road 1311 and a link with the Tusquitee Loop Trail.

From Wolf Creek Gap, the Choga Trail turns north, joining the Junaluska Creek and proceeding northeast, partly along an old road, back to Junaluska Gap.

Tusquitee Loop Trail — 8½ miles. The western end of this loop is on F.R. 1311 at Old Road Gap, about half a mile west of the spur trail that comes south from the Choga Trail on Wolf Creek. It runs south along the Cherokee-Macon County line uphill from an elevation of 3600 feet to 4794 feet in the first mile to reach Shinbone Ridge. It curves southeast along a ridge top of the Valley River Mountains about half a mile to a fork. The left fork will take you back to the road about a mile east of Old Road Gap. The right fork continues southeast another mile past Signal Bald to Tusquitee Bald (elevation about 5100 feet). This section of the Tusquitee Bald Trail that runs along the top of the Valley River Mountains is supposed to be part of a 27-mile Rim Trail the Forest Service hopes to get in shape for general use during the summer of 1975. (See section on Tusquitee District Trails). You can continue south from Tusquitee Bald as far as Potrock Bald (2½ miles), but there may be some downed timber to climb over.

Retrace your steps northwest past Signal Bald to the east half of the Tusquitee Loop Trail heading back downhill. It soon reaches the headwaters of Big Choga Creek and follows that stream all the way back to F.R. 1311 at the west end of Nantahala Lake. Walk west on the Forest Road half a mile to the spur trail that will take you back to the Choga Trail and eventually to the Apple Tree Group Camp.

Trails in the Highlands District
This district has a few short trails, none of them long enough to be of much interest to backpackers. We mention one of them. *Ellicotts Rock Trail,* 3½ miles, because it connects at its mid-point with the 16-mile *Foothills Trail* in South Carolina's Sumter National Forest (see South Carolina chapter).

Location and Description: Ellicotts Rock Trail begins at Forest Road 417 just south of the Ammons Picnic Area. It follows the Glade Creek Road south to cross Glade Branch. It curves east then and winds through a grove of young white pines to reach the Chattooga River at Ellicotts Rock, a scenic point that overlooks the river and the forests of North Carolina's Nantahala National Forest, Georgia's Chattahoochee and South Carolina's Sumter National Forest.

It winds west along the border for half a mile, then joins Ellicotts Road and follows it north to Forest Road 441 just west of Pleasant Grove Church about four miles east of the trail's westernmost point.

USGS Quad: Cashiers, N.C.

PISGAH NATIONAL FOREST

This 478,000-acre forest contains two National Wilderness Areas, Shining Rock and Linville Gorge, and a mountain range with 18 peaks rising over 6,000 feet in elevation. One of these, Mount Mitchell (elevation 6,684 feet), is the highest mountain in eastern North America.

Hiking trails in the Pisgah are numerous and well-maintained, thanks partly to the efforts of individual forest rangers who are responsive to increasing demands for this kind of recreation.

A private organization, the venerable Carolina Mountain Club, has also been instrumental in getting trails established and in keeping them maintained. A number of the trails in the Pisgah Forest, and even some of the mountain peaks, are named for past members of this club who were dedicated to preserving and encouraging an appreciation of the area. Address of the club is P.O. Box 68, Asheville, N.C. 28802. Individual dues for membership are $3.00 per year; family memberships are $3.50.

The Carolina Mountain Club also sells a well-researched guide to area trails written by one of its members, Mr. Bernard Elias of Asheville. The guide is called "100 Favorite Trails of the Great Smokies and Carolina Blue Ridge" and sells for $1.

Trails in the Pisgah District

Shining Rock Wilderness

Location: Southeast of Asheville, bordered by the Blue Ridge Parkway on the south and Interstate 40 on the north. Entrance from the Parkway is at Milepost 420.2, where Forest Road 816 runs 1½ miles north to a dead-end at a parking lot. Another entrance is near the Daniel Boone Boy Scout Camp, located off N.C. Route 215 near Sunburst. A third way in is from off U.S. Route 276 where it crosses the East Fork of the Pigeon River, about three miles northeast of the Blue Ridge Parkway.

Access to the Wilderness interior is by footpath only. Camping

permits can be obtained and reservations made by writing the
District Ranger, U.S. Forest Service, P.O. Box 8, Pisgah Forest,
N.C. 28768.

Length: The network of trails in Shining Rock Wilderness totals
25 miles.

USGS Quad: Shining Rock, N.C.

Description: This 13,600-acre preserve is named for the massive,
snow-white quartz rock outcrops that occur within it. The largest
and most visible of these is Shining Rock itself, located roughly at
the center of the area. Elevations vary from 3,500 feet near the
mouth of Dry Branch to 6,030 feet on Cold Mountain, an unusual-
looking cone-shaped peak at the north end of the Wilderness.
The Pigeon River, a major tributary of the Tennessee, has its
headwaters in Shining Rock.

This wilderness has very little dense woods. It is dominated
rather by flowering trees, shrubs, heath meadows, and scattered
trees, particularly at higher elevations. Waterfalls are frequent
along the creeks and rivers. Shining Rock is very different in appearance from the other National Wilderness in this district,
though they're only a few miles apart.

139 — Sorrell Creek Trail, 2½ miles. This trail begins on private
land at the mouth of Sorrell Creek where it flows into the East
Fork of the Pigeon River. It runs east along the creek, climbing
gradually from an elevation of 3200 feet at the road to 3600 feet
at the western boundary of Shining Rock Wilderness. Continue
along the creek and when it forks again, take the left fork. When
it forks once more, take the left fork again. Follow that steeply
uphill to the stream's headwaters, then continue by a series of
switchbacks to the ridgecrest of Cold Mountain at an elevation of
almost 5700 feet. Turn sharply east and proceed half a mile along
the ridge to the summit of Cold Mountain at an elevation of 6030
feet. The Art Loeb Trail, #141, has its northern terminus on the
Cold Mountain summit.

141 — Art Loeb Trail. The total length of this trail is 32 miles; 8.7
of them are within the Shining Rock Wilderness. This is one of
the trails named for a deceased member and officer of the Carolina Mountain Club.

If you're going to pick one trail to take in Shining Rock, this
one will give you the best and most typical look at the terrain.
The Art Loeb's northern terminus is on Cold Mountain. It descends from there 0.8 miles to Deep Gap at an elevation of 5000
feet. (A spur trail, *Crawford Trail,* #101, runs east two miles from
this point down the east slopes of the mountain by a series of

switchbacks to a road that leads east along Crawford Creek 2½ miles to U.S. 276).

The Art Loeb Trail continues south along the cliffs known as the Narrows, then up to the peak of Stairs Mountain (elevation 5869 feet). Distance from Deep Gap to Stairs Mountain is 2.5 miles. It reaches Shining Rock itself in another half mile. This white bare quartz outcrop has long been a landmark for airplane pilots. It can also be seen for some distance on the ground. You can circle Shining Rock by forking left (southeast) here and walking half a mile to Beech Spring Gap (and junction with Old Butt Knob Trail heading east), then turning right another half mile down to Shining Rock Gap. Or you can continue directly south along the Art Loeb Trail along the western side of the rock to Shining Rock Gap.

Several trails intersect here. One branch of the Art Loeb Trail turns east and descends by a series of sharp switchbacks to the headwaters of the North Prong of Shining Creek.

The main trail continues south, however, along the east side of Shining Rock Ledge 1.5 miles past Flower Knob, Flower Gap and Grassy Cove Top to Ivestor Gap and the southern boundary of the Wilderness. It continues south 2.6 miles across a jeep road, up Tennent Mountain, a grassy bald with an elevation of about 6000 feet, along a ridge to Black Balsam Knob and downhill to the Blue Ridge Parkway at Milepost 420. (See separate section for a description of the portion of this trail south of the Parkway).

The east fork of Art Loeb runs east from Shining Rock, follows the North Prong and then the main part of Shining Creek east to Shining Creek Gap and a junction with the Old Butt Knob Trail.

The distance from Shining Rock Gap to Shining Creek Gap is 3.5 miles. Average elevation along the creek is 3800 feet. From Shining Creek Gap this branch of the Art Loeb Trail turns north to reach the Pigeon River at U.S. Route 276 and the eastern boundary of Shining Rock Wilderness.

332 — Old Butt Knob Trail — 3 miles. This trail has its western terminus at Beech Spring Gap, just east of Shining Rock. It runs east up to Dog Loser Knob (elevation 5720 feet), then down to Spanish Oak Gap and back up to Old Butt Knob (elevation about 5560 feet). It turns southeast downhill from the knob, losing some 1700 feet of elevation in two miles to reach Shining Creek Gap and the junction with the Art Loeb Trail.

107 — Little East Fork Trail — 5.8 miles. This trail begins at the south end of a road at the western wilderness boundary that parallels the East Fork of the Pigeon River about a mile south of the mouth of Sorrell Creek.

It follows the river south about 3½ miles. When the river forks, the trail follows the left (northernmost) fork 1½ miles east to its headwaters at Shining Rock Ledge. A short spur trail leads left (north) 0.2 miles to the Art Loeb Trail, then another half mile to Shining Rock Gap.

The Little East Fork Trail turns south along the west side of Shining Rock Ledge paralleling the Art Loeb Trail south 1.3 miles to Ivestor Gap at the southern boundary of the wilderness.

The Art Loeb Trail runs straight south from Ivestor Gap. Another trail heads east and then south on the east slopes of Tennent Mountain on an old logging road. This trail is called *Graveyard Fields,* 4.5 miles. It proceeds across open fields on Graveyard Ridge and was a cross country hiking route before it was declared a formal trail. The trail crosses Yellowstone Prong Creek just downstream from a waterfall called Second Falls and upstream from another one called Yellowstone Falls. A few hundred yards south, it reaches the Blue Ridge Parkway just west of Oaklog Gap.

357 — Big East Fork of Pigeon River Trail — 4 miles. This trail leaves the Blue Ridge Parkway at Bridges Camp Gap and runs north to join the East Fork of Pigeon River near its headwaters. It follows the river north into the Wilderness, turns east, still along the river, at the mouth of Greasy Cove Prong. It skirts Nobreeches Ridge on its south side and curves north along the river past the mouth of Little Buckeye Cove on the left, Bennett Branch on the right, and Rocky Cove on the right to reach U.S. 276 and the eastern boundary of the Wilderness at Big East Fork.

109 — Fork Mountain Trail — 6 miles. This trail runs west along the southern boundary of the Wilderness from a point on the Art Loeb Trail just south of Ivestor Gap. It follows the ridge of Fork Mountain at an elevation of 5400 feet down gradually to 4800 feet — 6 miles to the park's western boundary.

Trails west of Fork Mountain

Location: This network of trails is contained in an area bounded (with two exceptions) by the Blue Ridge Parkway on the west and south, the West Fork of Pigeon River and N.C. Route 215 on the east. The Sunburst Recreation Area on Highway 215 makes a good base camp for exploring this region.

Length: The ten trails that interconnect here total 32 miles.

USGS Quad: Sam Knob, N.C.

Description: Three trails run south from Sunburst Recreation Area. Most of the other trails link these three from east to west.

115 — Bear Trail Ridge Trail — 3 miles. This trail begins at the south end of the recreation area on Forest Road 258 just south of its junction with Forest Road 97-B. It climbs gradually but consistently along the ridge southwest from an elevation of 3200 feet at Sunburst to 5800 feet at Reinhart Knob on the Blue Ridge Parkway. Very few of the trails which originate on the Parkway are signed; you will have to poke about a bit to find them. Most start from an auto pull-over area, however, at scenic vistas. So there are places to leave your car.

142 — Haywood Gap Trail — 5 miles. To reach this trail, walk south on a dirt road (F.R.258) from Sunburst Recreation area about two miles. The trail continues south from that road's dead-end just north of a junction with trails #117 and #112. The elevation at this point is 3860 feet. It follows the Middle Prong of the West Fork of Pigeon River south another two miles to a fork in the stream. Trail #126 (Buckeye Gap Trail) follows the easternmost fork; Haywood Gap Trail takes the west fork to a point near its headwaters, then climbs steeply to an elevation of 5200 feet at Haywood Gap and a junction with the Blue Ridge Parkway.

113 — Green Mountain Trail — 7 miles. This trail begins at the junction of N.C. Route 215 and F.R. 109 just south of the Sunburst Recreation area and runs south up to the crest of Fork Ridge where it intersects Trail #112, Coon Hollow Trail, heading west. It continues south to Green Mountain, continues along the ridge to Mount Hardy, and turns east to reach N.C. Route 215 at Forest Road 815. If you walk south on Highway 215 about a mile you will reach the Blue Ridge Parkway. Walk east on it a mile and meet Trail 128, Courthouse Trail, heading south.

128 — Courthouse Trail — 2 miles. From the Blue Ridge Parkway a mile east of Beech Gap, this trail follows Courthouse Creek downhill from an elevation of 5500 feet at the B.R.P. to 3800 feet at the junction with the north end of F.R.140. If you follow highway 140 south ½ mile you will reach the north end of Trail 129.

129 — Summey Cove Trail — 2 miles. This trail follows a ridge west of the road, then south and downhill to an elevation of 3200 ft. at the junction with N. C. Route 215 at Beartree Fork about a mile west of highway 140.

131 — Flat Laurel Trail — 2.5 miles. This trail runs east from N.C. Route 215 along Flat Laurel Creek; the peak you can see south of the creek is Little Sam Knob (elevation 5862 feet). The trail turns south, leaving the creek to climb and cross Pisgah Ridge at an elevation of 5800 feet. It descends the south side of the ridge and reaches the Blue Ridge Parkway at an elevation of about 4600 feet just east of Trail 128.

117 — Big Bear Trap Trail — 2.5 miles. The western terminus of this trail is on the Blue Ridge Parkway at Reinhart Gap. It runs east along Big Bear Trap Creek to the south end of Forest Road 258. Jog south a few hundred feet on this road to Trail #112 heading east and #142 heading south.

112 — Coon Hollow Trail — 2 miles. This trail heads east along the hollow, then up to the crest of Fork Ridge and intersection with Trail #113. It crosses that trail and descends from the ridge, crossing Tom Creek and turning north to reach N.C. Route 215.

126 — Buckeye Gap Trail — 4.5 miles. The south end of this trail is on the Blue Ridge Parkway at Buckeye Gap (elevation 5600 feet). It runs north along Grassy Ridge, then downhill (to 3900 feet) and west along a creek to intersect with Trail #142.

125 — Bearpen Gap Trail — 1.5 miles. This trail begins at Bearpen Gap on the Blue Ridge Parkway and runs east to join Trail 142 about a mile north of Haywood Gap.

Trails Around Cove Creek Group Camp

Location: Northwest of Brevard, west of U.S. Route 276, and south of the Blue Ridge Parkway.

Length: The trails in this area total 46 miles.

USGS Quad: Shining Rock, N.C.

Description: The *Art Loeb Trail* (#141) circles around the south side of all these trails and connects at its east end with trails around Black Mountain. We already described that part which lies in Shining Rock Wilderness and south of the Wilderness as far as the Blue Ridge Parkway. That part was 8.7 miles long; the part we will now describe is 23.3 miles.

From the Parkway, the trail heads south two miles to Farlow Gap where it meets the western terminus of Trail 106. It continues south (paralleling Forest Road 229 on its west side) one mile to Deep Gap where there is a trail shelter. In another ¼ mile, the trail passes Pilot Mountain Lookout Tower (elevation about 5,000 feet).

It turns east then and proceeds down a ridge one mile to Gloucester Gap (elevation 3400 feet). F.R. 229 comes from the north to end at this point. F.R. 471 continues east. Another forest road goes north. The Art Loeb Trail continues east, along Forest Road 471 for a short distance, then northeast 1½ miles to Chestnut Mountain (elevation 3400 feet).

The trail heads south ¼ mile to Low Gap, then around the south slopes of a mountain and back north to another trail shelter at Butter Gap and a junction with Trail #123 heading north. There are two routes from Butter Gap east to Sandy Gap. One circles the south slopes of Cedar Rock Mountain to reach the gap in one mile. The other heads straight east across the top of the mountain (elevation 4056 feet) to reach Sandy Gap in ½ mile. Head northeast ½ mile to Cat Gap and a junction with trails 151, 120, and 124. Continue east ½ mile past Chestnut Knob, then Stony Knob in another mile. The trail angles northeast ½ mile to Neil Gap and east down Shut-In Ridge past the Sycamore Flats Recreation Area, to trail's end at a barn on U.S. Route 64 just south of its junction with 276.

106 — Farlow Gap Trail — 5.3 miles. This trail heads east from a junction with the Art Loeb Trail and Forest Road 229 at Farlow Gap, east across the south ends of Shuck Ridge, Daniel Ridge, and Fork River Ridge two miles to junction with Trail #330, *Daniel Ridge Trail*, which heads south 1.1 mile, partly along a road, to a forest service fish rearing station. It continues east 3.3 miles southeast across the slopes of a ridge to Cove Creek Group Camp and a junction with Trails #120 and #151. A spur trail, #361, leads south ¼ mile to the Davidson River.

Cove Creek Trail — 4 miles. Runs north along Cove Creek from the Cove Creek Group Camp and joins with the Farlow Gap Trail (#106) and Caney Bottom Trail (#329) to the west end of Forest Road 225. If you walk northeast along this road less than half a mile you will notice Caney Bottom Trail heading south.

329 — Caney Bottom Trail — 2 miles. This trail follows Caney Bottom Creek south to the group camp.

123 — Butter Gap Trail — 3 miles. It runs north from the trail shelter at Butter Gap on the Art Loeb Trail along Grogan Creek to its mouth at Cedar Rock creek and a junction with Trail #120, Cat Gap Trail, heading south.

120 — Cat Gap Trail — 2.4 miles. This trail begins at Cat Gap on the Art Loeb Trail (Horse Cove Trail, #151, also begins there). It heads northwest along Cedar Rock Creek to the old U.S. Fish Hatchery at John Rock on the Davidson River and F.R. 475 — about a mile west of U.S.Route 276.

151 — Horse Cove Trail — 2 miles. From Cat Gap (elevation about 3400 feet) this trail runs north around the east side of John Rock Mountain, down Horse Cove and then east in Fate Ostein Cove to the John Rock Fish Hatchery.

124 — Kings Creek Trail — 2 miles. This trail follows Kings Creek southeast from the Art Loeb Trail at Cat Gap to end at a road on Mine Creek about ½ mile northwest of Brevard.

Looking Glass Rock Trail — 5 miles. This one runs north from Forest Road 476 (Davidson River Road) just east of U.S. 276 and the

Coontree Campground. It climbs from an elevation of 2200 feet at the road to 3969 feet at Looking Glass Rock. This rock is a granite monolith. It received its name from its glistening sides, caused by water seeping from a forest cover on top. The rock's north face is nearly vertical — a sheer drop of some 400 feet.

Black Mountain and South Fork Mills River Trail Networks

Location: You can probably find these trails easiest if you remember they are all just south of the Cradle of Forestry in America area and its adjacent Pink Beds Recreation Area. The first school of forestry was established here at the turn of the century and the first active forest management was practiced in this area of the Pisgah National Forest. The old school has been reconstructed, and displays tell the history of forest management in this country. "Pink beds" are a local name given to the big, open patches of laurel, rhododendron, and azaleas that occur so frequently in the Appalachians.

Length: The network of trails around Black Mountain totals 22 miles; those around the South Fork of Mills River total 31 miles.

USGS Quads: Dunsmore Mountain, N.C.; Pisgah Forest, N.C.

Description: **322 — Sharpy Mountain Trail —** 7 miles. Links the two trail networks, so it should probably be described first. Its western end is on Black Mountain (elevation 4286 feet) where it connects with Trail #122 and #127. It heads east on a ridge that descends gradually in elevation from west to east, past Deep Gap, Poplar Lick Gap, McCall Mountain, Wagon Road Gap, and Sandy Gap to Sharpy Mountain (elevation 3280 feet). It continues east from there ¼ mile to a trail shelter at Simpson Gap, then another ¼ mile to Turkey Pen Road (F.R. 297) just south of the South Fork of Mills River and north of the Boylston Highway (N.C. Route 280) at Boylston Creek Church.

Trails Around Black Mountain

122 — Buckwheat Knob Trail — 5 miles. Runs northwest from the west end of Trail 322 at Black Mountain along a ridgecrest with fantastic views to Clawhammer Mountain. It continues northwest to Buckhorn Gap where it intersects Trail 103 heading south. It crosses Soapstone Ridge and reaches a trail fork. The left fork is the main trail, leading southwest. The right fork continues northwest (Soapstone Ridge Trail, #149) 1.3 miles to the Pink Beds Recreation Area. The trail names we have used here come from U.S. Forest Service inventories. The Carolina Mountain Club guide refers to both of these trails as the Black Mountain Trail. The Forest Service calls Trail #127, which heads south from Black

Mountain, the Black Mountain Trail. Both agree, however, that this northernmost trail is marked with orange blazes.

The Buckwheat Knob Trail heads southwest from Soapstone Ridge one mile to Club Gap, where it intersects Trail #105. It continues south across a dirt road to Saddle Gap, where it intersects Trail #144, *Coon Tree Mountain Trail*. This spur heads south 2 miles to Coontree Recreation Area on U.S. 276.

The Buckwheat Knob Trail runs east from that intersection to Avery Creek, then south to Bearpen Mountain and east again to intersect Trail 127 about two miles north of U.S. 276 at the Pisgah Work Center.

127 — Black Mountain Trail — 4.5 miles. From Black Mountain this trail runs south and downhill two miles to Pressley Gap and Hickory Knob (elevation 3500 feet), then southwest 1½ miles to Little Hickory Knob (elevation 2800 feet) and the headwaters of Thrift Cove Creek. It follows the creek south to its mouth at the Davidson River and U.S. Highway 276 just east of the Pisgah Work Center.

103 — Buckhorn Trail — 2.7 miles. This trail runs south from Trail 122 at Buckhorn Gap to the headwaters of Henry Branch, then along that creek to a junction with Trail 105 at Avery Creek. (Elevation change 3000 feet to 2600 feet).

105 — Club Gap Trail — 3 miles. Its north end is at the Pink Beds Recreation Area on U.S. 276. It runs south ¼ mile to Club Gap and an intersection with Trail 122, then south a mile to Avery Creek and a junction with Trail #103. It continues south along Avery Creek to join Trail #122 just north of Bearpen Mountain.

Trails in the South Fork of Mills River Area

133 — South Mills River Trail — 11 miles. This trail heads southeast from Wolf Ford at the south end of F.R. 476 (a mile south of Yellow Gap Road). It follows the South Fork of Mills River at an elevation of about 3,000 feet for five miles to Cantrell Creek Lodge, one of three lodges in this district owned originally by the Vanderbilt family. It is privately owned and not for general use.

148 — Cantrell Creek Trail — 2.2 miles, runs north along Cantrell Creek from the lodge to Trail #147.

The South Mills River Trail continues southeast and then east along the river another two miles to a junction with *Pounding Mill Trail* (#349), 1.5 miles. This trail runs north along Pounding Mill Branch to Trail 147 at Laurel Mountain.

In another mile, you will intersect the *Mullinax Trail* (#326), one mile, heading north to Trail 147 at Mullinax Gap. This is the official end of Trail 133. Turkey Pen Road heads south from here across the river to the Boylston Highway (N.C.280) at Boylston Creek Church. If you're approaching the trail from this end you can recognize it by remembering that it begins left across the road from a housing development sign that says Turkey Pen Gap.

South of the trailhead about ¼ mile on Turkey Pen Road, you will intersect another trail, heading right. This is the Sharpy Mountain Trail, #322, described previously. It is just ¼ mile south along that trail from Turkey Pen Road to a trail shelter.

Another trail heads north from Turkey Pen Road at this point. This is the *Vineyard Gap Trail* (#324). It leads northwest 3 miles to Vineyard Gap.

147 — Squirrel Gap Trail — 7.9 miles. This trail, like #133, begins at Wolf Ford. It turns north to reach and then parallel Glady Branch for half a mile to that stream's headwaters. The trail continues north past Squirrel Gap, then turns east and crosses two prongs of Laurel Brook. It heads east around the south slopes of a mountain and meets a spur trail that crosses east along Horse Cove Gap to Trail 146 on Cantrell Creek, about 1½ miles south of the lodge.

Squirrel Gap Trail turns north along the east slopes of a ridge to the headwaters of Cantrell Creek and a junction with Trail 146 about two miles north of the lodge. It continues west, then south, now on the west slopes of a ridge overlooking Cantrell Creek.

About two miles from the Cantrell Creek junction, it reaches Laurel Mountain and the junction with Pounding Mill Trail, #349. In another half mile it passes the Mullinax Trail, also heading south (see previous description).

The trail reaches the head of Pea Branch shortly after passing the Mullinax Trail and follows the branch about a mile east to its mouth at Bradley Creek. The trail ends here at the junction with Trail 351 at Pea Gap.

351 — Old Bradley Creek Gap Trail — 4.2 miles. This trail begins at the Yellow Gap Road (F.R. 142) about half a mile west of Yellow Gap and the east end of the Laurel Mountain Trail (#121). It runs south along Bradley Creek east of Grindstone Ridge, through a flat, wooded area with several clearings to Pea Gap and the junction with Trail 147. It continues south another mile to reach the South Fork of Mills River. It turns west to parallel the river about ¼ mile, then crosses the river just north of Vineyard Gap and follows a small stream south to connect with Trail 324.

North of Yellow Gap Road and east of the Blue Ridge Parkway in this area is another group of trails; these are referred to locally as "the trails around Pisgah Inn," for the lodge located on the Parkway just south of Buck Spring Gap.

Trails Around Pisgah Inn

Location: South of Ferrin Knob, east of the Blue Ridge Parkway, and north of Yellow Gap Road.

Length: The trails in this area total about 25 miles.

USGS Quad: Dunsmore Mountain, N.C.

Description: **102 — Big Creek Trail —** 5 miles. The west end of this trail is at the Blue Ridge Parkway at Little Pisgah Ridge Tunnel which cuts through Little Pisgah Mountain just north of Buck Spring Gap. Elevation at the road is about 5000 feet. The trail runs east down Little Pisgah Ridge two miles to the headwaters of Big Creek at an elevation of 3100 feet.

You cross Bee Branch, flowing into Big Creek from the north, at this point. This is one of numerous stream crossings on this trail. Average elevation is 2600 feet. The ridge to your north between Bee Branch and Horse Cove Creek is Beetree Ridge. Shortly after Horse Cove Creek flows into Big Creek, another stream, Boby Cove Creek, comes in from the south. Continue east along fairly wide, flat banks for the next mile. The mountains begin to slope more steeply toward the creek as you approach Rich Cove Creek cascading down a draw from Rich Gap Mountain to the south. In another mile you will reach trail's end at the Hendersonville Reservoir and Hendersonville Reservoir Road. Trail 142 continues east from here and Trail 146 heads north.

142 — North Mills River Trail — 2 miles. This trail continues east from Trail 102 across Henderson Reservoir on a road bridge, follows the road right along the North Fork of Mills River for half a mile to the mouth of Long Branch Creek. It heads northeast uphill (2600 to 3000 feet) 1½ miles then to join Trail 354 on Trace Ridge.

146 — Spencer Branch Trail — 2.3 miles. This one heads north from the Henderson Reservoir along Fletcher Creek through a narrow band of open land called Fletcher Fields. After half a mile a trail branches left to follow Middle Fork Creek northwest 2 miles to a point near its headwaters. This trail had not been recently maintained when we checked. If you hike it, allow plenty of time for working your way through rhododendron and fallen timber. Just before you reach the mouth of Spencer Creek the trail forks. The left branch follows Fletcher Creek for another mile to a point near its headwaters. The right branch heads up Spencer Branch then and angles right to join Trail 354 on Trace Ridge.

354 — Trace Ridge Trail — 3 miles. The north end of this trail is at the Blue Ridge Parkway at Beaverdam Dam, just east of Ferrin Fire Tower. It follows the ridge crest south along Old Trace Ridge Road at an elevation of 3400 feet dropping gradually to about 2800 as you head south. Cross Hendersonville Reservoir Road and continue south to the North Mills River Recreation Area.

121 — Laurel Mountain Trail — 8.4 miles. It follows the crest of Laurel Mountain from the Blue Ridge Parkway north of the Pisgah Inn and just south of the Buck Spring Tunnel east to Yellow Gap on F.R. 478. From the Parkway it heads south first along the ridge at about 5000 feet to the north and east slopes of Little Bald Mountain. It curves east to pass Turkey Spring Gap, Good Enough Gap and Sassafras Gap at elevations of about 4400 feet. It circles Johnson Knob on its south slopes, passes Johnson Gap and then Rich Gap Mountain, also on south slopes. It descends to 3600 feet at Rich Gap and continues at that elevation, still on the ridgetop for another mile before dropping down to Yellow Gap and Yellow Gap Road at an elevation of 3202 feet.

132 and 321 — Thompson Ridge Trail and Pilot Rock Trail — 4 miles. These trails make a loop that provides an easy day hike from Yellow Gap Road just east of the Pink Beds and Cradle of Forestry area. Thompson Ridge Trail runs north on the slopes of a ridge on the west side of Thompson Creek 1½ miles before turning east along the south slopes of Little Bald Mountain half a mile to join Pilot Rock Trail. The elevation at the junction is 5000 feet. Turn south and descend a mile to Pilot Rock (elevation 4000 feet). Continue winding down the mountain for another mile to reach the road at Grassy Lot Gap (elevation 3300 feet).

Trails in the Toecane District

Location: In Yancey County north of the towns of Black Mountain and Old Fort, north and west of the Blue Ridge Parkway between Blackstock Knob and Little Switzerland.

Length: The trails in this area around Mt. Mitchell total 43 miles

USGS Quads: Mt. Mitchell, N.C.; Celo, N.C.; Montreat, N.C.

Description: We hiked a few trails in this district, but most of the information we have comes from District Ranger Johnny McClain, one of those rangers we mentioned earlier who has a strong personal interest in backpacking, who believes it is one of the biggest areas of demand in forest recreation today, and who, therefore, has managed with limited funds to see that his district has numerous and well-maintained trails.

The South Toe River has its beginnings in this district. The river's tributaries flow down from the Black Mountains, highest range in eastern North America. These mountains have 18 peaks over 6,300 feet in elevation.

The Black Mountains get their name from the evergreen forest of spruce and fir that mantle the top of the range. Along the crest of the mountains grows the largest remaining stand of Fraser Fir in the United States.

The quest for virgin spruce and fir timber along the top of the Blacks brought the timbermen around 1900. They built railroads up both the east and west sides of the range to haul out the huge logs to their sawmills in the valley. By 1915 the railroads were abandoned, leaving much of the timber on the west slopes uncut. Today most of this virgin spruce and fir still remains on National Forest land.

The most prominent peak in the Black Mountains is Mt. Mitchell (elevation 6684 feet). The mountain was named for Dr. Elisha Mitchell, a professor of mathematics at the University of North Carolina. Dr. Mitchell established that Black Dome, later to be named Mount Mitchell, was the highest peak in the east, though a personal feud developed for some years between him and a former student, Senator Thomas Lanier Clingman, who insisted that Clingman's Dome in the Great Smoky Mountains was highest.

Dr. Mitchell was killed on June 27, 1857 after leaving Black Dome for Big Tom Wilson's home on the headwaters of the Cane River. He became lost in the dark as he made his way down the mountain and fell to his death over what is now known as Mitchell Falls. Dr. Mitchell's body was found 10 days later by Big Tom Wilson, a famous hunter and skilled mountaineer in the area. A mountain peak now also bears Big Tom's name.

In 1913 the National Forest Service began buying lands that now make up the South Toe River basin on the Pisgah National Forest. These lands, comprising about 25,000 acres, were purchased to protect the watershed and to help maintain a continuing supply of timber for a rapidly growing nation.

In 1915, the Mount Mitchell State Park was established on the crest of the range. More than 1450 acres were purchased by the state and set aside to honor Dr. Mitchell for his work and to preserve the natural beauty of the highest peaks in eastern North America.

190 — Mount Mitchell Trail — 5.6 miles. Beginning at Black Mountain Campground, (elevation 3200 feet), this trail climbs through virgin stands of hardwood, crossing numerous lively streams and seeps. Above 4500 feet the trail enters old growth stands of red spruce and Fraser fir. The density of these stands gives a park-like appearance. At 3.9 miles the trail intersects with the Maple Camp Bald Trail and at 4 miles the trail reaches the Camp Alice trail shelter.

This shelter contains 10 wire bunks and a fireplace. There are pit toilets, a horse corral, and a small separate shelter for cooking nearby. Water is available at the intersection of the Maple Camp Bald Trail.

From the shelter the trail leaves the old roadway and enters the woods, climbing through young stands of spruce, fir and yellow birch. The dead trees you will notice as the trail nears the mountaintop result from a balsam wooly aphid epidemic. At 5.2 miles a trail intersects from the right. It leads to a parking lot in Mt. Mitchell State Park. At 5.4 miles the trail intersects the Mt. Mitchell tower trail. At this point the blue blazes end and the trail descends 0.2 miles to the parking lot on Mount Mitchell.

179 — Black Mountain Trail — 6.5 miles. The southern half of this trail begins at the parking lot on top of Mt. Mitchell and runs north to the Deep Gap Trail Shelter. The northern half begins at Deep Gap and runs north, still along the mountain crest, to Celo Knob. Elevation varies from 6550 to 6645 feet.

This trail is an ungraded one that offers the hiker spectacular views as it crosses Mount Craig (elevation 6645 feet), Big Tom Mountain (elevation 6558 feet), Balsam Cone (elevation 6611 feet), and skirts along the rim of the Middle Creek Natural Area.

At 3.0 miles the trail crosses Potato Hill (elevation 6440) and descends steeply into Deep Gap. At 3.5 miles the trail reaches the Deep Gap Trail shelter. The shelter has four wood bunks and floor space that will sleep six. There's a spring 400 feet down the mountain on a blue blaze spur trail.

From Deep Gap the trail continues north along the mountain crest at the border between national forest land (east of you) and private land (west). In one mile you will reach Winter Star Mountain (elevation 6203) at the top of Colberts Ridge. Two miles farther north you will pass over Gibbs Mountain, then continue ¼ mile to Horse Rock. In another half mile you will rech Celo Knob (elevation 6327 feet).

178 — Colberts Ridge Trail — 3.7 miles. This trail begins on the Colberts Creek Road and terminates in Deep Gap at the trail shelter. To reach the trail head take Colberts Creek Road west from Ballew's Store on N.C. Route 80 just north of the Carolina Hemlocks Recreation Area. Proceed 0.6 miles along the road to a sign on the right that says "Colberts Creek Trail — Deep Gap 3 miles." There is a place to park your car on the left just before you get to the trail.

The trail ascends gently for the first half mile, and then more steeply as it climbs slowly toward Deep Gap. There are occasional rock outcrops that give the hiker good views of the crest of the Black Mountain Range and the South Toe River Valley. On clear days you can even see such faraway peaks as Roan Mountain, Grandfather Mountain, and Table Rock.

At 3.6 miles the trail reaches Deep Gap and intersects the Celo Knob Trail. At 4.7 miles it reaches the Deep Gap Trail Shelter. It continues four miles to reach the entrance to Mt. Mitchell State Park.

Bald Knob Ridge Trail — 2.8 miles. This trail begins on Forest Road 472 about three miles south of Black Mountain Campground and climbs west to the Blue Ridge Parkway at Bald Knob. It ascends steeply for the first mile, then more gently through stands of virgin spruce and Fraser fir. Some water is available along the upper reaches of the trail.

This trail is considered one of the most scenic along the Black Mountain range because of the park-like appearance as you pass through the virgin stands of conifers. About eight hours' hiking time should be planned for the trip up and back to the South Toe River Road (F.R. 472).

Buncombe Horse Range Trail — 8 miles. This trail, white blazed, also begins on F.R. 472 south of Black Mountain campground. It terminates at the Camp Alice trail shelter. As it leaves the road, it ascends on an old logging road for two miles on a moderate grade. Here the trail leaves the old logging road and passes along the side of a field and enters the woods. It passes through open glades and spruce-fir forest as it winds up the mountain. At 4.2 miles it reaches an old railroad tramway. For the next 3.8 miles the trail follows the path of this old tramway. At 7.4 miles a dirt road comes in from the left. This road leads to the entrance of Mt. Mitchell State Park, a distance of 1.5 miles. At 8 miles the trail reaches the Camp Alice trail shelter.

182 — Lost Cove Ridge Trail — 3.1 miles. This trail begins at Black Mountain Campground and runs east to terminate at the Green Knob lookout tower on the Blue Ridge Parkway. Elevation at the campground is 3200 feet. Elevation at Greenknob Tower is 5070 feet. No water is available on this trail.

It climbs steeply from Black Mountain Campground for 0.6 miles and more moderately following a ridge line to Greenknob Lookout Tower at 2.8 miles. From there it descends for .3 miles to the Parkway. About 10 hours' hiking time should be allowed for a round trip.

Trail 211 continues south from Green Knob across the Parkway to connect with a network of trails in the Grandfather District. We have not included these trails in our guide because we were advised they may be discontinued since they lie in a watershed that supplies city water to the town of Marion. They are neither maintained nor signed.

Maple Camp Bald Trail — 7 miles. This trail begins on the Colberts Creek Road (about ¼ mile west of the Colberts Ridge Trail head) and terminates at the Camp Alice trail shelter. It is white blazed. Average hiking time is 6 hours up, 4½ hours down. elevation is 2920 on the Colberts Creek Road, 5782 at the Camp Alice Shelter. Horse back travel is permitted.

The trail ascends moderately to steeply, following an old logging road for two miles where it enters a graded trail. For the next two miles the trail climbs through old bald areas that afford excellent views of the Middle Creek Natural Area and the South Toe River Valley. At 3.5 miles the trail enters a burned-over area. This area was burned by the Forest Service for eagle habitat improvement in the spring of 1974.

At 4 miles the trail reaches an old railroad tramway. For the next 3 miles it follows this old railroad right-of-way to the Camp Alice Trail shelter. At 4.9 miles it passes through a small grassy opening on a ridge line. This opening was constructed as an emergency helicopter landing pad by the Forest Service. From this point you look into the south fork of Rock Creek where two natural landslides occurred during the fall of 1973 following heavy rainfalls. As the trail traverses the Rock Creek drainage, one is afforded good views from several rock outcrops.

At 6.5 miles the trail passes directly above one fork of the 1973 landslide. At 6.9 miles the Mt. Mitchell Trail comes in from the left and at 7 miles the trail reaches the Camp Alice shelter. The shelter is 200 feet to the left of the old railroad tramway. Water is available along most of this trail.

161 — Big Butt Trail — 7 miles. Ranger McClain notes that if this mountain peak occurred in the West, it would be called a butte. Appalachian mountaineers are more plain-spoken.

This trail follows the crest of Brush Fence Ridge west of Mt. Mitchell and the valley of the Cane River. Its southern terminus is at Balsam Gap on the Blue Ridge Parkway and its northern end is on North Carolina Route 197 at Coxcomb Mountain.

About halfway, you will pass Flat Springs Gap, where a stream provides a water source. This is also a good camping spot. The trail climbs steeply from Balsam Gap to the ridge crest, then continues on more or less level ground.

There are several more primitive trails in this district. They are not maintained, signed, or blazed, and they are recommended only for experienced woodsmen. One of these lies in the newly-designated Craggy Mountain Wilderness Study Area. If you're interested in trying any of these, visit the ranger office in Burnsville for directions.

Trails in the Grandfather District

There are a number of trails in this district. Unfortunately for hikers, nearly all of them either already have been or are about to be converted to dirt tracks for motorcycles. An exception is the network of trails in Linville Gorge, one of only three national wilderness areas which existed east of the Rockies before the new Eastern Wilderness bill became law in the winter of 1974-75. Linville Gorge is certainly a good reason all by itself for visiting the Grandfather District.

Grandfather Mountain is the most dominant peak in the mountains of this district and is also worth a visit. From its summit, you can get an idea of the terrain of the entire region. Foot travel was once the only way to reach Grandfather Mountain. Now, however, a paved road leads to it from the Blue Ridge Parkway, and there are no hiking trails of any substantial length in the vicinity. The short trail that does lead to the summit from the parking lot requires strenuous effort, however. You will use ten ladders, some of them scaling sheer cliffs.

Trails in Linville Gorge

Location: In Burke and McDowell Counties, about 20 miles north of Marion and just east of U.S. 221 on N.C. Route 183 at the town of Linville Falls. Two gravel roads parallel the gorge along the ridges just outside the wilderness boundaries. N.C. Route 105 is the one on the west side; Forest Road 210 is on the east. Trails into the gorge begin on these roads, and there are spaces for parking cars at the trailheads.

To hike or camp in Linville Gorge you must get a permit from the district ranger (P.O. Box 519, Marion, N.C.). During summer or bear hunting season in October it is a good idea to apply at least three weeks in advance.

Length: The network of footpaths totals 20¾ miles. The longest trail is the Shortoff Mountain Trail which follows Jonas Ridge east of the Linville River through the southern half of the park's eastern boundary. The main trail along the river is the Linville Gorge Trail,

3½ miles; most of the other trails are spurs leading off this trail to the roads uphill on either side. These spur trails are divided into two categories: primitive and developed. The primitive ones consist mainly of blazes on trees and proceed directly down the mountainsides. The developed ones are wide and well-constructed, generally employing numerous switchbacks to ease your climb or descent.

USGS Quad: Linville Falls, N.C.

Description: This wilderness consists of 7600 acres along a 20-mile chasm formed by the swift-running, powerful Linville River. The sound this river makes as you walk along its banks makes you think it must still be cutting rock away at the rate of about two tons a week. The river descends 2000 feet in elevation through the gorge before breaking into the open flats of Catawba Valley.

It is a long, narrow canyon; the river runs through it almost directly from north to south. Linville Mountain is the ridge on the river's west side; Jonas Ridge is on the east. Laurel Knob on Linville Mountain has an elevation of 4040 feet at its highest point, more than 1640 feet above the river. Along the edge of Jonas Ridge is an assortment of rock formations including Sitting Bear, Hawksbill, Tablerock and the Chimneys.

The name Hawksbill well describes that peak, particularly the profile as seen from the east or west. From any direction, Table Rock suggests a giant fortress built by some ancient king. Immediately south from Table Rock are the Chimneys, a jumble of spires, fissures, massive irregular boulders, and overhanging cliffs. In places, the chimney formations drop down to the river in sheer six-hundred-foot descents. The ridge continues past Chimney Gap to Shortoff, a once-rounded monolith, whose western face has been left precipitous and scarred by centuries of weathering.

There is a great variety of plant life along the river banks and throughout the gorge, including numerous rare species. Mountain laurel, sand myrtle, and four native rhododendron species bloom here. Red chokeberry, yellow root, ninebark, alder, and the evergreen drooping leucothoe (dog hobble) grow from cracks in the rock shelf. Timber cutters avoided this inaccessible area, and trails now pass through virgin forest containing a variety of Appalachian hardwoods and pines.

The main trail along the river is called *Pine Gap Trail* (#247), 2½ miles, at its northern end. This trail leaves state road 105 at the northern boundary of the wilderness, about half a mile south of that road's junction with N.C. Route 183 in the town of Linville Falls. The road has not yet climbed up onto Linville Mountain at this point; elevation is about 3300 feet. The trail reaches the river almost immediately and follows it southeast half a mile before intersecting the Bynum Bluff Trail.

241 — Bynum Bluff Trail — ½ mile, developed trail descends from an elevation of 3480 feet on state highway 105, about half a mile south of the Pine Gap Trailhead at a northeasterly angle to join the Pine Gap Trail at the river where the elevation is about 3000 feet.

The Pine Gap Trail curves southwest with the river just south of the Bynum Bluff Trail and proceeds in that direction half a mile before turning southeast for half a mile to a junction with the Cabin Trail.

246 — Cabin Trail — ½ mile, primitive. This trail descends steeply from an elevation of 3800 feet at the road about half a mile south of the Bynum Bluff Trailhead. Elevation at the river is about 2800 feet.

The Pine Gap Trail continues along the river northeast around a curve and through a stretch of woods away from the river to a junction with the Babel Tower Trail.

240 — Babel Tower Trail — 2½ miles, developed, winds down Linville Mountain by a series of switchbacks through a deep woods of tall hemlocks and hardwood, losing about 800 feet of elevation between the road and the river.

Pine Gap Trail ends at the junction with Babel Tower Trail and the Linville Gorge Trail continues south along the river.

231 — Linville Gorge Trail — 3½ miles. This trail follows along slopes high above the river on its west side for the most part. It dips down occasionally for scenic waterfalls or good natural campsites. The elevation decreases very gradually from north to south. The swiftest water and most of the big waterfalls are in the northern part of the wilderness.

About a mile south of the Babel Tower Trail, you will see the Devils Hole Trail coming downhill on the river's east banks from south of Sitting Bear Mountain. It is possible to cross the river on rocks at this point if you want to explore a part of Jonas Ridge.

244 — Devils Hole Trail — 1 mile, primitive. This trail descends into the gorge from F.R. 210 about two miles south of that road's junction with N.C.Route 181. Elevation at the road is 3400 feet. You must climb over a small divide before beginning your descent. The trail parallels a small stream most of the way, making it fairly easy to keep from getting lost. Elevation at the river is 2600 feet.

Less than half a mile south of the junction of Devils Hole Trail at the river, you will reach the *Sandy Flats Trail* (#230) ½ mile, heading west. We hiked into the gorge on this trail. It, like the Devils Hole Trail, followed a small rivulet downhill through a very deep, tall hemlock forest. The rivulet was strewn with boulders and navigating was a little tricky with backpacks (fun, though). This trail was a little hard to follow in spots. Some hiker who preceded us had kindly torn an old muslin sheet into srips about eight inches long and tied them to trees to mark the route. We reached the river in a large flat area cleared of underbrush and sheltered by massive oak trees and a few hemlocks. This flat area overlooked the river from high slopes; there was a small waterfall.

The Linville Gorge Trail continues south on a ledge above the river for half a mile to intersect the Spence Ridge Trail heading east across the river to Forest Road 210.

233 — Spence Ridge Trail — 1½ miles, developed. This trail is the most civilized route into the gorge from the east side. It leaves the forest road about half way between Hawksbill and Tablerock Mountains and descends the ridge from an elevation of 2900 at the road to 2600 on the river. A log bridge crosses the river to connect with the Linville Gorge Trail.

242 — Tablerock Trail — 1 mile, developed, begins on F.R.210 at the same spot as the Spence Ridge Trail, but it runs south and uphill along the ridge to Table Mountain Lookout Tower (elevation about 3000 feet). Shortoff Mountain Trail continues south from this point along the eastern ridge overlooking the gorge.

235 — Shortoff Mountain Trail — 6 miles, developed. This trail along the ridgetop is a perfect complement to the Linville Gorge Trail. Hikes along both of them will give you a rather complete idea of what the area is like. This trail passes by several of the unusual rock formations and cliffs favored by rock-climbers. It reaches the Chimneys (elevation 3557 feet) about a mile south of Tablerock Mountain, and Chimney Gap in another 1½ miles. It curves southeast and then southwest from Chimney Gap along the eastern boundary of the Wilderness, 1½ miles to the southern boundary.

Shortoff Mountain rises from this southern boundary to an elevation of about 2960 feet (some 1600 feet above the Linville River). The trail follows the flat top of the mountain south about half a mile, then descends steeply on switchbacks to the northern end of Wolf Pit Road (F.R.117), elevation 1793 feet. Wolf Pit Road heads south 2½ miles to N.C.126.

The Linville Gorge Trail continues south from the Spence Ridge

Trail just one mile to its southern end and a beautiful campsite, at Conley Cove Trail.

229 — Conley Cove Trail — ¾ mile, developed, leads uphill by numerous switchbacks in a southwesterly direction to reach highway 105 about two miles south of the Sandy Flats Trail.

If you continue south on the highway three miles to the southern Wilderness Area boundary, you will reach the Pinch In Trail.

228 — Pinch In Trail — 1 mile, primitive. This trail follows the southern boundary line east and steeply downhill to a high bluff overlooking the Linville River. Shortoff Mountain is east and slightly south of you across the river. Elevation change along this trail is from 3200 feet at the road to 1400 feet at the river.

Trails in the French Broad District

Several short trails at the north end of this district in the Bald Mountains branch off the Appalachian Trail. They are of no interest to any backpackers except those hiking the A.T. and needing access to food or other supplies. Their locations are indicated on our Appalachian Trail maps for North Carolina.

There is one long trail in the district worth sampling:

314 — Pigeon River Trail — 8 miles.

USGS Quads: Waterville, N.C.; Lemon Cove Gap, N.C.; Cove Creep Gap, N.C.; Fines Creek.

This trail begins where Little Fall Branch crosses Forest Road 148 just south of the Appalachian Trail at Brown Gap. It heads south along Little Fall Branch, across Hurricane Ridge, down Hurricane Creek and along Hurricane Mountain to U.S. 40 at Waterville Lake on the Pigeon River immediately east of the Great Smoky Mountains National Park.

To reach this trail from the A.T., take Forest Road 148A south from Brown Gap about ¼ mile, turn left (east) on F.R.148, go another ¼ mile to the trailhead at Little Fall Branch. Elevation here is 2775 feet. The trail climbs to 3581 feet in about one mile. Elevation is 3800 feet at Hurricane Gap on Hurricane Ridge in the Harmon Dam Wildlife Management Area. The trail runs along Hurricane Ridge to Rathbone Cove, then heads south and west through a piece of private land in Horsepen Gap (elevation 3200 feet), south along Wilkins Creek. The trail follows an old logging road for awhile just before reaching U.S.40. Elevation at U.S.40 is 2600 feet.

GREAT SMOKY MOUNTAINS NATIONAL PARK

The Smokies are the culmination, the apotheosis of the southern Appalachians. Sixteen peaks within the park rise over 6000 feet. The highest, Clingman's Dome, is 6662 feet above sea level. Between the peaks, the crest of the main ridge of the Smokies stays continuously above 5000 feet for 34 miles.

In the park are preserved 500,000 acres of mountain land. Much of this land was once logged over, but there are stands of virgin timber scattered through the park. And the loggers never got to the forest of spruce and fir that caps the high ridges.

Parts of the Smokies were inhabited for generations, and the signs of this habitation are scattered around the park. Hikers following the creeks uphill come across old chimneys or even whole cabins that once housed a mountain family. Or they find a lilac bush or apple tree that once grew in somebody's yard.

In Cades Cove in the northwestern corner of the park, the park service has set up a living museum of mountain life. The broad fields of the cove are pasture for herds of cattle, and reconstructed cabins are scattered around the area. Outside of Cades Cove the land has been left alone so that it can return to its presettlement state.

The idea of turning the Smokies into a park dates back at least to the early years of this century, but it took years of patient effort to make the idea a reality. Money was a big problem. The states of North Carolina and Tennessee raised much of it, a project that took some doing, since these were not rich states in the twenties and thirties. John D. Rockefeller, Jr., gave several million to the project, and under the New Deal, the federal government came up with the rest.

Even with the money in hand, the problems of creating the park were a long way from over. The western parks, such as Yellowstone, had simply been set aside from lands in the public domain. But in the Smokies, negotiations had to be carried out with more than 6000 different land owners just to buy the land.

However, the problems were overcome, and on Labor Day, 1940, the park was officially dedicated. But the controversies about this park didn't end with the dedication. There have been intermittent fights ever since between those who wish to "develop" the park — especially with more roads — and those who want to preserve it as wild land.

The pro-wilderness people seem to have won now. It is currently proposed to formally designate most of the park as a wilderness area, and the park service has given up on an earlier plan to build a second trans-mountain road to supplement the one through Newfound Gap. However, the desire to build roads seems to burn very fiercely in some breasts, so we can never be absolutely sure that the fight is over.

The Smokies are a land of incredible profusion. The rich forests of the slopes are not only extraordinarily rich in species, but they also contain many trees of enormous size. Something in the environment of the Smokies is conducive to growing record size trees.

The beauty of this park and its proximity to a large share of the nation's population have made it our most visited national park. Millions come here every year, and about 350,000 people spend at least a little time on a park trail. Most of these hikers are looking for a brief walk, but about 60,000 of them are planning to camp out in the back country. These figures are taken from the Sierra Club Totebook on the Smokies. They were published in 1973 and probably represent 1972 levels. The figures have no doubt gone up since then.

Coping with all these visitors has created problems for the park service. The problems are compounded by the fact that a disproportionate number of these backpackers want to use the Appalachian Trail.

Extremely heavy use of the A.T. and its trail shelters has led to some environmental degeneration. The areas around the shelters have been picked clean by people seeking wood for campfires. When the downed wood is all gone, there are always a few idiots who will pull down saplings or tear branches off living trees. The fact that this green wood won't burn doesn't seem a deterrent.

The trail itself has suffered a certain amount of damage, especially in the area near the Newfound Gap Road. The trail is as broad as a sidewalk, and nearly all the top soil has been eroded. You walk on rocks. Along the edges of the trail, erosion has undermined tree roots, making some trailside trees too weak to stand up to mountain storms.

The park service has set up a system of rationing for the shelters along the A.T. and at Mount LeConte, Laurel Gap, Moore Spring, and Kephart Prong. You must acquire a permit to use these shelters, and permits are issued only up to the capacity of the shelters. No tent camping is allowed in the area of shelters.

Permits for rationed areas can be issued only after your arrival at the park, and then no more than 24 hours in advance of your departure on the trail. This means that you cannot really plan a trip on the A.T. or to one of the other rationed areas, since you won't know if you can go there until after you arrive at the park.

The purpose of these regulations is to discourage hikers from travelling the most heavily used routes, and we suggest that you help the regulations achieve their purpose. The Smokies have more than 500 miles of trails outside these rationed areas, and 95 backcountry campsites have been set up for use by backpackers. These campsites can be reserved in advance by mail, so you can plan your trip well ahead of your arrival at the park.

Setting off on foot with everything you need in the pack on your back is a way of getting out beyond the crowds we are usually surrounded with and experiencing something of the solitude of the wilderness. It seems absurd to struggle up a mountain all day with a huge weight on your back for the privilege of spending your night as part of a mob. If you want crowds, the park has excellent developed campgrounds that are set up to handle them.

In order to reserve a backcountry campsite, you need to tell the park service where you plan to start and end your hike, how many people will be in your party, and where you want to spend each night. They also want to know the purpose of your trip: hiking, or fishing, or whatever. If you don't get a permit by mail, you can get one at the park at any ranger station or visitors center or at park headquarters. For permits write the Park Superintendent, Great Smoky Mountains National Park, Gatlinburg, TN.

Facilities at the backcountry campsites vary. Some have picnic tables, privies, fireplaces, and bear-proof food caches. Others have nothing but tent space. Nearly all have a water supply.

If you are doing off-trail hiking, you may camp anywhere you wish, as long as you are at least a half mile from any trail and a mile from any road or developed area. However, you need a camping permit for off trail camping.

The park service has published a set of sensible rules for backcountry camping. They are:

1. All overnight hikers must have a camping permit.
2. Bicycles and motorized equipment are prohibited on trails; firearms are not permitted in the park.
3. All non-burnable trash packed in must be carried out with you. Never bury or throw this trash in pit toilets. Littering is prohibited.
4. Build fires at designated sites only. Never leave a fire unattended.
5. Only dead and down wood may be used for fires. Cutting of live trees and shrubs is prohibited.
6. Hitching horses within immediate vicinity of shelters or to trees is prohibited. Horses are prohibited on some trails.

7. Feeding of wildlife is prohibited.
8. Camping outside the sites and dates specified on the camping permit, or violating any of the above regulations is subject to prosecution.
9. Pets are not permitted on trails or cross-country hikes.

We should tack on to these our own suggestion that you avoid building a fire altogether, except in emergency conditions. The backpacker's stove is much easier to cook on, and it leaves no trace behind.

Between November 1 and March 31, the park service will not issue any camping permits until a ranger has inspected your clothing and equipment. Many people arrive at the Smokies apparently thinking that the winter time climate is balmy, and over the years, the rangers have had to go in and carry out a number of unfortunate campers. The park service has published a list of suggested equipment which we have included in our chapter on backpacking in the southern mountains.

The weather can be a problem in the Smokies at any time of year. The highest peaks get 90 inches of rain in the average year, making them the rainiest places in the U.S. outside the Pacific Northwest. You should be prepared with good rain gear, preferably something that covers your legs as well as your upper body. Wind and rain can combine even on a moderately cool day to chill you to a dangerous extent.

We talk more about bears in our introductory chapter, but the Smokies are where you are most likely to encounter one. Keep in mind that the bears, like everything else in this park — plants, animals, and rocks — are protected and are not to be molested in any way.

The Sierra Club, as part of its Totebook Series, has published a "Hiker's Guide to the Smokies," which we heartily recommend. It was compiled by Dick Murlless and Constance Stallings, and it provides detailed information on every trail in the park. An excellent topographic map of the park, on a scale of two miles to the inch comes with the book. The map has all the trails drawn in.

Sierra Club Totebooks are available in many outdoor equipment stores and in some bookstores. If you can't find a copy in your area, write to the Sierra Club, 1050 Mills Tower, San Francisco, Calif. 94104. Cost of the book is $7.95.

Since we simply do not have the space to do the sort of detailed account that Murlless and Stallings have done, and also because we are deliberately putting more emphasis on less well-known places, we will confine ourselves to a brief and somewhat general account of the trails in the park.

We will tell you how to get to each of the areas in the park, the mileage of trails in those areas, and some of the places of particular interest along the trails.

A note about maps: A number of good maps of the Smokies are available. We have mentioned the map that comes with the Sierra Club Totebook. The U.S. Geological Survey has a set of two maps (east half and west half) of the park drawn to a one inch to one mile scale. They are $1 each.

The 7½ minute quadranges for the whole park are, on the Tennessee side, west to east: Blockhouse, Calderwood, Tapoco, Kinzel Springs, Cades Cove, Wear Cove, Thunderhead Mountain, Gatlinburg, Silers Bald, Mount LeConte, Jones Cove, Mount Guyot, Clingman's Dome, and Luftee Knob.

On the North Carolina side, west to east, Fontana Dam, Tuskeegee, Noland Creek, Bryson City, Smokemont, Hartford, Bunches Bald, Waterville, Cove Creek Gap, and Dellwood.

Great Smoky Mountains National Park is a great oval lying athwart the Tennessee—North Carolina border. The major ridges of the mountain range run more or less east-west. The main ridge follows the long axis of the oval. It serves as the boundary between the two states, with Tennessee to the north of its crest and North Carolina to the south.

A single road cuts through the park from Gatlinburg, Tenn., in the north, to Cherokee, N.C., in the south. This is the Newfound Gap Road, which hits the main ridge of the mountains at Newfound Gap.

Newfound Gap is also the point where the road intercepts the Appalachian Trail. The trail follows the state line ridge through the park for nearly 70 miles beginning at Davenport Gap in the northeast. Just before leaving the park at Fontana Dam in the southwest, the trail turns away from the ridge to head south into North Carolina.

Most of the other trails in the park climb up to the main ridge from the lower ground around the perimeter of the park, following creek beds or spur ridges. This statement needs a great deal of qualification, since there are trails of some length running roughly parallel to the main ridge, in addition to many short trails that connect various major trails together.

We will begin our description with the Cades Cove area on the Tennessee side at the western end of the park. As we mentioned earlier, the park service has turned the Cove into a sort of museum of mountain life. An 11 mile one-way auto road takes visitors through this area. Cades Cove is also the site of a large, developed campground that can serve as a base for a number of interesting hikes. To get there, enter the park at Gatlinburg and take the Little River Road west to Cades Cove. You can also take Tennessee Route 73 east from Townsend into the park and the Little River Road.

The ranger station at Cades Cove campground can issue permits for back country camping. You can also get them at the Abrams Creek station, which is at the western edge of the park on the Happy Valley Road seven miles north of U.S. Route 129.

From Cades Cove, you have convenient access to nearly 70 miles of trails, not counting the Appalachian Trail mileage. There are a number of good day hikes available, and some 17 backcountry campsites are scattered through the area. A.T. trail shelters in this area include Russell Field, Mollies Ridge, and Moore Springs (actually just off the A.T.).

The flat floor of Cades Cove is just under 2000 feet, while Rich Gap on the main ridge of the Smokies is 4600 feet high, so you can do some considerable climbing in the area. If you want to stick to leveler ground, the Abrams Falls trail is a good one. The falls are quite impressive, and the stream is reputed to contain trout. Gregory Bald on the main ridge is a good example of the grassy bald. And it is also famed for its flame azalea displays in early summer.

The Elkmont—Tremont area extends from Cades Cove east to the Newfound Gap Road. The area includes 83 miles of trails, in addition to almost 25 miles of the A.T. on the ridge crest that forms the area's southern boundary.

The Elkmont campground along the Little River Road is the park's largest. You can get backcountry camping permits there, at the Sugarlands visitors center on the Newfound Gap Road just inside the park entrance, or at the Tremont Ranger Station off the Little River Road just west of the junction of that road with Tennessee Route 73. The area has 13 backcountry campsites.

If you are looking for a good climb on a short hike, try the trails up Road Prong or Chimney Tops. Both of these trails take off from the same parking area along Newfound Gap Road. If you are looking for a nice, relaxed walk in the woods without any hard work, the Cucumber Gap and Huskey Gap Trails near the Elkmont campground are the places to go.

On the .A.T. in this section, Spence Field offers open grassy areas, Thunderhead Mountain is an impressive heath bald, and Clingmans Dome is the highest point in the park.

The area east of the Newfound Gap Road in both Tennessee and North Carolina we will combine under the rather cumbersome title of Greenbrier—Cosby—Big Creek—Cataloochee area. This represents about a third of the park, and it offers some 250 miles of trails as well as 30 miles of the A.T. On the Tennessee side of this area, a developed campground is located at Cosby. It can be reached by taking Tennessee Route 32 south from the town of Cosby into the park. There is a ranger station just north of the campground and another in the Greenbrier area just inside the park off Tennessee Route 73 east of Gatlinburg. Camping permits can also be obtained at the Sugarlands visitors center on the Newfound Gap Road just into the northern boundary of the park.

On the North Carolina side, there are developed campgrounds at Balsam Mountain and Smokemont. The Balsam Mountain camp is on a spur road north from the Blue Ridge Parkway east of Cherokee. The Smokemont campground is just off the Newfound Gap Road near the park's southern boundary.

The North Carolina side also has two primitive campgrounds. One is at Big Creek just south of Waterville. Take I-40 to the Waterville exit. Cross the Pigeon River and turn left beyond the bridge. The park entrance is two miles away on this road, and the campground is just beyond the entrance.

The Cataloochee primitive campground is off North Carolina 284 about six miles north of Dellwood. Primitive campgrounds have pit toilets, but they are accessible for car camping.

Ranger stations in this area are near the Big Creek and Cataloochee primitive campgrounds and just inside the southern boundary of the park on the Newfound Gap Road.

This area has 20 backcountry campsites. Six of these, marked with asterisks on the map, are designed for horse parties, and one, the Towstring Horse Camp, No. 51, is for horse parties only. Rationed areas in this portion of the park include seven shelters on the A.T. as well as the shelters on Mount LeConte, Laurel Gap, and Kephart Prong.

This area is so large and various that it is difficult to characterize briefly. One of the most popular places is Mount LeConte, where the rationed shelter is supplemented by the Mount LeConte Lodge. The lodge is privately owned and operated under a contract with the Park Service. It is a small group of rustic cabins surrounding a main building with dining room. The cabins are lighted with kerosene lamps and heated with wood stoves. Rents at the time of our visit to the park were $12.00 a day for room and two meals. The lodge is open from mid-April through October and it is usually booked up way in advance. If you want to stay there, write the LeConte Lodge, Gatlinburg, Tenn. 37738. You can get to the lodge by hiking up the Alum Cave Trail or by the A.T. and Boulevard Trails, or by horse up the Rainbow Springs Trail from Gatlinburg.

Mount LeConte is not a place to seek the solitude of the wilderness. Hikers are numerous just about all year, but the place is extraordinarily beautiful. The sunrise from Myrtle Point is justly famous. It was for us the first time our senses agreed with Galileo. It is really the earth that moves, not the sun.

The Greenbrier Basin is a place for seeking solitude. It is a vast area almost without trails. However, one trail in the area follows a creek up to Ramsey Cascade, at 60 feet the highest waterfall in the park. Greenbrier Cove is an excellent example of a southern mountain cove hardwood forest.

To the west of Greenbrier, the area around Cosby campground has the views from Mount Cammerer and the Albright Grove along the Indian Creek Trail. The grove is a stand of virgin hemlock and yellow poplar.

Big Creek is a relatively undeveloped area which therefore receives less use than places like Mount LeConte. The area has over 20 miles of trails, many of which involve considerable climbs from the creek bottom up onto the high ridges of the Smokies. From Big Creek campground up to Mount Sterling, the climb is just over 4000 feet.

The North Carolina side of the park east of the Newfound Gap Road receives more use by equestrians than any other area. One place that you won't find horses is on Breakneck Ridge. The extremely steep, rough trail up the ridge is in an area that the park service wishes to keep in primitive condition. Horses are not allowed because they might bring in the seeds of alien plants in their droppings.

West of the Newfound Gap Road in North Carolina are the Deep Creek campground and ranger station, located about three miles north of Bryson City. The area has about 80 miles of trails and 10 backcountry campsites. The main trails are one up Deep Creek, and two ridge top trails: Thomas Divide and Noland Divide. These trails are also accessible from the Clingmans Dome Road at their upper ends.

The North Shore Road west from Deep Creek campground will take you to Noland Creek near its mouth and access to 12 miles of trails and seven backcountry campsites. One of these is reserved for horse parties. The main trail in this area goes up

Noland Creek and connects with a trail on Forney Ridge.

Immediately to the west, the Forney Creek watershed has about 38 miles of trails and 10 backcountry campsites. A trail up the creek climbs to meet the Forney Ridge Trail near its northern end, and the combined trails climb up to meet the end of the Clingmans Dome Road.

Hazel Creek is an area that is very popular with trout fishermen. The major trail in the area goes up Hazel Creek and climbs to the A.T. near Silers Bald. According to the Sierra Club Totebook, this area is noted for its pushy bears.

However, to the west is the Twentymile Creek area, which may be the least heavily used portion of the park, and consequently, probably an area where bear trouble is less likely. Access to this area is through the ranger station at the park boundary just north of North Carolina Route 28. Take U.S.129 to 38 and go east for about two miles to get to the road to the station.

The trail up Twentymile Creek starts out right near the ranger station, but Eagle Creek to the east has no road access at all. The last six miles of the A.T. in the Smokies are on Twentymile Ridge between Twentymile Creek and Eagle Creek.

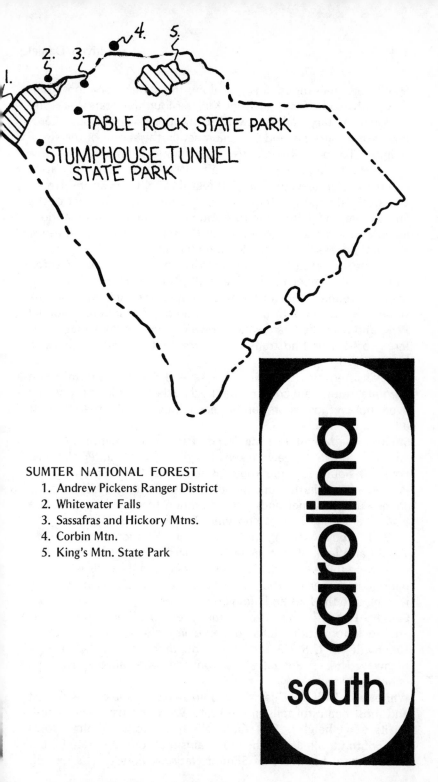

TABLE ROCK STATE PARK

STUMPHOUSE TUNNEL
STATE PARK

SUMTER NATIONAL FOREST
 1. Andrew Pickens Ranger District
 2. Whitewater Falls
 3. Sassafras and Hickory Mtns.
 4. Corbin Mtn.
 5. King's Mtn. State Park

carolina

south

South Carolina's mountains run along the state's common boundary with North Carolina from King's Mountain State Park and National Military Park westward to the point where South Carolina, North Carolina, and Georgia meet on the shores of the swift-running Chattooga River, a distance of some 100 miles.

The state's highest peak, Sassafras Mountain, is in this area, and rises to an elevation of 3550 feet. Hiking trails of any length are confined largely to the Andrew Pickens Ranger District of the Sumter National Forest and to a couple of state parks. Exceptions include short walks up to several of the region's most picturesque mountain peaks (Sassafras Mountain included).

We are indebted in our research of this state to Mr. Carlton Faubion, a member of the Greenville Natural History Club and South Carolina Chauvinist extraordinaire. We met him on the slopes of Mt. LeConte in the Great Smoky Mountains National Park, and when he heard what we were doing he immediately offered to help us find trails in his area that we might otherwise have missed.

He insisted also that there are several scenic spots in South Carolina's mountain country that backpackers would enjoy seeing even though those spots can be reached by car. We therefore list a few of them here.

Stumphouse Mountain Tunnel State Park — This park is near the entrance to the Andrew Pickens District of the Sumter National Forest on South Carolina Route 28 about eight miles northwest of Walhalla. The partly built tunnel represents an 1853 attempt to "hand" drill a tunnel under the mountain to provide a rail route from Charleston, S.C., to Knoxville, Tenn.

While you're visiting this park, Mr. Faubion suggests you should also look at **Isaqueena Falls,** named for a Cherokee princess (were there ever any Indians in state park legends who were mere commoners?) who is said to have escaped pursuit by leaping into the falls and hiding on a small ledge.

Caesar's Head — This is the name given to a line of high cliffs and rock formations located approximately 30 miles north of Greenville on U.S.276 and only a hundred yards or so off the highway. There are great views from the observation tower (elevation 3300 feet).

Whitewater Falls — This, Mr. Faubion says, is one of the highest and most beautiful falls in the east. (We don't have any figures on its exact height). The water falls from North Carolina down into South Carolina over the mountains that form the state border and northern boundary of Sumter National Forest. It is just off

South Carolina Route 107 (a highway which runs north through the Andrew Pickens District of the Sumter Forest north of Walhalla).

Foothills Trail

Location: Andrew Pickens Ranger District, Sumter National Forest. The trail's northern end is at Ellicott's Rock, a scenic point where the Nantahala National Forest of North Carolina, the Chattahoochee National Forest of Georgia, and the Sumter National Forest of South Carolina share a common boundary. The southern terminus is at Long Mountain Lookout Tower just west of Carolina Route 107 near Oconee State Park.

Length: 18 miles including a 2.5 mile spur trail from the Chattooga River to the Chattooga Recreation area.

USGS Quad: Tamassee, S.C.

Description: Oconee State Park makes a good overnight stop before embarking on this backpack trip. There's even a grocery store there in case a last-minute check of gear shows you've forgotten something crucial like candles or flashlight batteries. The park's 1165 acres lie entirely within the Sumter National Forest today. They were acquired by the state in 1935, primarily to preserve the stands of champion-size virgin hardwood trees. There are 140 campsites and 18 cabins. For further information, write: Oconee State Park, Walhalla, S.C.29691.

To reach the beginning point for your hike, drive east from the park to South Carolina Route 107. Continue east across that road, then north to the Long Mountain Lookout Tower. There's a designated campsite at the foot of the tower, too, in case you prefer it to the more civilized state park. Elevation on the mountain is about 2000 feet.

For the first half mile north you will stay on top of Long Mountain. Then there's a gentle drop down to an elevation of about 1600 feet and another designated campsite just south of the trail's crossing of Tamassee Creek near its headwaters.

The entire length of this trail runs through wild, unsettled country, almost entirely wooded and continuously mountainous. It seems appropriate that the area in general, and particularly that portion of the trail which follows the Chattooga River, was chosen for filming part of the movie *Deliverance*.

From Tamassee Creek, the trail climbs gently again to 2000 feet and closely parallels the state highway for about a mile. A short footpath leads west to the highway about a mile north of the creek.

The trail turns east then, heading uphill quickly to Dodge

Mountain (elevation 2400 feet) and proceeding parallel to and about half a mile south of, Tamassee Road, downhill very slowly for two miles to an elevation of 1200 feet at Townes Creek and another designated campsite. Tamassee Road, providing good trail access from highway 107, crosses the trail near this campsite.

The path from Townes Creek north to the next campground at Cherry Hill (and another junction with South Carolina Route 107) is 3.41 miles. For the first three miles you will be following the old Winding Stair Road steadily uphill to about 2300 feet. At the end of the first mile you should have a good view to the east of Towne's Creek Falls. There's another designated back country campsite at the end of the second mile.

Cherry Hill Campground is located at the junction of the trail with highway 107, Big Bend Road and Burrell's Ford Road. The trail leads north and west from here to reach the Chattooga River and state line at Big Bend in just over two miles.

The trail parallels Big Bend Road for the first half mile, then crosses it and heads north along Burrell's Ford Road for just under a mile. It turns west then and follows an old logging road to the base of Big Bend Mountain and another designated campsite.

The trail west continues to climb up Big Bend Mountain, passing beneath its crest at an elevation of about 2700 feet. Eight-tenths of a mile from the campground on the Big Bend Mountain, you will reach the spectacular Chattooga River at Big Bend (about ¼ mile north from Big Bend Falls). The trail follows the river and state line north from here all the way to Ellicott's Rock (about 5½ miles).

Four miles north of Big Bend along the river you will reach Burrell's Ford Campsite in a rare wide grassy expanse of riverbottom land. Half a mile north is Burrell's Ford across the river into Georgia.

The trail parallels Burrell's Ford Road north a short distance, then leaves it to follow the river (at an elevation of about 2100) about half a mile to a designated campsite. Another campsite is located half a mile farther on where East Fork Creek flows into the Chattooga.

A side trail from this creek confluence leads east 2.5 miles to the Chattooga Recreation Area. For the first mile, this side trail follows cliffs above the East Fork. These cliffs are approximately 70 feet high and are continuously wet with ground water seepage. The trail leaves the cliffs and joins an old logging road for about a mile, then continues cross country to the Recreation Area and Walhalla Fish Hatchery. Car access to the Recreation Area is about two miles of very curvy road from state route 107.

Back on the main trail, the path leads north along the Chattooga from the mouth of East Fork Creek about 1.7 miles to Ellicott's Rock and the state line. There's a designated campsite in the first half mile north of East Fork Creek. (See Nantahala Forest trails in North Carolina for another trail that leads to Ellicott's Rock from the north).

Kings Mountain State Park and National Military Park Trails

Location: 12 miles northwest of York on South Carolina Route 161.

Length: There are two long trails in this park and one short one. The first, providing a 5½ mile round trip, is primarily a horse trail and runs west from the stables at York Lake to the border with the adjacent Kings Mountain National Military Park. The second, three miles one way, runs west from the campground at Lake Crawford to the headquarters of the adjacent National Military Park. The short trail makes a 1½ mile loop around Crawford Lake.

USGS Quads: Kings Mountain, S.C.; Filbert, S.C.; and Grover, S.C.

Description: Kings Mountain was the site of a critical Revolutionary War battle which brought fame to a colorful backwoodsman named John Sevier, colonel in the North Carolina militia and later first governor of Tennessee. A good biography of Sevier and a lengthy description of the Battle of Kings Mountain can be found in a book by Michael Frome called *Strangers in High Places* (Doubleday & Co., Inc., $6.95).

The battle took place in September 1780 and might never have occurred at all if Colonel Patrick Ferguson, officer in charge of the occupying British troops in the region, had wisely left the hillfolk to their own business. He made a big point, instead, of ordering them to stop sheltering deserters and threatening to burn their houses and lands if they didn't stop the practice.

Some 600 angry hillmen assembled at Sycamore Shoals, N.C., on September 26, and, under command of Colonel Arthur Campbell with Sevier as one of the seconds-in-command, they began a march against a man they considered their personal enemy. The militiamen traveled lightly in buckskin shirts and homespun trousers with nothing to carry but small knapsacks, tomahawks and scalping knives, and lightweight hunting rifles made in Pennsylvania and famed for their long-distance accuracy. This group was joined by 300 more men before they reached Kings Mountain, where Ferguson had chosen to make his stand.

With their fierce drawn swords and bayonets, the British at first were able to chase the mountain men back into the woods. The settlers regrouped then, however, and fought Indian style, "darting from tree to tree, shouting war whoops and following their commanders into battle," according to Michael Frome. Sevier was said to have perfected a particularly blood-curdling yell himself. It may have contributed to the fact that he lived a charmed life, never once wounded in thirty-five engagements although he always rode at the head of his troops.

The British style of formal fighting was no match for the guerrilla warfare of the colonials, and their smooth-bore musket, the "Brown Bess", was no match for the New World long rifles.

Within an hour the Americans had gained the crest and killed Ferguson himself. The British suffered three hundred casualties; the remainder surrendered. Colonial casualties numbered less than one hundred. The battle of Kings Mountain was said to have revitalized a flagging colonial spirit and slowed the advance of General Cornwallis, contributing to his ultimate surrender at Yorktown the following year.

The current state park and national military park combined encompass some 11,000 acres. The countryside is quite wild and some of the park boundaries have never been ascertained precisely on the ground.

There's a campground on Lake Crawford, at the northern edge of the state park; cabins for group campers are located on York Lake in the southern part of the park. There is a trading post on Crawford Lake where one can purchase supplies, and there is a refreshment stand but no restaurant.

The trail from York Lake (a 5½ mile round trip) is designed mainly for horses and begins at the stables on York Lake. (The park does not rent horses; local individuals and saddle clubs bring their own. Stalls for 60 horses are provided). The trail is blazed with horseshoe symbols. It heads west and north up Long Branch Creek, then over a mountain at an elevation of about 750 feet along an old logging road.

It reaches a road where a sign identifies the trail at the border of the state park with the national military park. If you continue west along this road, you will reach the national park headquarters in another 2½ to 3 miles. If you turn east on the road, then turn right (south) at that road's first junction with another, you will arrive back on the trail very near Lake York in just over two miles.

A better trail for hikers begins at the Lake Crawford campground and heads west over the mountains in some very wild country to the headquarters and parking lot of the National Military Park.

This trail is three miles one way, and you must retrace your steps to get back to the campground. It proceeds gradually by a series of ascents and descents from an elevation of about 750 feet at the campground to a 945-foot peak well within the boundaries of the national military park.

After crossing that peak, the trail winds south past some graves of soldiers who died in the Battle of Kings Mountain, past two monuments erected by the National Park Service and into the parking lot near the park headquarters. Exhibits at the headquarters building describe details of the battle and terrain of the national park.

The park's third trail is called the Gold Nugget Trail and makes a 1½ mile loop of Lake Crawford from the campground. You will be able to see abandoned mine shafts at a number of locations in the park. The area was a major source of gold from Revolutionary times to well into the 19th century.

There are plans for another trail in the two parks. It will run for some 20 miles through both the state park and the national military park, then turn north across the border into North Carolina to join with other historic trails being planned in that state. Some back country campsites and shelters will be constructed along the route.

For up-to-date information before you visit Kings Mountain State Park, write the park headquarters at R.F.D.#2, Box 230, Blacksburg, S.C. 29702.

Table Rock State Park Trails

Location: 16 miles north of Pickens on South Carolina Route 11.
Length: 8 miles
USGS Quad: Table Rock, S.C.
Description: There are actually three long trails in this state park, but they combine to form a loop that makes a good day hike. They are well-blazed (each of the three in a different color) and well-maintained.

The first trail heads west and north from the campground at Pinnacle Lake four miles to the top of Pinnacle Mountain. Elevation change is from 1160 feet at the campground to 3425 feet on the peak.

For the first mile, the trail follows Carrick Creek west. There are a number of rapids and small waterfalls on this mountain stream. As the creek curves north the trail leaves it to continue west up gentle then steeper slopes by a series of switchbacks. The trail turns south along a slope at about 2600 feet elevation to a waterfall at the headwaters of Mill Creek. Then it winds north again and climbs to join with the Table Rock trail about a mile east of the Pinnacle Mountain summit. Between this junction and Pinnacle Mountain you will pass over the tops of three ridge peaks at elevations of about 3200 feet. The view from the Pinnacle is spectacular in all directions.

Retrace your steps to the junction, then continue east on a ridge top near the park's northern boundary to reach Table Rock Mountain at elevation 3124. When you pass the trail leading back downhill (right) to the campground, you'll know you have just another ¾ mile to go to reach Table Rock.

Both Table Rock and the Pinnacle dominate the landscape of this part of South Carolina. You can see them from miles away. Table Rock is a gigantic granite dome with a crew-cut of trees on top. Its north face of bare rock is particularly striking.

The trail from Panther Gap back to the campground leads south downhill by a series of hairpin switchbacks. It joins the Pinnacle Mountain trail in 2¼ miles at the northeast edge of the campground.

Table Rock State Park encloses 2860 acres of Blue Ridge Mountains south of Table Rock Reservoir. In addition to hiking trails, it has a 25-acre lake, 109 campsites, 12 cabins (they rent for $13 to $14 weekdays, $39 to $43 on week ends.) Capacity of the cabins varies from 6 to 12 persons. All have air conditioning and fireplaces; some also have central heat. There's a restaurant and a "trading post" which sells food, camping supplies, novelties and gift items.

For more information, write Table Rock State Park, Route 3, Pickens, S.C. 29671.

Corbin Mountain

Location: Drive approximately 30 miles north of Greenville on old U.S. Route 25; turn north at the state line on Gap Creek Road. Go west half a mile to the base of Corbin Mountain and park your car. The trail is actually an old fire road which leads to the lookout tower.

Length: 2 miles

USGS Quad: Zirconia, S.C.

Description: Corbin Mountain is located on the North Carolina-South Carolina state line. Elevation is 2900 feet. In clear weather you can see Greenville and the foothills of the Piedmont to the south. The climb to the fire tower is steady, from an elevation of 2280 feet at Gap Creek Road to 3025 feet on top.

Sassafras Mountain to Hickory Nut Mountain

Location: Take U.S. Route 178 16 miles north from Pickens, then

turn right at a sign marked Sassafras Mountain Tower and proceed five miles on a paved road to the summit.

Length: 2 miles

USGS Quad: Eastatoe Gap, S.C.

Description: The trail begins at the fire tower on Sassafras Mountain, highest peak in the state at 3554 feet. There's a spectacular
view of the Great Smoky Mountains to the northwest and of several blue-water lakes.

If you walk east from the tower about 150 yards into the woods,
you will reach an old logging road. Follow this road and an abandoned bare-wire phone line south by southwest along a ridge to
Hickory Nut Mountain (elevation 3483 feet).

No automobile road leads to Hickory Nut Mountain and few
people have ever even heard of it; yet it's the second highest
peak in South Carolina and provides some beautiful views of the
surrounding area.

The river you can see down in the valley about half a mile east
is the South Saluda. It parallels the trail and forms the boundary
here between Greenville and Pickens Counties. The top of Hickory Nut Mountain is narrow, long and level. Our friend Mr. Carlton Faubion from the Greenville Natural History Club is fond of
picking out resemblances and says this mountain looks like a
pork chop bone.

CHATTAHOOCHEE NATIONAL FOREST
1. Cohutta Ranger District
2. Chestatee (Cooper Creek) Ranger District
3. Brasstown Ranger District
4. Tallulah (Rabun Bald) Ranger District

In northern Georgia, the mountains of the Appalachian chain gradually give way to rolling hills. Most of the rugged high country lies within the boundaries of the Chattahoochee National Forest which stretches across the north end of the state from the South Carolina border on the east to U.S.411 on the west.

The Blue Ridge and Cohutta Ranges come together here, forming a large "V" with the Blue Ridge as eastern arm and the Cohutta as western. The highest point in Georgia lies along the Blue Ridge at Brasstown Bald with its elevation of 4784 feet.

The Appalachian Trail follows the Blue Ridge for 78 miles from Bly Gap at the North Carolina border southwestward to the southern terminus of the trail at Springer Mountain, elevation 3782. A six-mile approach trail runs from Amicalola Falls to Springer Mountain, providing access to the A.T.

The other trails described in this chapter lie in four separate sections of the Chattahoochee. In the east, the trails around Rabun Bald are located in the Warwoman Wildlife Management Area near Clayton, Ga. Brasstown Bald is a few miles southeast of Young Harris, Ga. The Cooper Creek Recreation Area lies in the Cooper's Creek Game Management Area, about 10 miles southwest of Blairstown, and the Cohutta trails are located within the Cohutta Wildlife Management Area northeast of Chatsworth.

For a map and general information about the Chattahoochee National Forest, contact the Supervisor's Office, U.S.Forest Service, P.O.Box 1437, Gainesville, Ga. 30501. The telephone number is 404/532-6366.

For information about specific trails, contact the district ranger offices listed in the text.

TRAILS AROUND RABUN BALD

William Bartram Trail

Location: The trailhead is at Warwoman Dell Picnic Area northeast of Clayton, Ga. Entering Clayton from either north or south on U.S. 23 and 441, turn east on Warwoman Road. The Heart of Raven Motel stands at the intersection. The picnic area is about four miles from the intersection.

Length: 8 to 9 miles.

USGS Quad: Rabun Bald, Ga.

Description: William Bartram was a Pennsylvania Quaker who traveled the Appalachians collecting and describing plants. He came through this area in 1775 on a trip from Charleston, S.C., that took him into North Carolina nearly as far as the Smokies. He was something of a pantheist, who saw God's hand in every aspect of nature — but particularly in plants. He traveled these mountains alone and unarmed.

An association has been formed to promote the development of a trail along the route that Bartram followed in 1775, as far as it can be reconstructed. Eventually, if all goes well, the trail will start in South Carolina, cut across this corner of Georgia and head north into North Carolina.

This short completed section heads north from the Warwoman Dell picnic area at 1800 feet. It follows the banks of a creek for just over a mile before climbing up onto Beck Ridge. The climb is fairly steep to about 2900 feet and then levels off as the trail follows- the ridge top. The trail turns north along the east slope of Rock Mountain to join with the Rabun Bald Trail which it follows up to the summit of Rabun Bald. Elevation at the junction is about 3200 feet. The trail continues north through Windy Gap, climbs to 3500 on Blacks Creek Knob and then turns east at Rattlesnake Knob.

From Rattlesnake Knob, the direction is northeast to Rabun Bald. The elevations along this ridge climb from Double Knob (3700 feet) to Flat Top (4100 feet) and then to Rabun Bald at 4696. However, the trail does not go across the highest points. It stays on the slopes of the ridges, passing Flat Top at 3800 feet.

However, past Saltrock Gap, the trail climbs quickly up to 4000 feet, then gradually up to 4200 feet before climbing the west slope of Rabun Bald in a series of switchbacks.

According to our informant at the Tallulah Ranger District Office in Clayton, there is a spring along the trail about one mile south of Rabun Bald. This is the only water source on the trail between the climb onto Beck Ridge and Rabun Bald.

Rabun Bald is a heath bald, but there is a grassy area around the old fire tower that is suitable for camping.

2 — Rabun Bald Trail

Location: The western end of the trail is on Forest Highway 23 just north of Clayton. The eastern end is on Forest Road 7. To reach this road, take Warwoman Road about 10 miles east from Clayton. Turn north on Forest Road 7 to the trail.

Length: 11 miles

USGS Quad: Rabun Bald, Ga.

Description: This trail illustrates some of the problems involved in putting together a guide such as this. The name of this trail and its location are taken from Forest Service engineering maps. According to these maps, the trail begins just east of Clayton, leaving the road at an elevation of about 2200 feet. It climbs quickly to 2900, skirting Raven Knob and Rock Mountain. Just beyond Rock Mountain, the Bartram Trail joins this one from the south. From there to the top of Rabun Bald, the new Bartram Trail follows the route of the Rabun Bald Trail.

From Rabun Bald eastward, according to Forest Service maps, the trail goes steeply downslope, crossing Coldspring Gap at about 3600 feet. It then drops quickly to about 2500 feet at Forest Road 7.

However, in *A Backpacking Guide to the Southern Mountains,* Samuel M. Blankenship describes a hike on a trail from Forest Road 7 to Rabun Bald, and he says the trail is identified by a roadside sign as "Three Forks Trail." To make matters more confusing, the trailhead, he says, is just north of a creek bridge over a stream marked "Addie Branch." However, he says the stream is actually Bailey Branch. On the USGS quad, Addie Branch is just north of Bailey Branch, but who made the mistake, the author or the Forest Service?

The safest course is probably to hike the Bartram Trail and check with the Ranger Station in Clayton first, if you are interested in some additional exploring. They can supply current information on the status of any other trails in the area.

8 — Big Ridge Trail

Location: Take Warwoman Road about eight miles east of Clayton. A dirt road branches off to the north. About 1½ miles up the road, it forks. The trail heads north from the fork. North end of the trail is at the Bartram Trail on the southwest slope of Rabun Bald. *Length:* 4 miles

USGS Quad: Rabun Bald, Ga.

Description: From the road at 2500 feet, the trail climbs up onto Big Ridge, rising steeply to just over 3000 feet. From there it rises steadily but less dramatically to 3800 feet. The last mile of the trail is a fairly steep climb up to 4400 feet at the trail junction.

For current information on the trails around Rabun Bald, contact the Tallulah Ranger District, Ranger Station, N. Main St., Clayton, Ga. 30525. The telephone number is 404/782-3320.

TRAILS AROUND BRASSTOWN BALD

Brasstown is a place name that turns up in a number of places in the southern Appalachians. Apparently it is based on a mistake. The Cherokees called some areas Itse'yi, meaning new green place or place of fresh green. Tin-eared settlers heard this as Untsaiyi (brass), and so we have Brasstown Bald as the highest place in Georgia.

The Forest Service has constructed a rather elaborate visitor's center on top of the Bald — elevation 4784 — and built a steep winding road up to it. This road is open from 8 a.m. to 6 p.m. every day. It starts at Georgia Route 180 about 10 miles east of U.S. 129 and 19 south of Blairsville, and climbs up to a parking lot located perhaps 200 feet below the summit. From there, you can walk up a steep, paved footpath, or pay to be hauled to the top in a little bus.

The visitors' center itself is a circular building with windows all around. Inside are exhibits about trees, animals, and Indians. During working hours, Forest Service people are in the building to give out information.

74 — Trail to Young Harris along Wolf Pen Ridge

Location: Just up the hill from the Brasstown Bald parking lot, a jeep road curves around the hill to the right (as you ascend). This is one end of the trail. The other is in the town of Young Harris where a jeep road hits U.S. Route 76 next to the Methodist Church and opposite a Union 76 gas station.

Length: 6 miles

USGS Quad: Hiawassee, Ga. (Note: the peak of Brasstown Bald itself is at the northern edge of the Jack's Gap quad, but it is not really necessary to have this quad to use this trail. The trail is shown as a jeep road on the quad.)

Description: We hiked this trail on a beautiful day in late October. The sky was a cloudless blue, the fall color was at its peak, and the cool autumn day was perfect for hiking.

The jeep road curves around the eastern side of Brasstown Bald through a stand of young birch trees. Once around to the north slope, the trail heads north, following the ridge. The trail is an old wagon road that was blasted out of the side of the mountain years ago. The drill holes for the dynamite are still visible in the sheer rock that borders the trail in many areas.

The trail follows the west slope of the ridge for a short distance, passing Little Bald Mountain, crosses through a gap in the ridge to the east side, and then crosses the ridge again to follow the west slope once more. After passing Chimney Top, the trail turns west along the south slope of Double Knob, rounding the west end of the mountain in a low gap that may have been dug out years ago. This first section is perhaps 2½ miles long. It is steadily and fairly gently downhill all the way, from about 4000 at Brasstown Bald down to 3200 feet where the trail rounds Double Knob. There are many beautiful views along this section.

Hugging the west slope of the ridge, the trail continues downhill, with the grade getting somewhat steeper. The trail is steadily angling westward, until it is going almost directly east-west where it ends in Young Harris. The elevation of the town is 2000 feet.

A short distance above the town, the trail forks. The north fork goes to a radio tower, while the south fork continues into town.

We saw water seeping from the rocks at many places along the trail. This was during a rather dry fall, so it is possible that some of these spots would be springs with enough flow to make them good water sources in wetter seasons. However, we found no actual water sources along the trail.

29 — Arkaguah or Track Rock Trail

Location: From the northwest corner of the parking lot at the Brasstown Bald visitors' center to the Track Rock Archeological site on Track Rock Road. Track Rock Road goes east from U.S. 129 and 19 about 2½ miles south of Blairsville. It angles east and north to join U.S. 76 just over a mile south of Young Harris. A sign on the highway directs you to Track Rock.

Length: 5.5 miles

USGS Quads: Hiawassee and Blairsville

Description: The signs at the Brasstown Bald trailhead were down when we were there. If they are still down, you can find the trail by looking for the toilets at the corner of the parking lot. The trail goes right past them.

The trail heads west on Locust Ridge, down from about 4500 feet at the parking lot through Rock Gap and Low Gap at 3500 feet. Crossing Locust Log ridge, it climbs slightly back up to 3600 feet, and then drops steeply down to 2200 feet where it ends at Track Rock Road.

Track Rock itself is covered by petroglyphs of Cherokee origin. An exhibit at the Brasstown Bald visitors' center explains these drawings.

45 — Jack's Knob

Location: From the south end of the Brasstown Bald parking lot to the Appalachian Trail at Jack's Knob.

Length: The Forest Service says 4.5 miles, the Appalachian Trail Conference says 5.5 miles

USGS Quad: Jack's Gap, Ga.

Description: From just over 4500 feet at the parking lot, the trail goes south on Wolfpen Ridge, losing altitude slowly at first, and then dropping steeply, dipping 1400 feet in less than a mile to Jack's Gap at 3000 feet.

At the Gap, the trail crosses Georgia Route 180 and then climbs up again along Hiawassee Ridge. Highest points on the ridge are

Henry Knob at 3530, Brookshire Top at 3552, and Eagle Knob at 3566. The trail divides on the north slope of Jack's Gap. One fork goes around the mountain to the right (west), while the other goes left (east). The right fork joins the Appalachian Trail at Chattahoochee Gap. A side trail runs about 125 yards down a steep slope from the A.T. to Chattahoochee Spring, source of the Chattahoochee River and of drinking water for hikers.

The left fork of the trail joins the A.T. at Red Clay Gap, east of Jack's Knob. The Rocky Knob trail shelter is on the A.T. one mile east of the trail junction. A spring lies about 150 yards downslope from the shelter.

For current information about the trails around Brasstown Bald, contact the Brasstown Ranger District, Ranger Station, Highway 76 West, Blairsville, Ga. 30512. The telephone number is 404/745-6259.

TRAILS IN THE COOPER CREEK RECREATION AREA
86 — Yellow Mountain Trail
Location: Cooper Creek Recreation Area campground off Forest Road 236 about two miles north of Georgia Route 60. Take Route 60 about seven miles northwest from the hamlet of Suches to reach 236. The other end is on Forest Road 33 about six miles west of Lake Winfield Scott Recreation Area on Georgia Route 180 and about five miles north of Suches.
Length: 2.5 miles
USGS Quad: Mulky Gap, Ga.
Description: One of the problems involved in producing a guide like this is maps. The standard tourist map of the Chattahoochee National Forest — like the standard tourist maps of other National Forests — shows only a fraction of the roads on the forest. One that it doesn't show is Forest Road 33, the eastern terminus of the Yellow Mountain Trail. However, it is there, according to engineering maps in the Atlanta regional office.

The trail starts at the Cooper Creek Recreation area at an elevation of 2200 feet and heads east in a gradual climb up the ridge of Yellow Mountain to 2900 feet. An easy downslope leads to Addie Gap at 2700 feet, and then the trail continues down to cross the Pretty Branch of Bryant Creek. The trail then turns south to cross Cooper Creek before reaching the road.
89 — Mill Shoal Trail
Location: The Mill Shoal Trail also begins at the Cooper Creek Recreation area and heads north and east. It crosses Forest Road 39 before climbing to the top of Spencer Ridge (or Spencer

Mountain, depending on the map you are using).
Length: 4 miles
USGS Quad: Mulky Gap
Description: The trail heads north out of the campground, climbing over the ridge of Yellow Mountain at 3800 feet. North of the ridge, the trail crosses Forest Road 39. Several streams lie athwart the trail, most notably Bryant Creek, which the trail follows for a short distance northward before turning westward around Hickory Knob and up to Spencer Mountain, elevation 3000 feet.

For current information on the trails around Cooper Creek, contact the Chestatee Ranger District, Corner of Warwick & N. Derrick St., Dahlonega, Ga. 30533. The telephone number is 404/864-2541.

TRAILS IN THE COHUTTA WILDLIFE MANAGEMENT AREA

The Cohutta district contains some of the wildest and most rugged country in the Georgia mountains. Forest Service gravel roads skirt the edges of the Wildlife Management Area, but only a few dirt roads cross through it. Now that 34,000 acres of these mountains have been set aside as a wilderness area, these roads will presumably be gated and seeded, and the land will be left alone for people to enjoy.

One of the roads that will probably be closed is Georgia Route 2, which crosses the Cohutta from east to west. However, the road will continue to provide access to the edges of the wilderness area.

Jack's River Trail
This trail is shown on the Forest Service tourist map following the course of the Jack's River across the Cohutta for about 11 miles. It is mainly on the bed of the narrow gauge railroad that was built into these mountains when the area was logged off.

We really can't recommend this trail. It crosses the river about 40 times all told, and the crossings can be difficult. In low water, you would have to wade in knee deep water at times, and at high water, you could find yourself waist deep in a very fast moving current. There are better ways to drown yourself.

However, we want to mention the trail, because the Jack's River is a good trout stream. If you are into fishing, you might want to take Georgia Route 2 east from Cisco, Ga., about 10 miles to the Shedd's Creek Rd., and then north for a short distance to the Jack's River Bridge. From there, you could follow the trail upstream to a good fishing spot.

12 — Rough Ridge Trail

Location: The south end of the trail leaves Georgia 2 about one mile north of the junction with Forest Road 64 and goes north to the Jack's River. Across the river, hikers can connect with an old logging road between Rock Wall and Penitentiary Creeks. This road leads up to Hemp Top tower and Forest Road 73.

Length: 7.5 miles (to the river)

USGS Quad: Hemp Top, Ga.

Description: The trail leaves the road just south of Cowpen Mountain at an elevation of 3700 feet, following Rough Ridge north. The ridge is narrow and steep sided, but the top is relatively level. As the trail nears the river, at 2800 feet elevation, the downslope becomes quite steep for a little less than a mile, dropping to the river at 1700 feet.

9 — Tearbritches Trail

Location: Take Forest Road 18 north from U.S. 76 about 20 miles east of Chatsworth, Ga. Then go right on Forest Road 68 and left on Forest Road 64. The trail head is about two miles from the 68-64 junction. The trail ends at the confluence of Tearbritches Creek and the Conasauga River.

Length: 3.5 miles

USGS Quad: The northern portion of the trail is on the Hemp Top, Ga. quad. The southern portion is in an area which has been surveyed but which is without a published map.

Description: See following

90 — Chestnut Creek Trail

Location: Goes north from Forest Road 64 between the 64-68 junction and the Tearbritches Trail. North end is at the confluence of the Conasauga River and Chestnut Creek.

Length: 2 miles

USGS Quad: Hemp Top, Ga.

Description: See following

11 — Conasauga River Trail

Location: Coming north from U.S. route 76 on Forest Road 18, go right on Forest Road 68, and then right again on Forest Road 64. The trailhead is about one mile north of the 68-64 junction.

Length: 4.5 miles

USGS Quad: Dyer Gap and Hemp Top, Ga.

Description: We made an overnight trip on the Conasauga, Chestnut Creek, and Tearbritches Trails, so it will be convenient to describe them together. We started on the Chestnut Creek Trail, going north from Forest Road 64. We turned northeast on the Conasauga River Trail, and then returned south on the Tearbritches Trail.

The road up to the trail was one of the more hair raising we encountered in the mountains. Narrow, with a long steep drop to one side, and a washboard surface rough enough to send the rear wheels of our car skittering.

The Chestnut Creek Trail was well marked with a sign visible from the road. If the sign hadn't been there, we could still have seen the area provided for parking cars along the north side of the road.

The trail is well marked with paint blazes, and it gets enough traffic to be easy to follow even without the blazes. It heads northeast from the trail head in a series of short switchbacks downhill, and then turns northwest down a long draw filled with tall, straight yellow poplars until it reaches Chestnut Creek. The elevation change in the first half mile or so is 600 feet: 3200 feet at the road and 2600 at the creek. However, the grades are not very steep.

The USGS quad shows three streams coming into the Conasauga River from the south in this area. None of these streams is named on the map, but Chestnut Creek is apparently the middle one.

The trail follows the creek to the Conasauga, crossing it five times along the way. The trail was very easy to follow, and we made all the crossings without getting our feet wet. However, we were there in a very dry autumn. The area had been without rain for weeks. But Chestnut Creek is probably not too formidable even in spring time.

It would certainly be beautiful in early summer. Rhododendron is everywhere along its course. When it blooms, the place must be spectacular. The forest here is mixed pine, hemlock, and hardwood, with yellow poplar the most common tree.

Chestnut Creek joins the Conasauga at about 2300 feet elevation. A large, flat, relatively open area where the two streams come together would make an excellent campsite. Families with small children could handle the Chestnut Creek trail for an overnight outing. It is only two miles from the road to the river, and the slopes are not very steep along the way.

Taking the Conasauga River Trail from Forest Road 64 to this junction would be an even easier walk, according to the map. We did not walk this portion of the trail, but it should be not much more than a mile in length.

We turned northwest along the Conasauga, following a trail that is rarely more than 100 feet from the river. It gets that far away only in a couple of places where the narrowness of the valley forces it up onto the hillside. We crossed the river nine times altogether, again managing to keep our feet dry with some judicious rock hopping.

Good campsites are fairly common at intervals along the creek. We stopped in a flat area on the bank that had enough soil to allow us to drive in our tent stakes.

Night out in the woods can be a magical experience. On this night, the sky was clear, dominated by a bright moon about one day from the full. We heard a screech owl around twilight and then silence except for the sound of the river nearby.

Moonlight is one of the casualties of modern urban life. We live surrounded by artificial light. Even in campgrounds, the trees are festooned with bright lanterns. But, the silver grey of moonlight on the pale trunks of the yellow poplars is worth the hike all by itself.

If you are looking for more practical reasons for walking the Conasauga, the trout might provide one. We had no fishing gear with us, but we saw a number of fish of keeper size in the river's many pools.

The Conasauga River Trail ends at the junction with the Tearbritches Trail. This junction is on an island of private land in the midst of the forest. A small metal sign tacked to a tree along the trail marked the forest boundary. If you miss that, note that the river turns from northwest to west and the trail climbs steeply up the spur of a hill on the south bank. About 100 feet above the river, the trail drops back down the other side of the hill and crosses a small creek that flows north into the Conasauga. This is Tearbritches Creek, and here the Tearbritches Trail begins.

The trail turns south along the creek for perhaps 50 yards before turning east, crossing the creek again, and starting uphill. Signs made all this clear when we were there, but it is unwise to count on the durability of signs.

The Tearbritches Trail climbs up on a ridge immediately east of the creek that gives it its name. It follows this ridge all the way to the trailhead at Forest Road 64. The first part of the climb is steep and long. With only one switchback to ease the grade, the trail goes from about 2000 feet at the creek to 3200 feet in less than one mile. The first half of this distance is the most difficult. Take it slow, because most of this trail is uphill. Once you hit 3200 feet, you keep going up at a somewhat slower rate until you reach the top of Bald Mountain, 4010 feet. From there, you follow a gentle downslope to the road.

Some fierce weather must hit the tops of these high ridges in winter. The trees — mostly oaks — look stunted, twisted, and gnarled. The trail takes you higher than most of the surrounding country, but the views are not all that good, largely because the tangle of stunted trees and shrubs blocks out most of the scene.

Less than a mile from the trail's beginning, we crossed a tiny rivulet. It held perhaps an inch of water standing virtually still. It may run a bit more in wetter weather. This is the only water along the Tearbritches Trail.

When we reached the road, we were about a mile and a half from where we had left our car at the Chestnut Creek trailhead. It is downhill most of the way, so it wouldn't have been a difficult walk. Fortunately, we caught a ride in the back of a pick up truck, and that made it even easier.

For current information on the trails in the Cohutta District, contact The Cohutta District Ranger Office, Chatsworth, Ga.

8.

9.

10.

11. KNOXVILLE

12. 13. 14.

TELLICO PLAINS

15.

CLEVELAND

7.

5.

4.

3.

2.

1.

6.

CHATTANOOGA

CHEROKEE NATIONAL FOREST
1. Ocoee Ranger District
2. Hiwassee Ranger District
3. Tellico Ranger District
4. Nolichucky Ranger District
5. Unaka Ranger District
6. Watauga Ranger District

7. **GREAT SMOKY MOUNTAINS NATIONAL PARK**

8. **PICKETT STATE PARK**

9. **HONEY CREEK WILDERNESS**

10. **BIG RIDGE STATE PARK**

11. **FROZEN HEAD STATE PARK**

12. **VIRGIN FALLS**

13. **NORTH RIDGE TRAIL OF OAK RIDGE**

14. **PINEY RIVER TRAIL**

15. **LAUREL-SNOW WILDERNESS**

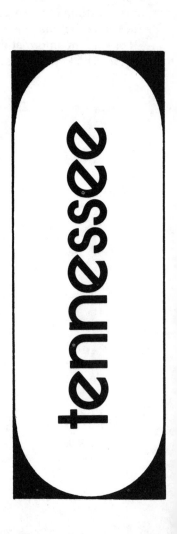

tennessee

This state is unique among those in the Southern Mountains in that its officials have made a concerted effort to coordinate their outdoor recreation facilities into an interrelated system. Now being developed is a series of seven long scenic trails that will incorporate many existing trails, campgrounds and scenic areas in state and city parks, the Cherokee National Forest, and the Great Smoky Mountains National Park. (See separate section for description of trails in the Smokies). From a total of 21 state parks existing in 1965, there are now more than 115 existing and proposed outdoor recreation areas.

The need for a wide distribution of trails of all types was recognized by the Tennessee Trails System Act of 1971. The Act provides the authority and guidelines for development of hiking, equestrian, and bicycle trails in and near urban areas and in the remote wilderness areas in the state.

Two trail systems were authorized by this Act. The Tennessee Recreation Trail System will be composed of relatively short, urban-oriented trails while the Tennessee Scenic Trail System will be made up of long distance trails located in the remote natural areas of the state.

A trails coordinator was hired by the state to plan routes and acquire land, and an umbrella Tennessee Trails Association was formed in 1968 to represent the various groups, both public and private, with an interest in trails. For up-to-date information, contact: Trails Administrator, Tennessee Department of Conservation, 2611 West End Avenue, Nashville, Tennessee 37203.

Big Ridge State Park Trails

Location: About 15 miles north from Knoxville on Tennessee Route 33 then west about three miles on Tennessee Route 61.

Length: There are a number of trails in this state park; two of them, Dark Hollow Trail and Indian Rock Trail, combine to make a good day hike of about 8 miles.

USGS Quads: White Hollow, Tenn., and Big Ridge Park, Tenn.

Description: This 3600-acre park is one of the oldest of those which surround the Tennessee Valley Authority's Norris Lake. The shores of the lake are heavily wooded for the most part; the breaks in the forest often turn out to be the sites of old pioneer villages. Dark Hollow and Indian Rock Trails lead to one of these sites called Sharp's Station.

The campground in Big Ridge Park offers 50 tent campsites and a handful of cabins. There is also a restaurant.

To reach the beginning point of Dark Hollow Trail, take the

campground road northeast past the ranger's residence and the cabins, and past a road that leads north to a group camp. You will see a sign announcing the trailhead.

The path climbs first over Pinnacle Ridge, from an elevation of 1000 feet to 1300 feet, then back down to 1200 feet in Dark Hollow. At about mile 1.5, you will pass by an old cemetery, referred to locally as Old Dark Hollow Graveyard and on U.S. Geological Survey maps as Langley Cemetery.

From the hollow the trail climbs up and over Big Ridge Mountain (elevation 1400 feet), then down into the flat area near the lake known as Big Valley. About a mile from Dark Hollow, you will come to the first junction with Indian Rock Trail. You can turn east there or wait for the other end of the loop. You'll reach it in another ¼ mile if you continue toward Norris Lake and the end of Dark Hollow Trail. The entire loop of Indian Hollow Trail is just over two miles.

If you turn right at this second junction, you will reach, in a few hundred yards, the two giant boulders known as Indian Rocks. A settler named Peter Graves was ambushed by Indians here in 1794. His slaying was thought to be an act of retaliation for Indians killed in an earlier battle by Graves and the other men of nearby Sharp's Station Fort. A few months' after Graves' death, the fort itself was attacked, but the settlers warded off the onslaught and nobody was even injured.

In another half mile you will reach the site of the old fort itself. It was thought to have been built in 1784 or 1785; no one is certain about those dates. The first session of Knox County Court, however, meeting at White's Fort (now Knoxville) in 1792, ordered a road built from that place to Sharp's Station. There are mentions of several members of the Sharp family in Knoxville newspapers of that period, and there are descendents of that same family working at Big Ridge State Park today.

From the fort the trail continues right to make a wide loop and rejoin Dark Hollow Trail in just over a mile.

For up-to-date information, write Big Ridge State Park, Maynardville, Tennessee 37807.

Frozen Head State Park Trails
Location: 12 miles west of Oak Ridge or 5½ miles east of Wartburg on Tennessee Route 62.
Length: The longest trail in this park is 35 miles and follows the boundaries of the old Morgan State Forest, predecessor to Frozen Head State Park before new acreage was added. Shorter trails,

still long enough for a day hike or overnight trip, cut across the park's interior from west to east to connect with the boundary trail at various points. They include: a trail that follows an old jeep road from the campground northeast to Peach Orchard Gap, four miles; Panther Branch Trail, 2½ miles; North Mac Mountain Trail, three miles; and Spicewood Trail, 2½ miles.

USGS Quads: Fork Mountain, Tenn.; Petros, Tenn.; and a tiny corner of Camp Austin, Tenn.

Description: This 10,218-acre park was transferred from state forest ownership to state park ownership in 1971. The name was changed at that time from Morgan State Forest to Frozen Head State Park. (Your geological survey maps will still say Morgan State Forest). The new name was derived from the dominant mountain in the park, elevation 3324 feet. New acreage has been added to this public property in recent years, but the Boundary Trail still follows the old perimeters.

Frozen Head encompasses some unusually wild country (not typical of state parks), and the trails — when we checked on them in January 1975 — were not in uniformly good condition. It was possible to follow them without getting lost, however, and the state Department of Conservation was trying to arrange for a maintenance crew to get them in shape before summer.

The Boundary Trail begins by crossing the road that leads to the campground and heading south across Rough Ridge (climbing from an elevation of about 1400 feet at the campground to 2200 feet on top of the ridge, not quite a mile south of the road).

From the ridge, the trail climbs down to reach Rocky Fork Branch at 1600 feet. It follows that stream uphill to its headwaters and then farther up to the peak of Chimney Top Mountain, elevation more than 3000 feet. If you look northeast from Chimney Top you will see a long ridge of mountains across a wide gap and at the north end of that ridge is Frozen Head Mountain. If you continue along the Boundary Trail you will soon curve around to follow the ridge and you will reach Frozen Head Lookout Tower in another 4½ miles.

Meanwhile, the trail continues south and downhill in easy stages to the southwest corner of the park and then east to reach an old logging road that parallels Beech Fork Creek about two miles (as the trail winds, not as the crow flies) from Chimney Top.

The trail follows the road north to its end where a creek flows through Lowgap Hollow to cross the trail. It climbs up Little Fork Mountain and reaches Mart Fields, one of those high, treeless glades for which the Appalachians are famous. Mart Fields makes a good natural campsite or at the very least, a long lunch and siesta break. The elevation is 3100 feet.

At the eastern end of Mart Fields, a short spur trail branches off to the left (northwest) to connect with Spicewood Trail. Spicewood combines with this southern section of the Boundary Trail to make a nice loop of nine miles that begins and ends at the campground.

If you continue north along the Boundary Trail, you will come to another spur trail leading west to Spicewood in about ¼ mile. Both these spurs are about ¼ mile long.

In another half mile, you will reach the peak of Frozen Head Mountain, located almost at the exact center of the park. The elevation at the lookout tower is 3324 feet. Directly east of you and just outside the park boundary is the town of Fork Mountain and the mountain for which the town was named. The ribbon of water that flows through Fork Mountain and on to the eastern horizon is the New River.

From Frozen Head the trail continues north along a ridge top for the most scenic section of the trail three miles to Cold Gap and the Garden Spot along the top of the Tennessee Valley Divide at the park's northeastern boundary.

About a mile north of Frozen Head you will meet the North Mac Mountain Trail coming in from the west. In another ¼ mile you will reach Cherry Log Gap. Elevation is still close to 3,000 feet and it never gets lower than 2800 feet on this entire stretch. You will cross Little Fork Mountain and then at Peach Orchard Gap you will meet the jeep road that leads north one mile to Emory Mountain and then southwest three miles to the campground.

If you stay on the Boundary Trail past Peach Orchard Gap you will curve east and reach Coffin Springs in another mile. Shortly afterward, you will come to Cold Gap and the Garden Spot and turn west.

The trail west along the park's northern boundary extends for some 3½ miles from the Garden Spot to Phillips Creek.

On the way you will cross the top of Bald Knob, elevation 3248 feet, it offers views every bit as good as those from Frozen Head. A mile west of Bald Knob you will cross several branches of Rayder Creek near its headwaters. The trail west of Rayder Creek crosses Jury Ridge and then drops down to 1400 feet above sea level at Phillips Creek before turning sharply south.

The distance from Phillips Creek to the campground is two miles. The route will take you along the creek to its head, up and over the long ridge of Bird Mountain at about 3000 feet, and finally downhill again in a mile-long descent to the campground on the North Prong of Flat Fork Creek.

Four good day hikes or week end trails lead east from the campground across the interior of the park to connect with the Boundary Trail at various points.

The northernmost of these is actually a *jeep road* but is seldom used by motor vehicles and makes a good walk of four miles northeast along the south slopes of Bird Mountain to Emory Mountain and then south across a Squire Knob to join the Boundary Trail at Peach Orchard Gap.

The second trail is called *Panther Branch*. This one also follows an old road, at least for the first mile and a half, upstream along the banks of the North Prong of Flat Fork Creek. The road ends where Emory Gap Branch and Panther Branch flow into the North Prong. The trail angles south along Panther Branch for half a mile then curves sharply west to join the North Mac Mountain Trail near the top of Old Mac Mountain at an elevation of about 2500 feet. A loop that begins at the campground and combines Panther Branch Trail with part of the North Mac Mountain Trail is about five miles long and makes an excellent week end backpacking excursion.

The *North Mac Mountain Trail* by itself begins just south of the road leading to the campground where the Boundary Trail crosses that road. It leads east and very gradually but consistently uphill from 1600 feet to 2900 feet at a junction with the Boundary Trail about a mile north of the Frozen Head Lookout Tower. A good loop that combines the North Mac Mountain Trail, Boundary Trail, and Spicewood Trail would give you a trip of seven miles.

Spicewood Trail branches east off the Boundary Trail about an eighth of a mile south of the Boundary Trail junction with North Mac Mountain Trail. It follows the northern slopes of Chimney Top Mountain just south of Spicewood Branch to a crossing of Spicewood Banch near that stream's headwaters. The trail branches soon after the creek crossing. The right branch leads ¼ mile to meet the Boundary Trail at Mart Fields, and the left branch meets the Boundary Trail about ¼ mile north of Mart Fields and ½ mile south of the Frozen Head Lookout Tower.

For current information, write Frozen Head State Park, Petros, Tenn., or call 615/346-3318.

Pickett State Park
Location: On the Kentucky-Tennessee border about 15 miles northeast of Jamestown on Tennessee Route 154.

Length: This 11,754-acre state park has a number of short hiking trails which can be linked for somewhat longer trails. Total trail length in the park is 58 miles. We have described two of the longer ones where backpacking is allowed and which combine to make a trip of some 14 miles. We also note routes for a couple of good day trips.

USGS Quad: Sharp Place.

Description: Walk half a mile north of the park office on highway 154 to reach the beginning of the *Hidden Passage Trail* or proceed north from Pickett Lake across the natural bridge rock formation (that actually functions as a bridge for hikers) and east along the Bluff Trail (one mile) to reach the highway directly across from the Hidden Passage Trail.

Hidden Passage is eight miles long and marked with light green. It winds along the ridges above Thompson Creek at an elevation of between 1200 and 1400 feet and passes through many unusual sandstone formations. After about the fifth mile you will come to a short side trail leading to Double Falls.

At the park's eastern boundary, Hidden Passage Trail ends. Just before that ending, Rock Creek Trail intersects and heads back west six miles to Route 154.

Rock Creek Trail is marked with brown blazes; it crosses Rock Creek five times, proceeds at an elevation of about 1400 feet, and takes you by some beautiful sandstone bluffs. Its western end at the road is about three miles north of the park office.

You can make this loop an overnight one and you can camp anywhere along the trail as long as you secure permission first from the park office.

A good day hike in the park combines the Hazard Cave Trail (white blazes) with Indian Rock House Trail (orange blazes).

Proceed south from the lodge along the ridge line 1½ miles to Hazard Cave, said to have sheltered Indians and outlaws (of course!). Across highway 154 from the cave parking lot is a half mile walk to an old Indian Rock House.

Back at Hazard Cave, you can make a loop north another 1½ miles to join Ridge Trail just west of the picnic area.

Ridge Trail is three miles long and marked with light green blazes. It begins at the footbridge at the end of the Lake View Trail (¾ mile) on Pickett Lake or at the west end of the picnic area. It follows along or on the slopes above Natural Bridge Creek.

For further information, write Pickett State Park, Jamestown, Tennessee 38556.

North Ridge Trail of Oak Ridge

Location: Along a greenbelt that follows the northern boundary of the city of Oak Ridge. There are eight access points to the trail from the Outer Drive, a street that also parallels the northern city limits. The western edge of the trail is between Morningside Drive and Louisiana Avenue; the eastern terminus is at Endicott Lane.

Length: 7½ miles with several side trails of about ½ mile each providing access to the main trail.

USGS Quad: Clinton. (You can also get a city map of Oak Ridge which shows the North Ridge Trail by writing the Chamber of Commerce, 1400 Turnpike, Oak Ridge, Tennessee 37830).

Description: Oak Ridge, as you probably know, was built from scratch in a single season early in 1943 as a base for the Army's Manhattan Project, the building of the atomic bomb which would be dropped on Hiroshima, Japan, two years later.

Retail businesses operated from tents and trailers in the beginning, much like those which opened in the western gold rush boom towns of the previous century.

There was one major difference between the gold rush towns and Oak Ridge, however. Oak Ridge had a master plan, a detailed architectural design laid out by the Chicago firm of Skidmore, Owings and Merrill. The retail businesses might operate temporarily from trailers, but the location of those trailers would be zoned quite strictly.

Within that master plan was an idea now common but unique at that time — the designation of linear greenbelts and circular patches of woodland scattered throughout the city's residential areas. When the city was turned over to the public by the Atomic Energy Commission in 1955, the new city managers agreed to preserve the greenbelt concept.

In April 1969, a local conservation group called the Tennessee Citizens for Wilderness Planning received approval from the Oak Ridge City Council to develop hiking trails through the greenbelts, under supervision of the city landscape gardener. By autumn of that year, a 1½ mile circular trail was developed, and its availability was publicized throughout the city. The response of and use by the citizens of the city to this first trail encouraged the members of TCWP to proceed with the development of a longer footpath through the entire northern greenbelt city boundary.

It took two years of volunteer effort to build the North Ridge Trail. The wooded area it traverses encompasses 564 acres. At times the corridor on either side of the trail is 150 feet wide; in other places it is almost 2,000 feet. The area is not mowed, so the understory of grass and shrubs makes good habitat for wild animals. If you couldn't hear the sounds of traffic in the distance, it would be easy to believe you were walking on a path far from any city.

Stands of shortleaf, Virginia and white pine occur occasionally along the trail, but the forest consists mainly of hardwoods. Oaks and hickories predominate, although in watersheds along the slopes you can find beech, sugar and red maple, black cherry and yellow poplar. Typical wet-site species are sycamore, sweetgum, white ash, black willow and hackberry.

Wildflowers abound as they do in all southern mountains. Among the more common plants in the greenbelt are Jack-in-the-Pulpit, varieties of trillium, wild onion, Solomon-seal, lady slipper, rattlesnake orchid, buttercup, may-apple, bloodroot, wild ginger, and goldenrod. The blooming periods of these different flowers extend from early March to late October.

The path goes through varied terrain, passes numerous rock outcroppings, and generally avoids steep grades. Spring-fed creeks are crossed at several places. Roads interrupt the trail only twice — approximately one mile from its westernmost origin and near the center of the trail.

This second road-crossing is quite near one of Oak Ridge's city parks, which provides parking facilities and a ready access point to the trail.

In 1973 the North Ridge Trail was designated officially as a National Recreation Trail. The main trail is blazed white; access trails are blazed blue. Double blazes designate sharp turns in the trail.

A short description of the eight access points, prepared by the Environmental Quality Advisory Board of Oak Ridge, is reproduced here:

Access 1 — the westernmost, is about 1.4 miles west of Illinois Avenue (Tennessee Route 62) on West Outer Drive (just west of 852 West Outer Drive). The access trail follows the old Reservoir Road for about 320 yards and then enters the greenbelt via a log ramp on the right (eastern) side of the road. As it crosses Illinois Avenue, it bears slightly to the north (downhill) and then follows an asphalt-surfaced road, bearing right and then left around a hairpin curve. The trail enters the greenbelt again (on the east) about 30 yards past this curve.

Access 2 — is near the northeast corner of the service station property at the northeast corner of Illinois Avenue and West Outer Drive. A large sign that designates the trail is located near

Illinois Avenue at the northern edge of the service station; the entrance to the access trail itself is located about 60 yards east of this sign, near a smaller sign that says, "This is your trail." The blue-blazed access path goes downhill (rather steeply) for about 250 yards to the hairpin curve on the asphalt-surfaced road. After following the road (to the right) about 30 yards, the North Ridge Trail enters the wooded greenbelt (uphill, to the east) near a tree marked with two white blazes. After bearing uphill for about 100 yards, it turns sharply left for about 100 yards, then right across a power line right-of-way. The trail bears slightly uphill across this right-of-way and again enters the woods near a blazed tree.

Access 3 — is to the left (west) of the turn-around at the end of North Walker Lane. Between Access 3 and Access 4, the trail crosses the old Highland View Trail.

Access 4 — is where the North Ridge Trail crosses Key Springs Road at a point about 100 yards above (south of) the entrance to Key Springs Park. Key Springs Road enters Outer Drive about 0.1 mile west of New York Avenue. The trail crosses Key Springs Road about 0.65 mile from the intersection of Outer Drive and Key Springs Road. Cars can be parked at Key Springs Park.

Access 5 — is on Orchard Lane, at the intersection of Orkney Road and Orchard Lane; this access follows the old Cedar Hill Trail. Between Access 5 and Access 6, the trail crosses the old Orchard Trail.

Access 6 — is on Outer Drive at a point directly opposite Georgia Avenue. This access is up a dirt driveway, past a house, and follows the old Georgia Trail.

Access 7 — is approached from the west side of the city pumping station on Outer Drive at a point slightly west of Delaware Avenue. This access is also the access to the Delaware Trail. The actual entry to the access trail is located at the northeastern corner of the city property. Between Access 7 and Access 8, the trail crosses the old Englewood Road.

Access 8 — the easternmost access to North Ridge Trail, is on the extension of Endicott Lane to Reel Heights. A sign on the western side of the road marks the entrance.

Future development may include: (1) pedestrian crossing signs at the roads which cross the trail; (2) identification and information structures at the major trail access points; and (3) development of a nature trail concept, including plant identification, trail guides, and other devices.

Lookout Mountain Trails

Location: From downtown Chattanooga, take Broad Street (Tennessee Route 2) to the junction of Tennessee Route 11 and 148 (follow the signs to Lookout Mountain; there are plenty of them).

Length: There are a number of trails on Lookout Mountain, all designed to help you appreciate the natural history of the area and also to understand the historical significance of Civil War battles fought in the vicinity. The Boy Scouts have combined parts of several of these for one all-day hike they call the Blue Beaver Trail. It proceeds from the road junction to the peak via trails the National Military Park people call Skyuka, Hardy, Earthworks, Cravens, and Bluff Trails. Total distance is 7⅓ miles. Elevation range is 700 feet to 2135 feet.

USGS Quads: Hooker and Fort Oglethorpe

Description: To appreciate this trail, it is necessary to digress with a bit of military history. First, we should explain that "Blue Beaver" does not refer to some extraordinary species of rodent found only in the vicinity of Chattanooga. "The Beavers in Blue" was a phrase coined by the Confederates to describe the activity of the Union soldiers bottled in Chattanooga during the summer of 1863, who were said to be always busy clearing trees for fuel, shelter, and fortifications.

These soldiers were forced to busy themselves with such defensive activities because their planned route south to Georgia was blocked by the Confederates, who had control of Lookout Mountain and Missionary Ridge.

A number of attempts by the Union to scale Lookout Mountain from the west side had been thwarted by Confederates stationed on nearby Signal Mountain who signaled information about the Union movements to their forces on Lookout. On the eventful day of November 23, 1863, a heavy fog capped the mountain, however, and signaling attempts were futile. By the end of the day, General Joe Hooker and his men were in command of the mountain, and the Confederates had been forced to flee.

So much for history. Here's the trail route:

It begins at a tourist attraction called Red Caboose No. 148 (remember, this is See Rock City country; it pays not to be surprised at anything). The Caboose is located at the junction of Highways 11 and 148. Hikers should follow blazes which say RR. This stands for Reflection Riding, a non-profit corporation that holds about 400 acres designed to preserve and maintain the natural beauty of the area. Trees, shrubs and flowers along the trail are marked for your information.

When you reach the park boundary on your climb (the park's official name is Chickamauga and Chattanooga National Military Park), you will notice historical markers that show how the Union forces lined up for their assault.

The major battle took place at Cravens House, about halfway up the mountain as the proverbial crow flies and about five miles of trail walking. This structure, which has been restored by the Association for Preservation of Tennessee Antiquities, is the oldest surviving building on the mountain. It was built in 1856 by Robert Cravens, pioneer ironmaster and one of the early industrialists in Chattanooga. During the Civil War, it was used as a Confederate field hospital.

Water is available for hikers at Cravens House.

The trail from the house weaves gradually back and forth until you reach the base of the escarpment. A sturdy iron stairway makes it possible to reach the actual peak and landscaped grounds of Point Park with ease.

From your vantage point you have an excellent view of the Chattanooga Valley, Tennessee River, and Missionary Ridge, that other strategic Confederate stronghold which held up the Union advance into the Confederacy.

For more detailed historical information and maps, write to the Chickamauga and Chattanooga National Military Park, Fort Oglethorpe, Georgia 30741.

Piney River Trail

Location: From Tennessee Route 68 in Spring City, take Shut-In Gap Road west one mile to the Piney River Picnic Area. The trail begins across the road and heads up the hill from the picnic area. Follow signs to the Twin Rocks Nature Trail.

Length: About 4 miles

USGS Quad: Pennine. (You can also purchase a topographical map for a nominal price from the Public Relations Department of Bowaters Southern Paper Corporation, Calhoun, Tennessee 37303. The number of their map which includes this trail is 1413.)

Description: This trail is one of several innovative recreation facilities developed by Bowaters Southern Paper Corporation and its subsidiary, the Hiwassee Land Company. Paper companies have traditionally provided campgrounds or public access to fishing lakes for good publicity and tax write-offs, but hiking trails are rare. We owe the existence of those developed by Bowaters mainly to a public relations officer named Clarence Streetman. He has been invited to speak on a number of occasions to other firms in the industry on his experience with (and the good publicity resulting from) the trail development. So hopefully we may see more trails on paper company lands in the future.

When we hiked the Piney River Trail in October 1974, it wasn't quite finished. It should be, however, by the time you read this. We were escorted by Bowaters forester Dave Rhyne, who planned the route and constructed much of the trail himself.

The trail was still so fresh in the fall that we encountered no litter at all. The only signs of human passing were the bottles of unopened Mountain Dew (the soft drink variety) Dave had hidden at every spring along the way and which were apparently his main source of body fuel for trail-blazing work.

Other outdoor experts on this trip included several naturalists from the Georgia Parks Department, two camping store owners, a forestry student, and the trails coordinator for the Tennessee Department of Conservation. None of this expertise, needless to say, prevented one of us from falling off a log and several of us from falling into streams. We had superior help, however, in identifying the plant species along our route.

The trail from Shut-In Gap Road climbs gently uphill for a few hundred yards before the short Twin Rocks Nature Trail curves off to the left and heads back to the road. Elevation at this point is 1000 feet. The main trail winds south to follow wooded slopes at an elevation of 1500 feet above the Piney River for about two miles. You will pass a small waterfall near the source of a mountain stream on the way.

We got a late start that first day, so we camped at the first point where the trail drops down to the river bank (elevation between 1100 and 1200 feet) about 2½ miles from the road.

Next morning, we crossed the river, hit an old railroad bed, and followed it for just over half a mile to reach a delightful little canyon where Rockhouse Branch tumbles down a mountain to join the river. There was a deep pool for swimming and big flat rocks good for spreading out picnic gear.

The trail eventually will head northwest up this branch on its south side, climbing about 400 feet (from an elevation of 1100 feet to 1500 feet) in approximately a mile before picking up an old road and following it out to another picnic area at the paper company's Stinging Fork Pocket Wilderness on Shut-In Gap Road. This point will be about four miles by road west of the Piney River Picnic Area where the trail begins. There are parking areas for cars in both places.

Because this last trail portion wasn't finished when we were there, we continued west along the railroad bed, leaving the Piney River to follow bluffs above Duskin Creek for about two miles. We left the creek then, walking under a high rock overhang that compared scenically with Alum Cave Bluffs in the Great Smoky Mountains National Park, and then uphill (to about 1700 feet) to join an old logging road. On the road we proceeded past newly planted groves of loblolly pines and a heap of rusting abandoned stoves and washing machines (we knew then that we were approaching civilization) to a point near Shut-In Gap Road where we had parked some of our cars. From that spot back to the Piney River Picnic Area was about seven miles.

For up-to-date information on the status of this trail write the Hiwassee Land Company, P.O. Box 537, Spring City, TN 37381.

Laurel-Snow Pocket Wilderness Trail

Location: Take U.S. Highway 27 three miles north from Dayton, then turn left just after passing a hospital, continue 1½ miles, then turn right (there are signs that say Laurel-Snow Pocket Wilderness) for another mile and a half to reach the parking lot and picnic area.

Length: 8 miles

USGS Quad: Morgan Springs. (You can also order a topographical map from Bowaters Southern Paper Corporation, Calhoun, TN 37303. Their map number for this plot of ground is 1411).

Description: This is the largest of the Bowaters Southern Paper Corporation's "pocket wilderness" areas in Tennessee; it contains some 710 acres. The rugged landscape provides great scenery, including two waterfalls, for hikers. Bowaters has set aside its "pocket wildernesses" as areas where no timber cutting will be carried on. Development of the areas is limited to the creation of footpaths only.

You should allow six to eight hours one way for this trip if you plan to visit both falls.

The trail begins at the parking area and proceeds north along Richland Creek (at an elevation of about 1,000 feet) for about two miles. There are bluffs or steep slopes on both sides of the banks for most of this distance, although after the first ¾ mile, Morgan Creek comes into Richland Creek from the left (west) and flattens out the terrain in that spot.

At the two and a half mile point, where Laurel Creek flows into Richland Creek from the right (east), the trail splits. The right fork winds uphill by a series of switchbacks (from an elevation of 1100 feet to 1700 feet) about ¾ mile to reach Laurel Falls. This branch of the trail crosses the creek above the falls and winds back south and southwest along the ridgetop for some 2000 feet to Bryan Overlook. There are several good camping spots in this area. Use special caution with your footing near the overlook. This bluff is more than 100 feet high.

To see Snow Falls on Morgan Creek, you will have to retrace your steps back down to Richland Creek, follow it north a few hundred feet, then double back and uphill on the trail's left branch.

You will reach the broad, flat ridge top (this one is also 1700 feet above sea level) in just over a mile by a series of easy switchbacks. The trail at this point branches again. If you turn right (north), you will follow along the edge of the ridge for ¾ mile, curve left to cross the ridge and reach Snow Falls on Morgan Creek.

If you turn left when you first reach the ridgetop, the trail will take you to another overlook at Buzzard Point (just over half a mile). From this point you can retrace your steps back to the intersection or you can reach it by a short loop that takes you briefly west along the bluff edge, then north across the flat, wide mountain top before rejoining the trail.

Eventually all these trail branches will be connected to provide more loop trails.

The Laurel-Snow Trail has been designated by the Bureau of Outdoor Recreation and U.S. Department of the Interior as a National Recreation Trail. It has also been named by the Tennessee Department of Conservation as a State Recreation Trail.

Honey Creek Pocket Wilderness Trail

Location: In Scott County, at the junction of Honey Creek and Big South Fork River. From Elgin, take Tennessee Route 52 west about a mile, then turn right (north) on a country road and proceed four miles before turning left to cross Clear Fork River and proceed 3.8 miles to the parking area for the pocket wilderness.

Length: The trail is a loop covering about five miles. An alternate route bisects this one to provide a smaller loop of 2½ to 3 miles. You should plan from five to six hours for the entire hike.

USGS Quad: Honey Creek. (Or order Bowaters Southern Paper Corporation topographic map number 1211).

Description: The area features spectacular scenery, "rock houses" used by Indians, and except in very dry periods, numerous small waterfalls. At one point, the hiker has a view of the river from a vantage point some 250 feet above the stream.

Ladders of pressure-treated wood with safety cages are provided for scaling the bluff to the overlook.

If you begin your loop by taking the east fork at the parking lot, you will walk about 2500 feet on more or less flat terrain before reaching the actual boundaries of the pocket wilderness where no timber cutting is permitted.

Proceed northwest along the slopes of the mountain at an elevation of about 1200 feet. After half a mile, you will reach a side trail which branches off to an overlook then rejoins the main trail ¼ mile farther on at the junction with the short loop alternate trail which leads 1¼ miles back across gently rolling woods to the parking lot.

The main trail, meanwhile, passes by Echo Rock, then winds downhill for a good view of the South Fork River at an elevation of 1000 feet.

The path soon leaves the South Fork River to wind west on a slope above Honey Creek for half a mile. When Honey Creek curves sharply south, the trail continues west along Fork Creek for ¼ mile. It doubles back on itself then and moves uphill to pass by an Indian Rock House. It rejoins Honey Creek and continues to follow it upstream for all but the last few hundred yards of the trail.

Virgin Falls Pocket Wilderness Trail

Location: From DeRossett, on U.S. Route 70 some 17 miles west of Crossville, proceed due south 5.9 miles on a county road, then turn right on a gravel road (there should be a sign that says Virgin Falls) and proceed two miles to the parking area at the beginning of the trail.

Length: 8 miles

USGS Quad: Lonewood. (Or order topographic map number 1508 from Bowaters Southern Paper Corporation, Calhoun, TN 37309).

Description: The trail leads southwest from the parking area to cross Laurel Creek. It proceeds then along level ground for about a thousand feet before winding down the mountainside to reach Big Laurel Falls, your first of several spectacular pieces of scenery on this small trail (which takes about seven hours, one way, to traverse).

The entire pocket wilderness area which includes the trail contains 317 acres. No timber cutting is permitted within its boundaries, and some of the trees (mostly the hardwoods) are more than 200 years old.

From the falls (at an elevation of about 900 feet) you will proceed slightly uphill and follow the slopes of a hill at about 1200 feet southwest for about ¾ mile until the trail splits to form a loop. If you take the right fork first you will continue along the slope of the mountain at about the same elevation for just over half a mile to Sheep Cave. Along the way, if you look carefully, you may see some old abandoned moonshine stills just down the mountainside.

From Sheep Cave you will head south to cross Little Laurel Creek on its way to join the Caney Fork River. From the creek, the trail begins a gradual ascent to reach Virgin Falls. This fall is formed by a stream that flows from a cave, runs some 50 feet over a rock surface, then drops over a 110-foot cliff. The stream disappears into another cave at the bottom of the falls.

The trail from the falls heads downhill overland on much the same route the water is taking underground until it reaches the wide, flat north bank of Caney Fork River. Proceed along this riverbank for half a mile or so before angling sharply uphill and northeast again, making an elevation change of 300 feet in less than half a mile before reaching the end of the loop and a junction with the main trail back to Big Laurel Falls and the parking lot.

CHEROKEE NATIONAL FOREST — TENNESSEE

The Cherokee National Forest forms a long, narrow strip along the eastern border of Tennessee from Virginia to Georgia with its eastern boundary following the state line. The forest's 600,000 acres are split into two sections by the Great Smoky Mountains National Park.

North of the park, the mountains are long, narrow ridges running from northeast to southwest. Between the ridges are valleys wide enough to support some settlement. South of the park, the forest tends to be more rugged and sparsely inhabited. The Tellico Ranger District immediately south of the Smokies is particularly wild. Government owned land there is of considerable size. Together with the adjoining areas of the Nantahale National Forest in North Carolina, the Tellico forms one of the largest blocks of wild land in the Appalachians.

The Cherokee offers splended opportunities for hikers. Many trails follow its creeks and ridges, and some of these are seldom travelled. There are many trails suitable for day hikes, and trips of a week or more also can be arranged.

In order to present the trails of the Cherokee in a manageable form, we have divided the forest into its constituent ranger districts and described the trails in each district separately. We will present the trails south of the Smokies first, followed by those to the north.

Trails in the Tellico Ranger District

The Tellico Ranger District runs from the Little Tennessee River in the north to a point about five miles south of the town of Tellico Plains. It has few roads and fewer settlements, but many trails.

It also has the European wild boar, a distinction whose value is rather dubious. It seems that in the first decade of this century, an English company called Whiting Manufacturing bought some large tracts of timber in North Carolina, just across the state line from the Tellico.

The company's hired manager decided to start a hunting lodge on Hooper Bald, one of the peaks of the Snowbird range. He was apparently a man who didn't believe in going at things in a small way. He built an enclosure for buffalo that measured a mile around, and his boar pen covered 600 acres.

In 1912, he brought in his animals. In addition to boar and buffalo, they included elk, European brown bear, mule deer, wild turkeys, and a substantial number of ring-necked pheasant eggs. The boar soon learned to escape from their enclosure after the manner of pigs, but they didn't stray too far away, since they got fed regularly at home.

The lodge was apparently supposed to draw rich hunters to shoot these exotic animals, but in that it was a failure. The manager eventually sold off his elk and disposed of his buffalo. The boars were taken care of by local poachers, as were the turkeys. However, the boars were a different matter.

According to *Strangers in High Places* by Michael Frome, there was supposed to be one great big hunt to eliminate the penned-up boars. However, when dogs were turned loose on the pigs, they wiggled through their previously prepared holes in the fence, treed the putative hunters, and took off for the woods.

All this occurred around 1920, and from that time until 1936, boar hunting was completely uncontrolled. Hunters and dogs went out year around and got as many animals as they could. In spite of this hunting pressure, the boar increased its range.

In 1936, a regular season was established for the boar. The animals today are firmly established in the Tellico and adjoining areas in North Carolina as well as in substantial areas of the Smokies.

There are people who will not stray out of sight of their cars in areas harboring wild boars. The animals certainly seem formidable enough to justify that kind of caution. They can weigh anywhere from 200 to 400 pounds, and they are armed with razor-like tusks and very sharp hoofs. Their lean, agile bodies are a long way from the sluggish rotundity of your average barnyard pig.

However, these animals are also hunted for about two months of the year, and as a result they are likely to be extremely cautious about getting near people. They are generally nocturnal and tend to spend the day holed up out of sight in a rhododendron thicket or some similarly out-of-the-way spot.

Certainly, if you see a wild boar, you should give it a wide berth. Your changes of actually seeing one are fairly slim, although you may well see the rooted up earth that boars leave behind when they feed. However, boar hunters are a different matter. During the October and November boar season, you should stick to established trails and avoid trying any cross country exploring. While on the trails, wear something bright red or international orange. You should also do this during the November and December deer season.

Road access to this district is via the town of Tellico Plains, TN, on Tennessee Route 68. From there, proceed on Forest Roads.

For convenience of presentation, we have divided the Tellico into three sections. The first one will cover the northernmost area as far south as Sassafras Ridge and Forest Road 217. The second will extend from there south to Forest Road 210, and the third from 210 south to the district boundary.

In the northern section, a major trail runs north-south along the ridge that forms the Tennessee — North Carolina border. This trail connects on the slopes of Big Fodderstack Mountain with a jeep road that heads north to Farr Cap at the junction of Forest Roads 59 and 26. Several trails branch off from this trail, heading west either along spur ridges or down creek beds.

We made a three day trip through the Tellico on a loop hike that took us up the North Fork of Citico Creek heading east, north along the state line ridge to Fodderstack, and then back west on Pinestand Ridge over what is actually a motorcycle trail.

95 — Fodderstack Trail — The south end of this trail is actually on Bob Bald, a peak on the North Carolina side of the border. It connects there with trails in the Nantahala National Forest's Cheoah district (see North Carolina chapter for details). The north end of the hiking trail is at the junction with the Pinestand Ridge motorcycle trail at big Fodderstack. Road access from the north is through the jeep trail which ends at the junction of Forest Roads 26 and 59 about five miles north of the Double Camp Recreation Area.

Length: Total length from Bob Bald to Farr Gap is 11 miles. The hiking trail from Bob Bald to Big Fodderstack is about five miles.
USGS Quads: Big Junction, TN., and Whiteoak Flats, TN.
Description: The trail heads north from Bob Bald (5100 feet), heading downslope along the ridge line to Cherry Log Gap which is 4400 feet above sea level. The trail from the north Fork of Citico Creek comes in at the gap.

In this area, the trail often follows the state line. The trail itself is marked with white paint blazes shaped like large block "i's". The state boundary is marked with orange paint blazes on trees. Do not confuse the two marks, since the trail splits from the state line north of Cherry Log Gap.

Between Cherry Log Gap and Big Fodderstack, the trail changes little in elevation. It generally skirts the peaks — Chestnut Knob and Rockstack — on their western slopes, returning to the ridge line at the gaps. Lowest point along this section is 3800 feet in Harrison Gap, just south of Big Fodderstack.

We saw a few extremely large hemlocks and oaks along the trail here. There are numerous excellent views to both east and west.

We found no water along the trail from Cherry Log Gap to Fodderstack. In a few spots, there were some damp rocks that might produce enough flow to provide drinking water in wetter times, but during the dry fall weather of our visit they were no help.

The slopes above and below the trail where it circles around the peaks are too steep to allow for camping, but in the gaps there are flat areas large enough to put up a tent. Unfortunately, we were preceded in these areas by louts who had generously littered them. They had also left behind large sheets of clear plastic — which some people use in place of tents — spread out over much of the level ground. Under these sheets, the ground was sopping wet, and not really an inviting place to unroll your bedding.

In the gap immediately north of Big Fodderstack, another trail crosses the path. This is the Pinestand Ridge motorcycle trail. Take it to the left, and it leads down Pinestand Ridge to Citico Creek. Take it to the right, and it leads to the jeep road that heads north to Farr Gap.

Three hiking trails branch off from the jeep road north of Fodderstack. In order, south to north, they are the *Mill Branch Trail* (which goes west), the *Crowder Branch Trail* (which crosses), and the *Stiff Knee Trail* (which goes east). It is less than a mile from the Pinestand — Fodderstack Trail junction to the intersection with the Mill Branch Trail.

96 — Mill Branch Trail — Between the motorcycle trail north of Fodderstack to Forest Road 59 about 2½ miles north of Double Camp Recreation Area.

Length: 3.2 miles

USGS Quad: Whiteoak Flats

Description: This trail is not shown on the USGS Quad. Mills Branch is a creek running west from just below Big Stack Gap, which is 3400 feet high. Heading east the trail drops to 3250 in a few hundred yards, reaching the head of the stream at that altitude. About ½ mile downstream a tributary enters from the south, and another ¾ mile along, another stream enters from the same direction. Between these two streams, the trail drops about 700 feet, from 3000 feet to 2300. One mile beyond the second tributary, the trail meets Forest Road 59. Mill Branch flows into Doublecamp Creek just west of the road.

About one mile north of Mill Branch, a trail heads east from the jeep road down to Slickrock Creek. Just north of this, the Crowder Creek Trail goes west from an open area that was once a homestead site.

84 — Crowder Creek Trail — From jeep trail 59 west to Forest Road 59 about three miles north of Double Camp Recreation Area.

Length: 2.5 miles

USGS Quad: Whiteoak Flats, TN

Description: From the jeep road, the trail drops 200 feet in about ½ mile, hitting the head of Crowder Branch at 3100 feet. It follows the north bank of the stream for the next mile, and in the last mile, crosses the stream several times. Three tributary streams come in from the south along the trail.

The ground flattens out somewhat as Crowder Branch nears Doublecamp Creek. The west end of the trail strikes the road just south of the bridge over Double Camp. Elevation, 1900 feet.

106 — Stiff Knee — This trail heads east from Farr Gap where the Fodderstack Jeep Trail meets Forest Roads 59 and 26. It follows Slickrock Creek as far as the Little Tennessee River. See North Carolina, Cheoh District of the Nantahala National Forest for details on the eastern end of the trail.

Length: 4 miles

USGS Quad: Whiteoak Flats, TN; and Tapoco, N.C.

Description: The trail goes east along the slope of the ridge from Farr Gap, dropping gradually from 2800 feet to 2400. It then drops into the hollow and Slickrock Creek which it follows eastward.

Six separate trails fan out from Citico Creek and Forest Road 35 between Boundary Lake and Double Camp Recreation Areas. From north to south, they are:

100 — Rocky Flats — The north end of this trail is at Forest Road 59 about 2 miles north of the Double Camp Recreation Area. The south end is at Forest Road 35, ½ mile east of Double Camp.

Length: 3.4 miles

USGS Quad: Whiteoak Flats, TN

Description: The trail heads east from 59 between Mill Branch and Rocky Flats Branch at about 1850 feet. It goes southeast up-hill to 2300 feet and then back down to cross Rocky Flats Branch at 2100 feet about ½ mile from the trail head. Shortly, it crosses a prong of Rocky Flats Branch and then goes southwest back up the slope of Pine Ridge. It follows the 2300 foot contour along the ridge before dropping down a draw to Citico Creek and the road at 1500 feet.

Going north from Boundary Lake, Forest Road 35 winds down-hill into the valley of Citico Creek. Where it strikes the creek, a road branches off to the east, crossing the creek. This is Forest Road 29 which dead ends less than half a mile from its beginning. The remaining trails in this area branch off from 29. From north to south they are the Pinestand Ridge Trail, the North Fork Citico Trail, the Brush Mountain Trail, the South Fork Citico Trail, and the Grassy Branch Trail.

99 — Pinestand Ridge Trail — Between Forest Road 29 and the Fodderstack Trail.

Length: 5.1 miles

USGS Quad: Whiteoak Flats, TN

Description: This is the motorcycle trail we mentioned in our des-cription of the Fodderstack Trail. Since it is a motorcycle trail, it is likely to be an undesirable spot on summer weekends. How-ever, we hiked it on a week day in the fall and met nobody. It is the most direct route between Forest Road 29 and the Fodder-stack Trail.

From the dead end of 29, the trail crosses the creek heading northeast at about 1660 feet. Once across, it climbs rather quick-ly with several switchbacks up to over 2000 feet. It crosses a small creek just as it starts up the hill. This is the last water on the trail.

Once up on the ridge, the trail climbs steadily but gradually up to about 4000 feet at its junction with the Fodderstack Trail.

98 — North Fork of Citico Creek Trail — From Forest Road 29 to Fodderstack Trail.

Length: 3.5 miles

USGS Quad: Whiteoak Flats, TN.

Description: We hiked this trail and found it extremely beautiful and also extremely strenuous. It had been three years since a trail maintenance crew had been through here, and a lot can happen in the southern mountains in that amount of time. Rhododendron and laurel along with herbaceous growth of various kinds had obscured the trail in many areas. Apparently a wind storm had been through at least once, because downed timber on the upper creek was very common. In places the combination of fallen logs and rhododendron reduced the trail to a tunnel, and we had to crawl through on our bellies.

However, as we pointed out in our introductory chapter, you should be prepared for eventualities like this when you depart from the more commonly used trails. Altogether, it took us nine hours to negotiate the length of this trail. Fortunately, we had allowed ample time to complete the loop hike we had laid out for ourselves, so our long struggle up the creek didn't throw us off our schedule. Since we had only to follow the creek bed to get where we wanted to go, we couldn't get seriously lost even if we could not follow the exact route of the trail.

Water would be no problem, since we were walking along the bank of a stream, and even a serious delay would not have left us short of food. We had planned a three day hike, but we took along an extra day's food as an emergency ration.

The lower portion of the creek, about two miles long, gave us no warning of what was to be. Starting from 29, we crossed Citico Creek on a low water bridge. Just across the creek, the trail forked, and we took the northern fork to the left. Following along the creek for a few hundred yards, we came to the confluence of the North and South Forks of Citico Creek. Here the trail forks again, and we again took the northern fork. It led across an old bridge that may have been built to support a narrow gauge logging railroad. The bridge had a concrete and steel structure, but it was covered with old planking that was beginning to rot out.

Beyond the bridge, the trail follows what is apparently an old road bed or railroad bed. It is broad and level and easy to follow. Block "i" blazes in white on tree trunks are frequent and easily visible. After about a mile and a quarter, a tributary stream comes in from the north, and a half mile farther along, there is another one. Between these two, two streams come in from the south.

A few hundred yards beyond the last tributary, two streams, the Indian Valley Branch and another unnamed creek, flow into the Citico from the North. Up to this point, good campsites have been common, but beyond here, the creek banks get steeper and the hollow gets narrower, and campsites are scarce.

We camped just beyond Indian Valley Branch.

When we started out the next morning, things changed quickly. The slopes of the hollow get steeper and closer together. There were a lot of hemlock trees and ferns, and the air was a bit damp. The white blazes disappeared, to be replaced by red plastic ribbons tied around tree trunks.

The guy who had tied these streamers up had been very frugal. He wasn't going to waste any plastic, so he tied them about 200 yards apart. Also, they had been tied on a long time ago, and long exposure to the weather had bleached them out to a powdery gray that almost matched the trunks of the yellow poplars they were often wrapped around.

The only way to operate in these situations is slowly. Rushing ahead if you are going wrong will only make you wronger faster. If you can see no trail ahead, stop and look around. If you still can't see anything, take your pack off and lean it against a tree. Backtrack a little ways; investigate in a couple of directions.

If you still can't find anything that looks like a trail, but you know you are supposed to keep following the stream bank, then it is time to treat the whole excursion like a cross country hike. Just pick out the easiest looking route in the direction you want to go.

Taking it slow in a sense is armchair advice. When you are picking your way over slippery, moss covered rocks, struggling through the rhododendron patches, and scrambling up steep slopes, there ain't no way to go but slow.

Alertness is a quality that should be cultivated by hikers. It is very easy when you are strolling along a smooth path to start day dreaming, to amble along with your head miles away. But when the trail ahead is obscure and the terrain demands that you watch where you put your feet, you will find yourself noticing a lot of other things too: the tiny wildflower on the forest floor or the wren flitting about in the underbrush. It's a great way to clean out your senses.

In the two miles beyond Indian Valley Branch, a tributary comes into Citico from the north, then three come in from the south, another from the north, and a fourth from the south. You are climbing all this time, from 2200 feet at Indian Branch to over 3000 at the last tributary. The creek tumbles over two rather spectacular waterfalls along this stretch, the highest having a single drop of perhaps 40 feet.

A few hundred yards beyond that fourth southern tributary, the creek forks, and the trail follows the north fork to the left. The rhododendron virtually enclosed the narrow stream at this point, and the trail simply follows the rocks of the creek bed uphill. If you are going on to hike along the Fodderstack Trail, you should fill your canteens before you leave the creek behind.

The trail ends at Cherry Log Gap, where we actually saw a downed cherry log. We also saw the Fodderstack Trail running north-south as well as signs identifying the land to the east as a North Carolina bear sanctuary. We had arrived.

97 — Brush Mountain Trail — From Forest Road 29 to Forest Road 217-H. 217-H is basically not navigable by ordinary automobiles. However, one can drive a short distance north from Forest Road 217 at Beech Gap along this route. The condition of the road will depend a lot on the weather, but since the weather can change rather rapidly, it is best to err on the side of caution and do less driving and more walking.

Length: 6 miles

USGS Quads: Big Junction, TN, and Whiteoak Flats, TN.

Description: At the dead end of Forest Road 29, cross Citico Creek on the low water bridge. Follow the trail along the creek to the left until you reach the bridge where the two forks of Citico Creek flow together. Turn right there and follow the south fork of the creek. Less than ½ mile south of this point, Ike Camp Branch flows into Citico Creek from the southeast. The trail forks here, and you will follow the left fork up Ike Camp Branch. The elevation here is about 1900 feet, and the trail climbs steadily along the creek. Two tributaries come in from the north, then about 1½ miles from the creek mouth, the stream forks. The trail follows the left fork uphill, passing the head of the creek at 3300 feet and climbing steeply up onto Brush Mountain at 3600 feet.

Turning southeast, the trail climbs slowly along the ridge top, reaching 4000 feet in about ½ mile. Where the trail ends at the road, it is possible to turn north, follow 217-H to its end, and then head east to hit the Fodderstack Trail at the state line near Cherry Log Gap.

105 — South Fork of Citico Creek Trail — From Forest Road 29 to Forest Road 217-G and Forest Road 217-H. 217-G is another short dead end road that heads north from 217-I. It is also reasonably passable in good weather, but not really recommended for travel in an ordinary passenger car. According to rangers at the Tellico district station, the first mile of the road north of 217-I is all right, but it is pushing your luck to try to drive beyond that point unless you have a four-wheel drive vehicle.

Length: 7.8 miles

USGS Quads: Whiteoak Flats, TN; and Big Junction, TN.

Description: From the dead end of Forest Road 29, cross Citico Creek on the low water bridge and follow it around to the left for a few hundred yards. Where the north and south forks of Citico Creek come together, turn south along the west bank of the south fork. After ½ mile, the Brush Mountain trail branches off to the left.

The Citico Creek Trail continues south just over a mile to where Eagle Branch flows in from the south and the South Fork of Citico turns east. In that mile, three tributaries flow in from the west. About ¾ mile east of this turn, the trail climbs up on the ridge along the north bank, rising about 400 feet in ½ mile. It follows the 2800 foot contour southeast, continuing on the slope for about ¾ mile, and climbing up to 3000 feet at the top of a narrow, steepsided gorge.

The trail crosses a tributary that comes in from the northeast and then turns southeast for a mile, crossing another tributary from the southwest and one from the northeast. Where a second tributary comes in from the southwest, a branch of the trail leads up it for ½ mile to the end of Forest Road 217-G.

A few yards beyond the branch, another stream comes in from the northeast. The trail then goes through a narrow gorge and then out onto a wider, flatter area where the trail stays south of the creek. The creek then divides and the trail follows the south (right) fork.

The trail follows the stream uphill to about 3600 feet, and then beyond the head of the creek goes steeply up the draw, climbing about 650 feet in just over ½ mile, crossing 217-H and ending at the state line.

91 — Grassy Branch Trail — From Forest Road 29 to Forest Road 217-I.

Length: 4.5 miles

USGS Quads: Whiteoak Flats, TN; and Big Junction, TN.

Description: While Forest Road 29 provides road access from the north, this trail actually begins where Eagle Branch flows into the South Fork of Citico Creek. From there at an altitude of 2200 feet, the trail goes south climbing slowly along the creek to 2400 feet where Eagle Branch and Grassy Branch fork. Grassy Branch is the fork to the east (left). The trail follows it for about a mile and a half, goes through a narrow draw and past a tributary at 3150 feet. The creek then forks again, with the trail following the western fork about ⅓ mile north to the head of the creek. From there it is an easy climb for about 200 yards to 217-I.

102 — Flats Mountain Trail — From Forest Road 217-I just west of the Hemlock Knob Fire Tower north to Forest Road 35 about one mile north of the turn off to the Indian Boundary Recreation Area.

Length: 6.5 miles

USGS Quads: Whiteoak Flats, TN; and Big Junction, TN.

Description: The trail begins with a short climb from 217-I up to the ridge of Flats Mountain, a narrow north-south ridge that forms the trail route for most of its length. Reaching the crest of the ridge at 3800 feet, the trail heads north, reaching the high point of Flats Mountain (3853 feet) in about ½ mile. The trail continues north past the head of Footes Creek to Forest Road 35.

The area between Forest Road 217-I and Forest Road 210 which parallels the Tellico River, contains six hiking trails. All of them follow creeks over most of their length.

103 — The Long Branch Trail — From Forest Road 217-2 about ½ mile north of Forest Road 210. The trail dead ends at the right of way of the proposed Forest Road 217, a highway that was laid out to travel along Sassafras Ridge into North Carolina. Complaints by environmental groups have been successful in stopping the construction of the road, and the Forest Service is currently looking for an alternate route which will have less impact on the semi-wilderness character of the Tellico area.

Length: 2.7 miles

USGS Quad: Big Junction, TN.

Description: The trail heads north from the North River Road at about 1700 feet, following the banks of Long Branch Creek. It climbs to 1800 feet and continues along the west bank of the creek. After 1 to 1½ miles, the trail leaves the creek to head uphill toward Sassafras Ridge, climbing from 2000 feet at the head of the creek to 3200 at the ridge.

101 — Hemlock Trail — From 217-2 about 1½ miles north of Forest Road 210 to the Hemlock Knob tower. The tower is just south of Forest Road 217-1.

Length: 3.5 miles

USGS Quads: Big Junction, TN, and Bald River Falls, TN.

Description: The trail follows Hemlock Creek north from the road, beginning at an altitude of 1800 feet. Tributaries come into Hemlock from the northwest at ⅓ mile, the northeast at one mile, and from the northwest again in another ½ mile. About ¼ mile beyond this last tributary, the creek forks, and the trail follows the right or east fork. From there, at 2100 feet, the trail climbs steeply for about 2 miles up to Hemlock tower at 4019 feet. The road lies just to the north about 150 feet below the tower.

92 — McNabb Creek Trail — From Grassy Gap on Forest Road 217-1 south to 217-2 about 1 mile west of the North River Recreation Area. The Grassy Branch Trail ends just across from this trail at 217-1.

Length: 3.7 miles

USGS Quads: Big Junction, TN, and Bald River Falls, TN.

Description: Heading south from Grassy Gap, the trail heads downhill quickly to the head of McNabb Creek which it follows for the remainder of its length.

In the first mile, you will descend 600 feet from 3400 to 2800. At 2800 feet, major tributaries come into the creek from east and west. In the next mile, the trail descends another 600 feet as the banks gradually widen out.

For the next 1¼ miles, the altitude drops gradually from 2200 to 2000 feet. Hampton Lead is the long mountain to the west, and Brushy Ridge parallels the creek to the east. The last ¼ mile of the trail is a gradual downslope to 1900 feet.

93 — Laurel Branch Trail — From Forest Road 217-2 about three miles north of the North River Recreation Area. The trail ends at Forest Road 217-1.

Length: 3.1 miles

USGS Quad: Big Junction, TN

Description: The trail leaves the road headed north at about 2000 feet following Laurel Branch upstream. A tributary comes in from the west at about ¼ mile, another at one mile, and a third at 1½ miles. Two more streams come in from the west with the next mile. Beyond this last, a tributary comes in from the east, and the trail takes the left fork. The altitude here is about 2700 feet. The trail follows the creek up to about 3000 feet and then leaves it to climb rather steeply up to 3800 feet to Sassafras Ridge.

137 — Big Cove Branch Trail — Follow Forest Road 217-2 about five miles beyond the point where it splits off from Forest Road 210. The trail ends at jeep trail 86 about two miles north of Forest Road 210.

Length: 3.2 miles

USGS Quad: Big Junction, TN

Description: The trail crosses the North River, heading southeast from Forest Road 217-2 at 2000 feet. The trail skirts the hillside for a short distance and then follows Big Cove Branch. It follows the creek for about two miles and then, at 3000 feet, climbs Whigg Ridge to Deep Gap at 3500 feet and then goes quickly downslope to the Sycamore jeep trail at 3000 feet.

89 — Sugar Cove Trail — North from Forest Road 217-2 about six miles beyond its junction with Forest Road 210. Ends at the state line.

Length: 2.4 miles

USGS Quad: Big Junction, TN

Description: The trail follows the hillside above Sugar Cove, climbing from 2700 feet at the trailhead up to 4320 at Beech Gap along the state line ridge.

There are five trails on the Tellico south of Forest Road 210:

88 — Bald River Trail — The north end of the trail is at Forest Road 210 just west of the Bald River Falls Recreation Area. The south end is at Forest Road 126 immediately west of Holly Flats Recreation Area at the bridge over Little Cove Branch.

88-A — Cow Camp Trail — This one-mile trail connects the Bald River Falls Recreation Area with Forest Road 210 over a low hill.

Length: The Bald River Trail is 5.6 miles. Cow Camp Trail is one mile.

USGS Quad: Bald River Falls, TN

Description: The trail follows the river for its entire length. The elevation is 1400 feet where the Bald River flows into the Tellico and 1840 where the Little Cove Branch crosses Forest Road 126.

107 — Henderson Mountain Trail — The trail begins at Forest Road 210 about five miles east of the Bald River Falls campground. It ends at the Sugar Mountain motorcycle trail (Trail 90) on Sugar Mountain.

Length: 5.7 miles

USGS Quads: Bald River Falls, TN; and Big Junction, TN.

Description: This trail actually begins on the south bank of the Tellico River across from Forest Road 210, so there is no direct road access from this end. The trail crosses a low hill, climbing from 1600 to 1920 feet, and then drops back to 1760 where it hits Panther Branch which it follows for about two miles.

Leaving the creek, the trail climbs up to Henderson Top, 2800 feet and then goes southeast along Camp Lead, crossing Forest Road 126 at 2600 feet and then going up Maple Lead to the summit of Sugar Mountain, 3600 feet.

Just beyond the summit to the east, the trail ends at the Sugar Mountain motorcycle trail which can be followed north for just over a mile to Forest Road 210 near Davis Creek or Davis Branch campground.

90-A — Brookshire Trail — The trail starts at Forest Road 126 about two miles south of Forest Road 210 and ends at Sugar Mountain motorcycle trail on Sugar Mountain Lead.

Length: 3 miles

USGS Quads: Bald River Falls, TN; and Big Junction, TN.

Description: The trail heads south from 126 at 2600 feet, climbing to 2900 to cross Chinquapin Ridge. It goes down off the ridge to the Bald River at the end of the Upper Bald River motorcycle trail.

From here there is disagreement about the route. According to maps in the Forest Service's Regional Headquarters in Atlanta, the trail goes northeast along Bryson Branch, climbing from 2200 feet at the Bald River up to 2800 feet at the head of the creek and then to 3600 feet on Sugar Mountain.

According to ranger district maps, it follows the Bald River eastward for about one mile and then turns northeast up the slope of Sugar Mountain Lead to the motorcycle trail. Bryson Branch and the Bald River are roughly parallel about ½ mile apart.

85 — Kirkland Creek — The north end of the trail is at Forest Road 126 about one mile east of the Holly Flats Recreation Area. The south end is at Sandy Gap at the state line where a logging road continues south.

Length: 4.5 miles

USGS Quad: Bald River Falls, TN

Description: The trail crosses Henderson Branch just south of the road and then heads south along Kirkland Creek. At ½ mile, a tributary comes in from the west and at one mile, creeks come into the main channel from both sides. At 1¼ miles a stream comes in from the east, and about two miles south of the road, Waucheese Creek flows in from the west and an unnamed creek comes in from the east. Within ½ mile, streams again come in from both sides.

Finally, the creek forks and the trail follows the north fork to the right for a short distance before turning up a steep slope to Sandy Gap. The altitude at the road is 1900 feet. Sandy Gap is 2575 feet.

Trails in the Hiwassee District

The Hiwassee District is immediately south of the Tellico. We will describe four trails in this district.

104 — Chestnut Mountain Trail — There are Chestnut Mountains and Chestnut Mountain Trails all over the Appalachians, a rather bitter irony, since the blight has wiped out all the trees they were named for. This particular Chestnut Mountain Trail starts at Iron Gap on Forest Road 297 four to five miles west of Forest Road 14. 297 branches off from 14 about five miles north of Reliance, TN. The trail ends at motorcycle trail 2004 about 1½ miles north of the Lost Corral Recreation Area.

Length: 3.5 miles

USGS Quads: Mecca, TN, Oswald Dome, TN.

Description: Heading south from Iron Gap, the hiking trail takes the east fork and the motorcycle trail the west fork. From 1600 feet at the Gap, the trail climbs up steeply to the southeast to 2200 feet on the ridge of Chestnut Mountain. It follows the southeast slope of the ridge, crossing the heads of two creeks before turning northwest to cross the ridge and join the motorcycle trail which you can follow into the campground at Lost Corral.

83 — Unicoi Mountain Trail — Starts at Forest Road 311 a few hundred yards southwest of the Buck Bald Fire Tower. Ends at the Hiwassee River about ½ mile east of the end of Forest Road 22. There is currently no direct road connection from this end of this trail. Eventually the John Muir Trail will be extended east along the river to hook up with this trail.

Length: 6 miles

USGS Quad: Farner, TN

Description: The folder issued by the Cherokee National Forest describing the trails on the Hiwassee shows a hiking trail going north from Bob Bald to Unicoi Gap at the state line (Trail number 82, 4.5 miles long). This trail is being converted to a motorcycle trail.

The Unicoi Mountain Trail begins just south of the Buck Bald tower which is at 2348 feet. The trail follows the ridge line southwest, gradually losing altitude to 1800 feet. Along the way, the trail crosses Tennessee Route 68. This is a new road which is not shown on the USGS Quad. The road shown as 68 on the quad is now Forest Road 311.

At the south end, the trail descends sharply in a series of switchbacks down to 1200 feet heading generally southeast. It then turns southwest again to drop steeply down to the river at 970 feet.

John Muir Trail — John Muir, the man who founded the Sierra Club, took a thousand mile walk shortly after the Civil War, heading south from Indiana to the Gulf. He came through this area. And someday, the John Muir Trail in the Cherokee will connect with a trail running from the Tennessee — Kentucky line into North Carolina. It will be awhile before that happens. In the meantime, this short stretch of trail along the Hiwassee River is a beginning. To get to it, cross the Hiwassee River at Reliance. Immediately north of the river, turn east on a dirt road, Forest Road 108. The road turns away from the river, and here the trail goes straight ahead following the bluffs along the river bank to where it rejoins Forest Road 108 to the east.

Length: 3 miles

USGS Quad: McFarland, TN

Trails in the Ocoee Ranger District

Back in the days when the isolated mountaineers of the southern Appalachians had to depend more or less completely on their own resources for food, the spring appearance of the ramp was a big event. The ramp is a particularly pungent member of the family of plants that includes garlic and onions, and the vitamins this fresh vegetable provided were very important to people who had been living on a rather monotonous winter diet.

In commemoration of the days when the ramp was a significant element in the mountain diet, people in Polk County, Tennessee have a "Ramp Tramp" every spring. A similar festival is celebrated in West Virginia. People head out into the mountains during the tramp looking for ramps. Outdoor dinners are cooked up for visitors with dishes featuring ramps.

We have never actually eaten a southern mountain ramp. We have sampled its northern cousins picked in the woods of Wisconsin. We found that one bulb about the size of a golf ball was sufficient to flavor a whole pot of stew. According to what we have heard, the Appalachian ramp will also flavor the eater for a couple of weeks. Some schools in West Virginia prohibit ramp-eaters for three days after sampling. It is not a food for weaklings.

If you are interested in joining in the festivities of the Ramp Tramp, we suggest you get in touch with the County Extension Agent in Benton, the seat of Polk County, TN. If you want to avoid the crowds, of course, it is a good idea to find out about the Ramp Tramp so you can schedule your trip for some other time.

The Ocoee district provides some excellent trails. North of the Ocoee River, there are some short paths around the Chilhowee Recreation Area and some longer trails around the Thunder Rock Recreation Area. Most of the trails are south of the river, especially around Big Frog Mountain. Big Frog is just north of the Georgia border. At 4200 feet, it is the highest peak in this area.

We will begin our description with the trails around Big Frog. Four fairly long trails connect Big Frog Mountain with Forest roads, while shorter trails provide connections between these trails. The easternmost of the longer trails is the Lick Log Trail.

65 — Lick Log Trail — The trail begins at Forest Road 221 just south of the Ocoee River about two miles north of Tumbling Creek Recreation Area. It ends on Big Frog Mountain at the junction with the Big Frog (64) and Wolf Ridge (66) Trails.

Length: 8 miles

USGS Quads: Caney Creek, TN, Ducktown, TN.

Description: Beginning at the road at 1700 feet, the trail climbs up onto Lick Log Ridge at 2500 feet. At about two miles, Trail 70 branches off to the right. Lick Log then heads southwest along the ridge, gradually climbing to 2950 at Lick Log Top. It continues to climb until it reaches Big Frog Mountain which is over 4200 feet.

64 — Big Frog Trail — From Forest Road 221 about one mile west of Forest Road 45 to Big Frog Mountain.

Length: 6.5 miles

USGS Quad: Caney Creek, TN

Description: The trail leaves the road at Low Gap at 1800 feet and heads southwest, climbing up Peavine Mountain to 2500 feet. At 1½ miles, the Rough Ridge Trail (70) comes in from the east (left). About one mile farther, both the Grassy Gap (67) and the Low Gap Trail meet Big Frog. The Frog turns sharply right at the intersection.

Continuing southwest on Peavine Ridge, the Big Frog Trail hits the Fork Ridge Trail in another mile and a half. This trail heads northeast at 3400 feet. A half mile beyond, the Big Creek Trail comes in from the right (west). Elevation here is 3600 feet. What follows is a steep climb to 4000 and a more gradual climb to 4200 at the peak and the intersection with the Lick Log and Wolf Ridge Trails.

68 — Big Creek Trail — From Forest Road 221 about six to seven miles west of Forest Road 45 to the Big Frog Trail.

Length: 6.4 miles

USGS Quad: Caney Creek, TN

Description: The trail heads south along Big Creek from the road at 1400 feet. It climbs as it follows the creek to 2600 feet where it turns northwest up the slope of Bark Logging Lead, doubles back southeast on the lead, and then goes southeast up Peavine Ridge to its junction with the Big Frog Trail at 3600 feet.

66 — Wolf Ridge Trail — From Forest Road 221 about three miles

east of its junction with Forest Road 62 south to a junction with Big Frog and Lick Log Trails.
Length: 7 miles
USGS Quad: Caney Creek
Description: The trail begins at Pace Gap at 1700 feet and heads up Wolf Ridge to the southeast. About ¾ mile from the road, the Pace Ridge Trail branches off to the east. The Wolf Ridge Trail continues southeast, striking the Grassy Gap (or Barklogging) Trail which goes off to the right in about another mile. In another ½ mile at 3000 feet, the Chestnut Mountain Trail branches off to the left heading southwest. The Wolf Ridge Trail swings in a more easterly direction along Blue Ridge to Big Frog Mountain. Between the Chestnut Mountain Trail and Big Frog you will come across a marble monument erected to John B. Curbow, one of the guiding spirits of the Ramp Tramp.

The cross trails in the Big Frog network are:
72 — Pace Ridge Trail — From the Wolf Ridge Trail east to the Big Creek Trail.
Length: 2 miles
USGS QUAD: Caney Creek, TN
Description: This short trail branches east from Wolf Ridge only about ½ mile south of Forest Road 221. The Pace Ridge Trail crosses Forest Road 221-E before dropping down to the Big Creek and its associated trail.
67 — Barklogging or Grassy Gap Trail — The Forest Service uses Barklogging for this trail, while the USGS Quad shows it as Grassy Gap. It begins at Wolf Ridge Trail in the west and goes northeast to end at the Big Frog Trail.
Length: 7 miles
USGS Quad: Caney Creek, TN
Description: The trail leaves Wolf Ridge at Grassy Gap at 2500 feet and heads southeast along the slope of the ridge to cross two prongs of Peter Camp Branch and three prongs of Penitentiary Branch. By going around the spurs of the ridges between the creek branches, the trail stays at about the same altitude. From 2400 feet it climbs up onto Bark Logging lead and then crosses the Big Creek and Big Creek Trail. It hugs the slope again as it crosses four more creeks before climbing up to 3600 feet at Low Gap on Peavine Ridge where it meets the Big Frog Trail, which comes in from the east and heads south, and the Low Gap Trail, which goes north.

63 — Chestnut Mountain — From Forest Road 62 about 10 miles east of Forest Road 221 to the Wolf Ridge Trail.
Length: 3 miles
USGS Quad: Caney Creek, TN; and Hemp Top, GA.
Description: Another point of access to the Big Frog Trail network. Starts about 2000 feet at road and climbs up ridge, meeting the Wolf Ridge Trail at 3000 feet.

69 — Fork Ridge Trail — From The Frog Mountain Trail to the Rough Creek Trail.
Length: 5 miles
USGS Quads: Caney Creek, TN, and Ducktown, TN.
Description: Starting on Peavine Ridge at the Big Frog Trail, it heads northeast along Fork Ridge, dropping from 3400 feet to 2400 feet and meeting the Rough Ridge Trail.

70 — Rough Creek — From Lick Log Trail to Big Frog Mountain Trail.
Length: 6.5 miles
USGS Quads: Ducktown, TN, Caney Creek, TN.
Description: A cross trail from Lock Log Ridge at 2700 feet down to Rough Creek, crossing at 1800 feet. It then climbs up Fork Ridge to 2300 feet and heads northwest down across the West Fork of Rough Creek at 1900. From there it climbs again, steeply, back up to 2200 and then more slowly to 2400 at the Big Frog Trail. The trail crosses Forest Road 221-G along Rough Creek and Forest Road 221-F along the North Fork of Rough Creek. These are the two forks of a single road that branches off from Forest Road 221.

Low Gap Trail — This is a short, unnumbered trail that heads north from the junction of the Big Frog and Grassy Gap Trails. It ends at a gated jeep road — 221-J — about one mile south of Forest Road 221.
Length: about one mile
USGS Quad: Caney Creek, TN.

Other trails south of the Ocoee River:
62 — Blue Ridge — From the intersection of Forest Roads 221 and 302 a few hundred yards south of the Sylco Recreation Area west past the forest boundary to Cookson Creek Road. The westernmost section of this trail is on private property, so we do not recommend that you hike it. The trail is also interrupted by Sawmill Branch jeep trail, so it might be a good idea to stick to the eastern section.
Length: 6.5 miles, overall

USGS Quads: Parksville, TN, and Caney Creek, TN.

Description: The trail leaves the road at about 1190 feet and climbs sharply to 1500 feet on the Blue Ridge. It heads west across the ridge, crossing Jack's Branch at about 1½ miles. The junction with the jeep trail is about four miles along the trail. Trail and jeep track follow the same route as far as Forest Road 67. Beyond the road, only the hiking trail continues. However, private property is not far ahead.

74 — Caney Creek Trail — Heads northeast from Forest Road 320 about 1½ miles north of Sylco Recreation Area. Ends at Ocoee River at the junction with the gated jeep trail 369, the Pace Gap Trail. This jeep trail is ½ mile long and connects with Forest Road 369 north of Forest Road 221.

Length: 7.8 miles

USGS Quads: Caney Creek, TN

Decription: From Forest Road 302 at 1100 feet, the trail heads north, crossing Dutch Branch just beyond the road. It later crosses Little Fall Branch, an unnamed creek, and three prongs of Fall Branch before climbing to the top of Hogback Ridge at 1400 feet. It continues north on the ridge to near the river and then meets jeep trail 369 which drops steeply down to 900 feet near the Ocoee Power Plant No. 2.

71 — Indian Flats Trail — From jeep trail 369 at the Ocoee Power Plant No. 2 to gated jeep road 221-K on Indian Flats ridge. 221-K goes south about two miles to Forest Road 221.

Length: 5.6 miles, according to the Forest Service, but the portion of it limited strictly to hiking is more like 1.5 miles (the rest is a motorcycle trail).

USGS Quad: Caney Creek, TN.

Description: This short trail goes south from the power station climbing Indian Flat Ridge, 900 feet up to 1400 feet, before meeting the jeep trail.

The Forest Service maintains a network of five separate color coded trails around the Chilhowee Recreation Area. The names, colors, and lengths are:

> *Azalea,* yellow, 3 miles
> *Arbutus,* white, 1
> *Benton* Falls, blue, 1½
> *Big Pine,* green, 1
> *Red Lead,* red, ½

USGS Quad: Oswald Dome, TN

79 — Clear Creek — From the Chilhowee Recreation Area to Tennessee Route 30 just north of the Parksville Lake Recreation Area.

Length: 4 miles
USGS Quads: Oswald Dome, TN, and Caney Creek, TN
Description: This trail branches off from the Chilhowee system and heads downhill to Parksville generally staying on the slopes of the ridge until it joins Clear Creek a short distance from Route 30.

76 — Dry Pond Lead — From Thunder Rock Recreation Area on U.S. Route 64 north to Forest Road 68 at Deep Gap about 1½ miles west of Sassafras Knob Tower.

Length: 6.5 miles
USGS Quad: Ducktown, TN
Description: Starting at 1145 feet at the campground, the trail climbs steeply to 1800 feet and then more gradually to 3840 along Dry Pond Lead. From that high point, the trail slopes down again to 2400 feet at its end. About 1½ miles north of the campground, the Rock Creek Trail branches off to the east.

125 — Rock Creek Tail — From Dry Pond Lead and Trail 76, east to U.S. Route 64 about three miles east of Thunder Rock campground.

Length: 6.6 miles
USGS Quad: Ducktown, TN
Description: The trail leaves Dry Pond Trail on the ridge and heads downhill to Rock Creek, which is also called Rock Camp Creek. It follows the creek upstream for about a mile and then starts winding south toward 64. It stays at 1800-2000 feet much of the way, crossing both Laurel Branch and Williams Creek along the way, finally sloping down to 1400 feet at the road. The trail head is between Williams Creek and Laurel Branch.

The Cherokee National Forest between Smoky Mountain National Park and the Virginia border has a different character than the areas to the south of the park. The mountains in the north are long ridges running northeast-southwest. Between the ridges are valleys broad enough to support considerable settlement.

The character of the country affects the possibilities for hiking. Much more of the land here is privately owned, making it more difficult to put together large networks of trails. The long ridges are generally publicly owned, and there are several trails of some length that follow these ridges. The other trails we will describe tend to be shorter trails that climb up a creek bed or a spur to the high points of the main ridges.

Trails in the Nolichucky Ranger District
6 — Meadow Creek Mountain Trail — Starts off Tennessee Route

107 just south of the Forest Boundary. A road brancnes off to the west of Beersheba Church and Cemetery, and the trail goes off to the left a short distance down this road. Ends at U.S. 70 just west of Del Rio where Shop Branch crosses the highway.

Length: 14.9 miles

USGS Quad: Paint Rock, TN., and Neddy Mountain, TN.

Description: From the road, the trail climbs quickly up on the spine of Meadow Creek Mountain. It follows the ridge southwest at altitudes ranging from 2600 to 3100 feet. About half way along, the trail crosses Forest Road 42 and less than a mile beyond, passes the Meadow Creek fire tower. From there the trail continues on the ridge before dropping down to follow Show Branch around to the south and U.S. 70.

5 — Gum Springs Trail — This short trail provides access to the Meadow Creek Mountain Trail from Tennessee Route 107 just west of the Houston Valley Recreation Area.

Length: 2.6 miles

USGS Quad: Paint Rock, TN

Description: It's uphill all the way to the intersection with the Meadow Creek Trail northeast of Forest Road 42.

21 — Big Jennings Creek — From the Old Forge Recreation Area on Forest Road 331 to Forest Road 88 on Round Knob. To get to Old Forge, take Tennessee Route 107 east about eight miles from Greeneville and turn south on Forest Road 94 about two miles to Forest Road 331. Forest Road 88 goes downhill into the hamlet of Greystone from which a road goes north to Forest Road 94 just south of Tennessee 107.

Length: 5 miles

USGS Quad: Greystone, TN

Description: The trail heads up Jennings Creek from 1900 feet to 2300 feet and then climbs up to 3400 at Round Knob. A short trail that ends on private property goes southwest and then northwest down Davis Creek.

8 — Wilson Level — From the Pigeon Valley Church in Hartford, TN. to Halltop tower at the end of Forest Road 207. 207 connects with Forest Road 147 about five miles south of Newport, TN.

Length: 6.8 miles

USGS Quad: Hartford, TN

Description: Starting from about 1500 feet at the church, the trail climbs up Devils Backbone to Halltop tower at about 3200 feet.

9 — Stone Mountain Trail — From a road that parallels the Pigeon River between Hartford, TN, and Denton, TN, to the Wilson Level Trail. Neither the road nor Denton are on road maps, making it somewhat difficult for us to supply concise directions.

Length: 4.3 miles

USGS Quad: Hartford, TN

Description: The trail leaves the road between Polecat Branch and Landin Cove and climbs up Rich Top to join the Wilson Level Trail on Devils Backbone.

Trails in the Unaka Ranger District

One of the attractions of this area is the Laurel Fork, a beautiful mountain stream complete with waterfall. The Appalachian Trail used to follow Laurel Fork, but it has been rerouted. It is still close enough to provide a good loop hike combining the A.T., the Laurel Fork Trail, and a short cross trail up Leonard Branch.

39 — Laurel Fork Trail — From Forest Road 50 at the Dennis Cove Recreation Area to Forest Road 50A on Cherry Flats Ridge. Take U.S. 321 east from Elizabethton to about ½ mile past Hampton. Forest Road 50 continues east from there. 50A, at the other end, joins 50 after one mile. From there, go east seven miles to U.S. 19E west of Roan Mountain.

Length: 6.1 miles

USGS Quads: White Rocks Mountain, TN, and Watauga Dam, TN

Description: The trail begins at Dennis Cove Recreation Area at 2600 feet and heads up Laurel Fork. At 2½ miles, the Laurel Fork jeep trail comes in from the north, and ½ mile farther, Leonard Branch and the Leonard Branch Trail come in from the south at about 2800 feet. About ½ mile farther up Laurel Branch, the trail arrives at the falls at 2978 feet.

From the falls, the trail continues up the creek to over 3200 feet and then turns north along 50A.

38 — Leonard Branch Trail — From the Laurel Branch Trail to the Appalachian Trail on White Rocks Mountain.

Length: 2.8 miles

USGS Quad: White Rocks Mountain, TN

Description: Climbing up the Leonard Branch from Laurel Branch, the trail follows the creek to its head at about 3600 feet and then continues up the draw to the A.T. at 3700 feet.

To make a loop trail, take the AT back northeast about three miles to Forest Road 50 about 1½ miles east of Dennis Cove Recreation Area.

113 — Patty Ridge Trail — Take Tennessee Route 81 three miles north of Erwin, TN, and turn south toward the hamlet of Embreeville. About ¾ mile south of Embreeville, jeep trail 190, the California Trail, branches off to the left. The hiking trail starts about one mile up the jeep trail.

The other end of the trail is also at jeep trail 190, but it is seven miles from there to the nearest auto road, so it is probably best to treat this trail as a dead end.

Length: 5 miles

USGS Quad: Erwin, TN

Description: The trail heads south from 1600 feet along Patty Creek. It climbs to 3000 feet and then heads southeast across a divide at 3400 feet, goes down to 3000 feet, then southwest up Broad Shoal Creek to end at 3200 feet at the jeep trail.

30 — Limestone Cove — From the Limestone Cove Recreation Area on Tennessee Route 107 about five miles east of Unicoi. Dead ends on Stamping Ground ridge.

Length: 4.3 miles

USGS Quad: Unicoi, TN

Description: Starting at 2200 feet at the campground, the trail heads southeast. It crosses a stream and then climbs steadily up to 4709 on Stamping Ground.

Trails in the Watauga Ranger District

40 — Pond Mountain Trail — From Tennessee Route 67 just north of the Watauga Scenic Area. The trail loops around to hit 67 again south of the Scenic Area between Dry Branch and Tigue Branch.

Length: 7.9 miles

USGS Quads: Watauga Dam, TN, and White Rocks Mountain, TN

Description: From 2000 feet at the scenic area, the trail climbs to 3000 feet quickly and then more slowly to 3200. Then it is up again sharply to 4000 feet. The trail heads south along the ridge to Pond Mountain top at 4329. A jeep trail goes southeast from Pond Mountain, while the hiking trail swings around to the northwest to follow the ridge between Dry Branch and Rat Branch downslope steeply to 3400 feet and then more slowly to 3000. From there, it is steep downhill to 2000 feet at the road.

41 — Little Pond Mountain — The trail starts at U.S. 321 2½ miles west of Elk Mills, TN. Ends at Forest Road 39 about six miles south of Watauga Point Recreation Area.

Length: 3.5 miles

USGS Quad: Watauga Dam, TN

Description: The trail starts up Row Branch from the road, following the creek for almost 2½ miles. Three tributaries come in from the south and two from the north in this distance, and the elevation goes from 2150 to 3000. Past the head of the creek, the trail climbs to Plot Gap at 3300 feet and then goes south to Goodwin Field Gap. There it forks, with the left fork going down

Scrawls Branch to private property. The right fork goes about ½ mile to Forest Road 39.

44 — Holston Trail — The trail is in two segments. One starts at the Appalachian Trail at Rich Knob and goes south as far as the Holston Knob fire tower to end at Forest Road 202. From there, the trail follows 202 southwest past the Low Gap Recreation Area to Holston High Point. From there it goes south to end at Forest Road 87 about five miles north of Biltmore, TN.

Length: 12 miles, overall

USGA Quads: Shady Valley, Carter, and Keenburg, TN (north to south).

Description: The trail leaves the Appalachian Trail at 4100 feet on the west slope of Rich Knob and stays around 4000 feet on the ridge heading southwest. It drops gradually to 3400 feet at Flint Mill Gap. From there it climbs steadily up to 4160 at Holston High Knob fire tower.

From there, the trail follows Forest Road 202 for about 4.5 miles. The second segment continues on the ridge from 4300 feet at Holston High Point going steadily down to 3000 feet to where the trail forks. The trail takes the west (right) fork, going steeply down to 2100 feet at Forest Road 87.

50 — Josiah Creek Trail — From Forest Road 87 along the east shore of Holston Lake to the Holston Trail.

Length: 3 miles

USGS Quad: Holston Valley, TN

Description: A spur trail of the Holston Mountain Trail. Starts northeast of the mouth of Josiah Creek at 1772 and climbs slowly along the creek. It climbs up onto the ridge about half way between Rich Knob and Holston Knob.

49 — Flint Mill Trail — From Forest Road 87 to Holston Mountain Trail at Flint Mill Gap.

Length: 2.2 miles

USGS Quad: Carter, TN

Description: Goes up Flint Mill Creek to about 2400 feet and then switchbacks steeply up to the Holston Trail at 3300 feet.

47 — Morrill Trail — From Forest Road 202 along the Holston Trail to Forest Road 87.

Length: 2 miles

USGS Quad: Carter, TN

Description: Another spur from 87 to the Holston Trail.

48 — Short Spur — From Forest Road 87 to Holston Mountain along Forest Road 202.

Length: 2.5 miles

USGS Quad: Keenburg, TN

Description: Another spur trail up Holston Mountain from 87.

54 — Iron Mountain Trail — In the north, access is by Tennessee Route 91 and Camp A-Hi-S-Ta-Di about three miles north of Laurel Bloomery. The trail ends at Forest Road 53 between Tennessee Routes 91 and 67. 53 goes west from 67 about five miles south of Mountain City.

Length: 20 miles

USGS Quads: (north to south) Laurel Bloomery, TN, Shady Valley, TN, Doe, TN.

Description: From the camp at 2200 feet, the trail climbs steeply up Butt Mountain to 3400 feet. It then heads southwest along the ridge for the rest of its length. Elevations along the ridge range from 3900 to 3600 with one climb to Grindstone Knob where the trail crosses U.S. Route 421. At the trail's south end, hikers can walk west for about one mile along Forest Road 53 and pick up the Appalachian Trail.

Three short side trails climb up to the Iron Mountain Trail. They all have their lower ends on private property.

For additional information: write Forest Supervisor, Cherokee National Forest, P.O. Box 400, Cleveland, TN 37311.

The Forest Supervisor can supply a map of the forest and also separate maps of each ranger district showing trails in the district. If you look over these maps and decide on a visit to a particular district, it is a good idea to contact the district ranger office, which has up-to-date information on the condition of individual trails; also, Rangers like to know when people are setting off into the back country in their district.

The addresses of the individual ranger districts in the Cherokee are:

Tellico Ranger District, Route 3, Tellico Plains, TN 37385

Hiwassee Ranger District, P.O. Box 349, Etowah, TN 37331

Ocoee Ranger District, Route 1, Benton, TN 37307

Nolichucky Ranger District, 1231A Tusculum Blvd., Greeneville, TN 37743

Unaka Ranger District, Main and Elm Sts., Erwin, TN 37650 and, Watauga Ranger District, P.O. Box 431, Elizabethton, TN 37643

PROPOSED SCENIC TRAILS FOR TENNESSEE

The Tennessee Trails System Act of 1971 authorized the development of seven scenic trails. Portions of these were completed as this book was being written, but public use was not being encouraged (except, of course, on the Appalachian Trail) until camping and picnic facilities were completed, blazing and mapping was finished, and arrangements with private landowners were final. For most current information, write the Trails Administrator, Tennessee Department of Conservation, 2611 West End Avenue, Nashville, TN.

The trails are:

1. The Appalachian Trail — which runs from the Virginia state line near the town of Damascus southeast to U.S. Route 19E near the Tennessee-North Carolina state line to Doe Knob in the Great Smoky Mountains (see description and maps in a separate section).

2. The Cumberland Trail — which is planned to run roughly from the Tennessee-Georgia state line near the border between Marion and Hamilton Counties north through Sequatchie, Bledsoe and Cumberland Counties, then northeast through Morgan, Anderson, Campbell and Claiborne Counties, reaching the border with Kentucky and Virginia at Cumberland Gap State Park. On the way, it will pass through Frozen Head State Park and Prentice-Cooper State Forest.

3. The Trail of Tears — running roughly from south of Cleveland near Red Clay, across the Hiwassee River, then the Tennessee River, intersecting the Cumberland Trail and passing through Fall Creek Falls State Park, continuing on to Cedars of Lebanon State Park and thence northwestward to Paris Landing State Park.

4. The John Muir Trail — running roughly from the mouth of Wolf River in northern Tennessee's Fentress County, joining Pickett State Park, and continuing south along the scenic south fork of the Cumberland River to Frozen Head State Park where it will intersect the Cumberland Trail.

From that junction, it will head southeastward to the Hiwassee Scenic River where TVA Reservoir property can be utilized. The last portion of the trail will either head south through Bradley County to the Georgia state line or hook up with an existing trail in the Hiwassee District of the Cherokee National Forest.

5. Trail of the Lonesome Pine — beginning near Corryton in Knox County and running northeastward through Grainger and Hawkins County, following closely the scenic gorges and escarpments of the Clinch Mountain Range.

6. Chickasaw Bluffs Trail — This trail and the following one are the only proposed scenic trails not located in the mountains. It will follow Mississippi River bluff tops for the most part, north from T.O. Fuller State Park south of Memphis to the proposed

Fort Pillow State Park in Lauderdale County and continue north-ward to terminate at Reelfoot Lake State Park.

7. **Natchez Trace Trail** — will parallel the Natchez Trace Park-way from the Tennessee-Alabama state line in Wayne County north to Nashville in the vicinity of Tennessee State Route 100. This trail will be designed for use both by foot and horseback travelers.

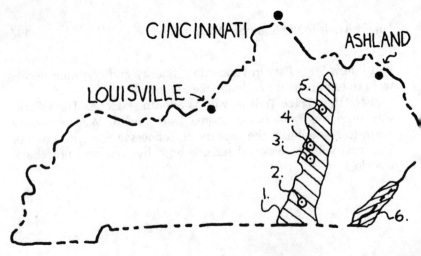

1. DANIEL BOONE NATIONAL FOREST
   2. Cumberland Falls State Park
   3. Natural Bridge State Park
   4. Red River Gorge Area
   5. Pioneer Weapons Hunting Area

6. CUMBERLAND GAP NATIONAL
   HISTORICAL PARK

kentucky

The best hiking in the mountains of eastern Kentucky is in the Daniel Boone National Forest, which extends 140 miles in a narrow strip from the state's northeast corner to the border with Tennessee at Pickett State Park. The forest encloses some 585,000 acres and contains more than 140 miles of trails.

Many of the trails are short and lead to particular scenic attractions. Networks of longer trails do exist, however, in the Primitive Weapons Hunting Area of the Morehead District and the Red River Gorge Area of the Stanton District. There are also two major isolated trails, the Big Limestone and the Moonbow; and there are trails in Cumberland Falls State Park, located within forest boundaries.

There are plans for a 223-mile trail, to be called the Daniel Boone Trace, but when we researched this book in the fall of 1974 no actual construction had begun. The trail will stretch the length of the forest and provide links with major recreation areas such as Cave Run Lake, Laurel River Lake, Cumberland Lake, Natural Bridge State Park, and Cumberland Falls. It will sample four wild river areas — Red, Rockcastle, Upper Cumberland, and the Big South Fork of the Cumberland. Eventually it will connect with other planned national scenic trails like the North Country Trail that will run through Ohio and the John Muir Trail in Tennessee. (Contact the Forest Supervisor at 100 Vaught Road, Winchester, Ky., 40391 for a status report on this trail).

Cumberland Gap National Historical Park contains some 40 miles of hiking trails, including a spectacular 16-mile trail that stretches the length of the park along the spine of Cumberland Mountain.

A Kentucky Trails Association has recently been formed of individuals and agencies concerned with promoting hiking in the state. Hugh Thomason, the association's current president, was a great help to us in our Kentucky research. If you would like to know more about this group or wish to join, you can write them c/o P.O. Box 784, Louisville, Ky., 40201. Individual memberships are $3 and student memberships are $1.

DANIEL BOONE NATIONAL FOREST
Morehead District

Trails in the Pioneer Weapons Hunting Area
Location: Take U.S. 60 ten miles west from Morehead; turn south at the town of Salt Lick on Kentucky Route 211 and proceed one mile to junction with state route 129. Turn left (east) on 129

another mile to the campground at Clear Creek and entrance to the hunting area.

Length: The network of trails in the area totals about 20 miles.

USGS Quad: Salt Lick.

Description: This unusual 7300-acre tract of national forest has been set aside for hunting wild turkey, white-tailed deer, ruffed grouse and other small game only with weapons our pioneer ancestors might have used. Specifically, the tools allowed are: longbow, crossbow, flintlock rifle, percussion cap rifle, muzzle-loading shotgun and pistol.

The trails are designed mainly for use by hunters, and as you walk you will frequently pass through open meadows that have been created purposely by the Forest Service to encourage wildlife.

Several of the trails begin at or near the campground in the Clear Creek Recreation Area. One of them, *Carrington Rocks Trail,* heads 2½ miles southwest and uphill from an elevation of 767 feet to 1140 feet in the first 1¼ miles, downhill to cross a small branch of Salt Lick Creek at its headwaters, uphill again to cross a ridge at an elevation of 1100 feet, down to 800 feet at Carrington Branch and up again to 1100 feet at a scenic overlook called Carrington Rocks.

Buck Branch Trail, 1½ miles, leads north up the creek for which it was named, past the creek's headwaters to connect with Trail #111, *Cedar Cliffs Trail.*

The right branch of Cedar Cliffs Trail leads south one mile along a ridge that forms the boundary between Bath and Menifee Counties (at an elevation of between 1000 and 1100 feet) to a junction with Forest Road 918 about half a mile east of the campground.

The left branch of Cedar Cliffs Trail heads north from its junction with the Buck Branch Trail to the cliffs for which it was named. Then it heads east for 1¼ miles along a ridge top to junction with Forest Road 918.

Turn left on the forest road and follow it about a mile until you see a sign that indicates a trail and directs you to the Tater Knob Lookout Tower. This last portion of the Cedar Cliffs Trail takes you to the tower (elevation 1388 feet) and continues east ¾ mile to the headwaters of McIntosh Branch.

If you have a good compass and topographical map and feel like trying a little cross country hiking, you can follow the McIntosh River east to a dirt road in the old town of Yale (now just a few houses and a cemetery). If you walk west on that dirt road you will come to a primitive campsite in about a mile and a half.

Proceed west from the campground on the *Buck Creek Trail* (2.6 miles) to a junction with a spur trail that leads up the mountain (north) to Tater Knob Tower. Buck Creek Trail runs through stands of bottomland hardwoods and pine and, at intervals, the open meadows designed to give the "edge effect" that attracts wildlife. (Many more species of animals congregate at the edge of a woods than are found deep inside a forest because of the greater variety of food available).

The entire loop from Tater Knob Tower, including the cross-country stretch down McIntosh Creek, is about 7½ miles. If you make this trip, plan an overnight stop at the primitive campground.

A separate network of trails in the Pioneer Weapons area begins in its northern section near two primitive campsites on State Highway 826 just south of the Licking River. These trails look like spokes of a wheel on the map, with the center of the wheel being a water hole frequented by game.

112 — Cave Run Trail, 3 miles, winds south from a point just south of the northernmost campground uphill to a peak 1153 feet in elevation. It follows the eastern slopes of a ridge through an oak-hickory forest to the water hole, then descends in a south-easterly direction about 200 feet to a wildlife opening on Big Cave Creek.

It proceeds east on this creek to another wildlife opening at the mouth of Peter Cave Run Creek. The trail turns south and then southeast for about a mile along a ridgetop to a junction with Forest Road 918 at the curve halfway between the two off-road sections of the Cedar Cliffs Trail (#111).

If you want to return to the campground by a different route, walk west on the road to Cedar Cliffs Trail and take that to a junction with the *Crossover Trail.*

107 — Crossover Trail, heads north 0.9 miles on a ridgetop to the water hole and a junction with the other trails.

Proceed east on Hogpen Trail along a ridgetop for two miles and then down into Hogpen Hollow at state highway 826 about a mile south of the campground where you started.

The part of Hogpen Trail that runs west from the watering hole goes downhill to the headwaters of a small stream that leads down to Trough Lick Branch. The trail follows that stream to Trough Lick and an elevation of 800 feet.

Big Limestone Trail

Location: This isolated trail is also in the Morehead Ranger District. To reach its northern terminus, take U.S. Route 60 west four miles from the town of Morehead then south one mile on Hungry

Mother Road. The trail begins where the road comes to a dead end. (Caution: The road, located along the banks of Hungry Mother Creek, is unimproved dirt surface and may be impassable in wet weather).

The southern end of the trail can be reached by taking Kentucky Route 801 four miles south from Farmers (and past the lake known as Cove Run Reservoir), then north from the Alfred Church four miles on Lockegee Rock Road.

Length: 6 miles

USGS Quads: Morehead, Ky.; Bangor, Ky.; and Farmers, Ky.

Description: The easiest direction to walk this trail is from east to west; otherwise there is a rather steep climb up from Hungry Mother Creek.

The walk begins at Lockegee Rock, a scenic overlook with an elevation of 1200 feet and a good view south down Lockegee Creek and into the bottomlands of Ramey Creek. The major river you can see to the southwest is Licking River.

Lockegee Rock is also the southeastern edge of a long ridge, and the trail follows this ridge (almost always at an elevation close to 1200 feet) for most of its length. You will reach the southern slopes of Limestone Knob in about three miles; a short but steep climb to its top would put you at an elevation of 1435 feet.

From Limestone Knob the trail descends to the headwaters of Hungry Mother Creek at an elevation of 900 feet, then follows the creek to the road and trail's end.

Stanton District

Trails in the Red River Gorge Area

Location: This area is bound on the north by the Red River and Kentucky Route 77 and on the south by the Mountain Parkway. The Koomer Ridge Recreation Area, main developed campground in this gorge, is east of the Parkway's Slade interchange and west of the Pine Ridge exit.

Length: There are 33½ miles of trails in the Red River Gorge. The Forest Service has combined most of them to make two major trips for backpackers. One of them, the Long Hunters Trek, is 13.1 miles; the other, Triple Arch Trek, is 14.4 miles.

USGS Quads: Slade and Pomeroyton.

Description: This area is best known for its abundance of natural bridges, those unusual rock formations that develop when a soft under-stratum is worn away by water and weather, leaving a harder layer of rock on top intact. There are 20 natural stone arches in the Red River Gorge Area of the Daniel Boone National Forest. More than a dozen other arches can be found on private land within the area. We will describe one trail which contains three.

Triple Arch Trek — This 14.4 mile hike begins at the Rock Bridge Picnic Area on Swift Camp Creek. The natural bridge here is still forming; it is said to be the only one in Kentucky under which an active stream is flowing.

The trail proceeds north along the west bank of the creek at an elevation of 900 feet about 6 miles before turning west to cross Kentucky Route 715. About half a mile north from Rock Bridge you will come to the second natural bridge, called Turtle Back Arch. Watch carefully for the trail as you ford Dog Fork (it is slightly downstream from your point of entry). A mile and a quarter north from Rock Bridge you will reach Timmons Arch and junction with the *Wildcat Trail* (1¼ miles). The arch here is across the creek on its east banks. (Wildcat Trail runs west upstream on Wildcat Creek past its headwaters at 1100 ft., and then along the ridgetop to Kentucky Route 715, about ¾ mile south of the point where the main Triple Arch Trek crosses the road near Angel Windows).

Continue north along Swift Camp Creek a mile north of Wildcat Creek, then head west to cross highway 715. A short trail leads directly west across the road to another unusual rock formation, called Angel Windows; but the main Triple Arch Trail follows the road north about 100 yards, then turns left (west) at a sign that reads "No. 221 — Rough Trail." The trail will take you across Parched Corn Creek near its headwaters, then uphill just over ½ mile to Chimney Top Scenic Drive (Forest Road 10), elevation 1200 feet. Turn left (south) and follow Chimney Top Drive about 1½ miles to Kentucky Route 715. Turn right (south) and walk on the shoulder of the road another 1½ miles to Rock Bridge Road. Turn left (east) on this and proceed three miles to the picnic area where the trail began.

If you want an even longer trip, there is a trail (continuation of Rough Trail, #221) running west from Chimney Top Drive at the point where the Triple Arch Trek reached that road. This trail connects with the Long Hunters Trek network of trails at Chimney Top Creek.

We will describe the *Long Hunters Trek*, 13.1 miles, as a separate walk, however, beginning at its southern end in the Koomer Ridge Recreation Area.

(A short trail from the recreation area, not included in the Long

Hunters Trek, is the *Silvermine Arch Trail*, 1 mile. It leads north ¾ mile to the Silvermine Arch and south ¼ mile to a lookout tower.)

The main trail, however, heads north from the recreation area. Coming north into the recreation area from the Mountain Parkway Access Road, you would take the left fork to the trailhead, the right fork to the campground.

The first 8½ mile stretch is called Koomer Ridge Trail (#220) on Forest Service maps. It climbs to the flat top of the ridge and follows it north for about two miles before reaching a trail fork. Bear right and proceed north to Chimney Top Creek and a junction with Rough Trail (#221).

A sign at the junction reads "3.6 miles — Grey's Arch." The trail turns left (west) here. There are a number of good campsites in the next half mile. Then begins a 1½ mile ascent up "Pure Misery Hill" to junction with the Pinch 'Em Tight Trail on Pinch 'Em Tight Ridge at an elevation of 1200 feet. (These hills and ridges definitely were not named by real estate promoters).

Continue northwest on the Rough Trail (you'll get back to Pinch 'Em Tight Trail later), following a sign that says "Trail No. 221 — 2 miles Grey's Arch." The arch provides a scenic overlook of the Red River to your north.

The trail leads south from there about ¾ miles to a picnic area on Tunnel Ridge Road. On the west side of this picnic area, there's a sign that says "Trail 1770 — D. Boone Hut Trail." The hut, an old log cabin, is enclosed by a wire fence and is located just a few hundred feet down the trail.

Retrace your steps to the picnic area and walk east on a gravel road to a sign that reads "Trail 223 — 3.9 miles Koomer Ridge Picnic Area." Follow Trail 223 (this is Pinch 'Em Tight Trail) about a mile along a ridge top (elevation between 1200 and 1280 feet) to a junction with Buck Trail, #226. Bear right onto Buck Trail which dead-ends into Trail 220 (Koomer Ridge Trail). Bear right on Trail 220, following a sign that says "1 mile to Koomer Ridge Picnic Area." The trail ends at its starting point.

Natural Bridge State Park

This park is separated from the rest of the Red River Gorge area by the Mountain Parkway. A short, two-mile trail, called *Whittington Branch Trail* connects the two. It runs north from the end of the short road across from Hemlock Lodge and follows Whittington Branch past its headwaters to cross the Parkway on Tunnel Road. If you walk east on access road 15 you will reach the Koomer Ridge Recreation Area in just over a mile. If you walk north on Tunnel Road you will reach the Grey's Arch Picnic Area in just over half a mile.

Another group of trails in the Red River Gorge is located at the north end of Tunnel Road (4½ miles north of the Parkway). The trails lead to Double Arch, Courthouse Rock, and Haystack Rock. A loop that will take you to all these scenic spots, using a couple of short spur trails, is about 4½ miles long. It proceeds north to a spur trail leading west to Double Arch, continues north to Haystack Rock and even farther north via a spur trail to Courthouse Rock, back south across Auxier Ridge and then either west on a shortcut back to trail's beginning at Double Arch or south another mile to Tunnel Road. If you walk north on Tunnel Road from that point you will reach the place where you parked the car in ¾ mile.

Elevations in this area are about 1000 feet, and Courthouse Rock offers a good view of the Red River to your north.

London District
Moonbow Trail [*and its access trails*]
Location: This trail begins in Cumberland Falls State Park and runs north to a picnic area at the mouth of the Laurel River where it flows into the Cumberland. To reach Mouth of the Laurel Picnic Area by road, take U.S. Route 25W south six miles from Corbin and turn right (west) on Kentucky Route 1277. To reach the state park by road continue south on U.S. 25W another three miles from the junction with 1277 to a junction with Kentucky Route 90. Take route 90 west four miles to Cumberland Falls.
Length: 10 miles (plus two side trails: Dog Slaughter Trail, 3 miles; and Bark Camp Creek Trail, 3 miles).
Description: The trail gets its name from a peculiar nighttime rainbow effect on Cumberland Falls. It can be seen about seven days a month when the moon is full, if the weather is clear.

9 — Daniel Boone Forest
The path follows the east banks of the Cumberland River for its entire length. Average elevation is 850 feet. Average hiking time is six hours. At times you will be on sand bars or flat rocky banks of the river; occasionally you will climb to cliffs or slopes above the stream. Stands of cove hardwoods are interspersed with hemlocks on the north slopes, Virginia and shortleaf pines on the south slopes. Wildflowers and ferns are plentiful.

A mile north from the park campground you will reach Center Rock Rapids. In another mile and a half you will cross Dog Slaughter Creek and the junction with Dog Slaughter Trail, which runs east three miles to Forest Road 95.

From Dog Slaughter Creek to Bark Camp Creek, where there's an Adirondack shelter, is four miles. A second side trail leads east along Bark Camp Creek three miles to Forest Road 193.

Trail's end at Mouth of the Laurel picnic area is another 3½ miles north. Half a mile south of the picnic area you will cross Fishing Creek. In times of heavy rains, you may get your feet wet wading across it.

Trails Within Cumberland Falls State Park

Since this park occurs right in the middle of the Daniel Boone National Forest's London District, we will describe its trails at this point.

Location: (See preceding description of Moonbow Trail location).

Length: There are a number of short trails in this park, some of them interconnecting. Their total length is about 18 miles.

Description: Circuit trails are indicated by even numbers, blazed yellow, and make a circuit back to their starting point. Numbers are painted on trees about eight feet off the ground. Connecting trails are indicated by odd numbers, painted red, and interconnect the circuit trails and points of interest. Short connecting trails not numbered are marked with a red "C".

Circuit Trails

Trail 2 — circles the park, following the inside curve of the river for four miles along the southern, western, and northern sides of the park. It completes the circuit by crossing some private property and part of the Daniel Boone National Forest. Total trail length is 7 miles.

Trail 4 — 1 mile, runs from the Lodge to near Cabin Group 2 and returns.

Trail 6 — features a fine view of the river and Gatliff Bridge from the overlook, goes past Cabin Group 1. It is a mile in length and is reached by a short connecting trail from in front and to the left of the Lodge. A short connecting trail leads to the falls.

Trail 8 — crosses Highway 90 twice in its mile and a half length; just east of the Hitching Post store and at the park boundary.

Trail 10 — can be either a 1.1 or a 2-mile hike. It is 2 miles if the hiker starts from Trail 9 at the footbridge and hikes to the shelter building overlooking the falls and returns the same way. It is 1.1 miles if he takes the steep descent from the shelter building downhill to Trail 9. From DuPont Lodge to the start of Trail 10 and back to the lodge is a round trip of 2.6 miles.

Trail 12 — 1.25 miles, runs east or west from the trailer campground and along a ledge above the river and returns to the other side of the camping area. It connects with Trail 3 and provides a good view of Eagle Falls across the river.

Connecting Trails

Trail 1 — is the Moonbow Trail; see previous description.

Trail 3 — ½ mile, provides a view of Eagle Falls across the river. It branches off and returns to Trail 12.

Trail 5 — connects Cabin Group 2 and the east end of Trail 4 with Park Circuit Trail 2 at the river ¼ mile away. There is a long stairway down the ledge.

Trail 7 — is actually a series of interconnecting trails affording a choice of route in transferring between circuit trails 2, 8, and 12, and Highway 90. Distance varies with the route chosen but the maximum length is ½ mile.

Trail 9 — is an old trail connecting #10 and Eagle Falls. From the highway to Trail 10 is about ⅓ mile. Round trip to Eagle Falls and back is 1.6 miles. Trail 9 branches, one path going below Eagle Falls, the other above and downstream.

Trail 11 — about 2 miles, runs east from the park boundary. It can be reached from highway 90 just beyond the park sign or by the connecting trail leading off the horse trail to the shelter above the highway. There is also a trail around the hill below the shelter which provides a third access to Trail 11. From any of these approaches the trail runs downhill, crosses the horse trails and a mountain stream and then climbs to Pinnacle Knob Firetower and the Firetower Road.

The elevation at Pinnacle Knob is about 1200 feet. Average elevation of the park is 1000 feet, and elevation on the Cumberland River at Cumberland Falls is 780 feet.

For more information on Cumberland Falls, write the park headquarters in Corbin, Ky. 40701. For more information about the Daniel Boone National Forest write the Forest Supervisor, 100 Vaught Road, Winchester, KY 40391.

Cumberland Gap National Historical Park Trails

Location: The western end of this 20,000-acre park is at Middlesboro, Ky., near the tri-state border of Kentucky, Tennessee, and Virginia. The park follows the Virginia-Kentucky line east to Ewing, Va. About two miles south of the park, Virginia Route 58 runs parallel to the park boundary from Middlesboro to Ewing.

Length: Some 40 miles of trails are maintained by the park rangers. We will describe the longest of these (*Ridge Trail*, 16 miles) and six side trails that branch off it (*Sugar Run Trail*, 2.25 miles; *Lewis Hollow Trail*, 1.68 miles; *Woodson Gap Trail*, 2.25 miles; *Gibson Gap Trail*, 5 miles; *Chadwell Gap Trail*, 2.3 miles; and

Ewing Trail, 3.9 miles). We will also say a few words about the 14-mile *Wilderness Road Trail*, which has fallen into disuse.

USGS Quads: Middlesboro South, Ky.; Middlesboro North, Ky.; Varilla, Ky.; and Ewing, Va.

Description: Cumberland Gap marks the historic break in the Alleghenies through which the pioneers poured from the Eastern Seaboard to conquer the West. The Indians had a road through the gap, too, however, long before European explorers ever saw the region. They called it the Warriors' Path because a number of battles took place in the area between Cherokees who passed through on hunting trips to Kentucky and other tribes who came south, also to hunt, from north of the Ohio River.

Dr. Thomas Walker was the first colonial settler to see the gap, on April 13, 1750. He and five companions were in the process of locating an 800,000-acre grant for the Loyal Land Company when they stumbled on the natural passage through the mountain barrier. Walker called the place Cave Gap for a large cave, with a spring flowing through it, which he found there. He named the nearby Cumberland River in honor of the Duke of Cumberland, son of King George II and Queen Caroline of England, and later that name was also given to the gap and to the entire mountain range.

The French and Indian War (1754-60) and Pontiac's Rebellion (1763-65) prevented any immediate attempt to follow Walker's lead, but when peace returned, small parties of hunters began passing through the gap to find and explore Kentucky's fertile bluegrass country. One of these early explorers was Daniel Boone, who first saw the gap in 1769 and who subsequently spent two years ranging through the woods and grasslands of Kentucky.

In 1775, Judge Richard Henderson bought the Cherokee claim to 20 million acres south of the Kentucky River and engaged Boone to blaze a trail through the gap. It took him, with a crew of 30, only three weeks to cut the "Wilderness Road" from Long Island of the Holston (now Kingsport, Tenn.) to the Kentucky River, 208 miles from their starting point.

When the road was finished, settlers began to pour through the gap and by 1792, when Kentucky joined the Union, the state had a population of 100,000. By 1800 it was more than 220,000.

Geologically speaking, Cumberland Gap is a saddle, or notch, cut into a ridge of resistant rock by former stream activity. Such notches, frequently found in the Appalachians, are known as wind gaps.

This region has been subjected to great earth stresses, producing folded and faulted rocks. Stresses were so great that older rocks from the southeast were thrust for miles over younger rocks to the northwest. Erosion of rocks of varying hardness and different angles of folding have formed the present topography.

The gap is in a zone of fractured rock where the ridge was most easily attacked by erosion. Presumably, a southward-flowing stream crossed what is now the ridge. However, the Middlesboro Basin, to the northwest, was more rapidly and more deeply quarried than the gap area. This resulted in the diversion of the stream northward into the Cumberland River. The ridge became the water divide, and the former stream course became the gap.

A visit to the national park should begin with a trip to the Visitor Center on U.S. 25E just south of Middlesboro near the park entrance.

Camping is available at the Wilderness Road Campground and in the back country at Martin's Fork Cabin and campsites. No other camping is permitted.

Campfire permits are required for campfires other than those in the Wilderness Road Campground. During periods of high fire danger, "no smoking" signs are posted throughout the trail system and this regulation is strictly enforced. Reservations for the Martin's Fork Cabin may be made by writing Cumberland Gap National Historical Park, P.O. Box 840, Middlesboro, Kentucky 40965.

The Ridge Trail, 16 miles, begins from a scenic overlook on a mountain called the Pinnacle, just north of the actual gap; the trail follows the ridge top of the Cumberland Mountain on the state line almost exactly through the middle of the park from west to east.

To get to the Pinnacle, take the Skyland Road (also known as Pinnacle Road) 4½ miles east from the Visitor Center to a parking area. On the way you will pass Fort McCook, part of a network of small earthen Civil War forts, built by Union troops early in the war to guard this important passageway through the Cumberland Mountains.

The Pinnacle is at an elevation of about 2500 feet, and the trail which starts there continues at approximately that elevation for the first three or four miles. The ridgeline increases gradually in elevation through the park to reach 3500 feet at White Rocks near the park's eastern terminus north of Ewing. The terrain is wooded generally, but there are occasional cleared spaces that offer panoramic views.

Less than a mile from the Pinnacle, you will meet the *Sugar*

Run Trail which runs 2.25 miles north (and gradually downhill) to the Sugar Run Picnic Area at an elevation of 1235 feet. Much of this trail's route follows the banks of Sugar Run Creek.

An automobile road runs south from the Sugar Run Picnic Area four miles to the Visitor Center.

About half a mile east on the Ridge Trail from the junction with the Sugar Run Trail, you will reach a second side path, *Lewis Hollow Trail* (1.68 miles), which leads southeast down a draw from 2200 feet on the ridge to 1600 feet at the Wilderness Road Campground. This campground is actually the site of an old settlement called Robinson Station where pioneers bought provisions for their trek over the mountains.

Back on the main trail, you will proceed uphill about 200 feet in the next two miles before reaching a junction with a third side trail, *Woodson Gap Trail*. This one also leads south — and very sharply downhill — for a mile where it joins with the Gibson Gap Trail at an elevation of 1300 feet. If you turn right (west) on the Gibson Gap Trail you will reach the Wilderness Road Campground in another 1¼ miles.

Gibson Gap Trail joins the Ridge Trail about 1½ miles east of the junction with Woodson Gap Trail and angles southwest downhill at a gentler incline than the Woodson Gap Trail. This trail is five miles long.

Just east of the intersection with Gibson Gap Trail on the Ridge Trail you will come to a large flat rock formation called Goose Nest where sentries stood during the Civil War watching the valley below for signs of the enemy. From the edge of this natural sink, created by a cave collapse, you can view virgin trees over a hundred feet tall.

The trail climbs in the next three miles to an altitude of 3,000 feet at Indian Rocks. This is a vast littered area of flint and stone where the Cherokee and Shawnee once flaked their arrows and spears for hunting.

Just past Indian Rocks you will reach a short side trail which leads north to the Hensley Settlement, an abandoned pioneer village from the early 19th century with 28 structures of log and stone still standing. The settlement is currently being restored by the Park Service. As you leave you may notice a small cemetery where 74 head and foot stones remain.

The Ridge Trail climbs to an elevation of more than 3300 feet in the next few miles before you reach the log cabin and campsites at Martin's Fork in Chadwell's Gap. This cabin was also abandoned by early settlers but has been renovated. One of its most interesting features is the large, old-fashioned fireplace.

There are natural springs near the cabin at the headwaters of Martin's Fork Creek.

Just past the campsite is a side trail (*Chadwell's Gap Trail*) that runs steeply downhill (from 3300 feet to 1800 feet in 2.3 miles) to connect with a road that leads three miles south to junction with U.S. 58 at Caylor, Va.

If you spend the night at Martin's Fork and continue east on the Ridge Trail next morning, you will reach Sand Cave in time for lunch (five miles). The opening of the cave is about 80 feet high and the entrance room encompasses about 1.25 acres. Next to the cave is a beautiful 100-foot waterfall, and a mile farther on is the trail's end at White Rocks lookout tower. The rocks were used as a landmark by the pioneers as they traveled over Boone's Wilderness Road.

If you had access to two cars on your hike of the Ridge Trail, you will have left one of them at Ewing. To reach it, take the trail that leads south from White Rocks 3.9 miles to connect with a road that leads another mile into town.

If you are retracing your steps to the Wilderness Road Campground you can make a loop around the White Rock Lookout Tower to rejoin the main trail near Sand Cave.

A few words about the Wilderness Road Trail:

This 14-mile national historical hiking trail used to begin in Cumberland Gap National Historical Park and proceed north to a mile south of Pineville, Ky., where it ended at the Bert Combs Forestry Building. The trail was designed to approximate part of the original Wilderness Road carved by Daniel Boone across Cumberland Gap and north to the Kentucky River.

We mention it because so many people have heard of it already. We are advised, however, by Mr. Albert Hawkins, superintendent of the Cumberland Gap National Historical Park, that "the Wilderness Road Trail has seen little use in recent years, and is practically impossible to follow in many places. It is not open to the general public, and we discourage use of this trail."

If you want more information or if you are interested in working to restore the trail, contact the Bluegrass Council of the Boy Scouts of America, 975 Liberty Road, Lexington, Kentucky 40505.

LOST VALLEY STATE PARK

BOSTON MTN.

1.

• RUSSELLVILLE

2.

• LITTLE ROCK

• HOT SPRINGS
NATIONAL PARK

MENA

1. OZARK NATIONAL FOREST
2. OUACHITA NATIONAL FOREST

arkansas

Stand on top of a ridge in northwest Arkansas' Boston Mountains, and you will inevitably notice, in the grandeur spread out before you, that most of the other ridges within sight are rather flat-topped and almost the same elevation as the spot where you are standing. The sharply upthrust peak standing above low gaps on either side that is so prominent a part of the landscape of the Appalachians is absent.

The rocks of these ridges were not spewed out of a volcano. They were not faulted, folded, compressed or twisted by mountain building movements of the earth. Indeed, strictly speaking, the Ozarks are not mountains at all. The Ozark Highlands is a plateau, an area of 55,000 square miles that was lifted as a unit above the surrounding country. The layers of rocks in its bluffs lie flat, except for a slight southward tilt of the entire plateau.

The geologic history of the Ozarks begins with a spate of volcanic activity that occurred between 1.2 and 1.5 billion years ago. Several different outbursts produced masses of rhyolite, granite, and basalt. This activity ceased about a billion years ago, and the entire area was uplifted and faulted again. The result was a series of low hills where the difference between the highest peaks and the deepest valleys was nowhere more than about 1000 feet.

The sea began to rise over this landscape some 525 million years ago. Algal reefs grew around the submerged areas, and sand settled on the edges. In time the algal reefs became limestone, the sand, sandstone. Where the lime sediment combined with magnesium from the sea water, dolomite was formed. Lead and zinc ore, still mined in the Ozarks, were created during this period. So was chert, a dense, quartzlike mineral that is everywhere in the Ozarks. The Indians used it to make scraping tools and arrowheads. You will probably encounter it the first time you try spreading a sleeping bag on a rocky Ozark hillside.

Through much of the Paleozoic Era, the Ozarks lay under the sea. Rich fossil deposits were built up in the rocks that were slowly forming at the bottom. As the seas receded, the area was subjected to uplift several times, the most significant occuring about 380 million years ago.

The land that rose above that ancient sea was basically flat, a thick accumulation of sediments from the sea bottom. And then the rivers went to work. Bit by bit, they cut their channels into the rock, eroding away the softer stone, digging their channels deeper and deeper below the more enduring rock that crowned the emerging ridge tops.

The present landscape of the Ozarks was created by the rivers. They cut the narrow, meandering, steep-sided valleys. They sculpted the spectacular bluffs that wall in the valleys. In places, they cut through the sedimentary rock down to the basalt and granite that underlay the plateau.

The waters also created the caves that honeycomb the Ozarks. Some of these have been decked out with largely spurious legends of Jesse James and opened to the public at so much a head. But the majority are known only to spelunkers — if they are known at all.

The Ozark caves exist because limestone is water soluble. Where a sandstone, for example, lies at the surface, water can percolate down through a crack in the rock to limestone below. The water dissolves the limestone and carries it away. If it goes on long enough, this process can produce the spectacular caverns of the Ozarks.

The porous nature of the Ozark rocks also removes water from the surface very rapidly. Valleys big enough to support a substantial stream elsewhere are often dry in the Ozarks, except after a heavy rain.

With so much water underground, springs — some producing an enormous amount of water — are common. Creeks and rivers sometimes simply disappear into the porous rock, only to reappear downstream. Natural bridges have been formed over many streams by water eroding away underlying strata while leaving surface strata relatively untouched.

The Ozarks are a meeting place for plant species from surrounding areas. More than 3,500 species of plants have been identified in the area. Northern plants, remnants of the ice-age, hang on in cool, sheltered creek bottoms. Southwestern plants inhabit hillsides with thin top soil where the porous rock sucks up rainfall like a sponge. The prickly pear cactus is fairly common.

The forest cover is mainly hardwood, with oak-hickory association predominating. Beeches and sycamores thrive along the stream banks. Maples, sweetgum, black gum, and dogwood add to the fall color.

The most common native conifer is the red cedar, though immigrant Mexican juniper, called in Arkansas the Ozark white cedar, finds a home along the White River and in a few places along the Buffalo River. The short-leaf pine was once uncommon, but it has been rather widely planted by the Forest Service in recent years.

Flowering trees include redbud, dogwood, red haw, wild plum

and crabapple, locust, silver bell, serviceberry, smoke tree, fringe tree, wax myrtle, and umbrella magnolia.

Of considerable interest along the Buffalo River are the "fern falls." On the cooler, moister north slopes óne finds cascades of ferns blanketing a precipitous, treeless incline, and from a distance appearing to be a green-tinted waterfall.

On dry, rocky slopes, one can find the "glades." Ozark glades are in fact patches of prairie interrupting the forest. They are covered with typical prairie grasses such as big and little bluestem, as well as prairie rose, rattlesnake master, and Indian paintbrush.

Forty-three species of mammals are native to the Ozarks, 13 of them bats living in the many caves. Many of the mammalianspecies that were once abundant here have been extirpated by hunting and habitat destruction. The elk, bison, and puma are gone. Bears and beavers disappeared for awhile, but they have been successfully reintroduced in a few areas.

Other species include bobcats, red and gray foxes, otters (a few), mink, muskrat, raccoon, oppossum, and skunk. The red wolf that once lived here is gone from the area (indeed, it may be extinct), but coyotes have become rather common.

Birds are generally those of the eastern woods, with some invasion by western species such as the scissor-tailed flycatcher. Birds of prey are much reduced — as they are almost everywhere — with such former breeders as the peregrine falcon altogether absent. Turkey vultures (locally known as Ozark eagles) seem slightly less common than robins.

The wild turkey, the ruffed grouse, and the prairie chicken were hunted out of the area, but recently the two former species have been reintroduced with some success.

Ozark rivers and caves harbor a number of species of amphibians and fish found nowhere else. Reptiles include the timber rattlesnake, the western cottonmouth, and the northern copperhead. Scorpions and tarantulas, animals usually associated with the southwest, are also found in the Ozarks.

Human settlement in the Ozarks goes back at least 9,000 years. A substantial number of archeological sites have been excavated in caves and rock shelters in the area. When Europeans arrived, the Osage Indians dominated the countryside. French traders entered the Ozarks in the late 17th century. Some place names still survive from that period.

The first settlers came after 1810, with many arriving in the 1830s and 1840s. The first to come were chiefly hunters who lived on the abundant game of the area. Later, farmers and miners moved in. The terrain dictated a pattern of settlement that saw farms spread out along the narrow valleys and on the flat ridge tops. The slopes were often too steep for settlement, and disastrous erosion often followed attempts to farm it.

This settlement pattern still exists in many areas, and it is important to hikers. Many streams running through wild land contain unsafe water because of cow pastures on the ridge top above the stream.

The timber of the Ozarks included many extremely valuable species such as white oak and black walnut. Except for isolated patches, the virgin timber was pretty well cut over by the 1930s.

The Ozarks cannot support a large population on a sustained basis. Many settlers found that the meager topsoil in their fields quickly washed into the rivers once the tree cover was gone. A steady outflow of population in the first 40 years of this century turned into a flood after World War II. In the Boston Mountains, the ruggedest area in the Ozarks, the road maps show numerous communities that no longer exist. What was a hamlet with houses, stores, and a grade school 40 years ago, may be nothing but a farmhouse today. As the people left, the Forest Service bought up the land, and the trees began to come back. Today, the Boston Mountains doubtlessly have more wild land than they did in 1925.

The Buffalo River flows through the Boston Mountains. Around 1905, there were 27,000 people living in its 1338-square mile watershed. By 1965, outmigration had reduced the area's population by half.

The flow is not entirely out, however. In some areas, extensive development of retirement homes has lured people from Chicago and St. Louis down into the mountains. Lately, frieks have been fleeing the city to set up communes and homesteads on little patches of land in the mountains.

The remains of past settlement give adventurous hikers some excellent opportunities for exploring. Old trails and traces of pioneer wagon roads can be found and followed in many areas. You may come across the remains of a settler's cabin in an isolated creek bottom. The old stone chimney and the rotting logs have become a piece of archeology, artifacts almost as exotic as the Indian arrowheads that still turn up regularly on Ozark hillsides.

OZARK HIKES

There are few established trails in the Ozarks, either within or outside the Ozark National Forest boundaries. Local people out for a weekend trek through the woods tend to follow the banks of streams. It is still possible, on a hike up one of these creeks, to discover a spectacular waterfall or rock formation that nobody has ever seen before (at least nobody who has ever bothered to tell the story). You may well find Indian arrowheads, and abandoned log cabins of early settlers can be a treasure trove for antique hunters.

There are remnants of old pioneer wagon trails in the mountains, but these are likely to peter out in some particularly inconvenient spot. Try to find them if you like; old geological survey maps occasionally show some of them. But be sure to take a compass along, and some means of boiling or purifying water. If you are planning an exploring trip of some duration, take an extra day's food along.

We have listed the few existing formal trails we know of and have made a personal selection of hikes up creek beds that we feel are particularly rewarding.

All but one of the hikes we describe are in the Boston Mountains, most rugged of the three geological subdivisions of the Ozark Plateau. We have given a short description of the Slyamore Ranger District, east of the Boston Mountains on the Salem Plateau; and we have recommended one hike in that district. (The third geological subdivision, in case you've been wondering, is the Springfield Plateau which, in Arkansas, forms a narrow band of relatively flat, good farming land between the Boston Mountains and the hills of the Salem Plateau).

The Forest Supervisor, Ozark National Forest, Box 340, Russellville, Ark. 72801, can supply maps and other information on the Ozark National Forest.

Hurricane Creek Trail

Location: From the grocery store at Sand Gap (also known as Pelsor) on Arkansas Route 7, take Arkansas Route 123 (gravel surface) west about 12 miles to a bridge across Big Piney Creek immediately east of Fort Douglas. The trail begins as a jeep road that heads right just west of the bridge.

(If you come to the sign that announces your arrival in Fort Douglas, you've gone too far. Like many other once-thriving villages in the Boston Mountains, this one is completely abandoned. Only a farm and a few tumbledown buildings remain).

In dry weather, you may be able to continue by car another mile up the jeep road to a curve by a large beech tree where the actual foot trail branches off to the right. There's a sign here, if it hasn't been vandalized, that says Hurricane Creek Trail.

Length: About 7 miles

USGS Quad: Treat and Mt. Judea, Arkansas.

Description: At the beginning of the trail, just past the beech tree, you will notice an old swinging foot bridge that crosses the creek. We don't advise you to try it. The fall to the creek would be a long one, and the bridge doesn't look very safe.

The first half mile or so of trail takes you through a wide valley, including a large meadow filled with wildflowers from spring through early fall. There are a couple of creek crossings where you are likely to get your feet wet. Elevation at the creek is about 800 feet.

Portions of this old trail follow an abandoned road, but at the first point where an intermittent stream comes down from the north to join Hurricane Creek, the trail leaves that road to clamber up the creekbed and then through a small red cedar woods. (To continue along the road here would require crossing a barbed wire fence, so you're not likely to become confused).

The trail climbs up to about a thousand feet, and if you watch carefully to your left you will see a small side trail leading up to a large rock overhang (it makes good shelter in a rainstorm) and a natural bridge in the limestone far above your head. In the autumn of 1974, there was a small sign on the main trail directing you to the natural bridge.

A few hundred yards farther on, a massive jumble of rocks has been given the name of Devil's Den. (Shallow caves are sometimes also called Devil's Den in Ozark terminology).

The trail continues to wind along the steep wooded slope about a hundred feet above the creek for the remainder of the first three miles. Then you reach a broad, grassy bank and the remnants of old homesteads at the mouth of Greasy Creek. This is an ideal spot for a picnic and for some nosing around to find old tools and household implements in the ruins. (This is still possible on Ozark trails; the traffic is extremely light. We seldom met other hikers).

The trail west and north of Greasy Creek hugs the banks of Hurricane Creek for most of the rest of your trip. This bank gradually becomes wider, and the high bluffs and wooded slopes recede. You are following the old road now all the time. Intermittent streams or "draws" become more frequent. The stream is a fast-running one. There are no spectacular waterfalls but plenty of small shoals.

The trail passes by the remnants of swings and a merry-go-round and portions of the old schoolhouse in Chancel, another of those mountain towns that's listed still on maps but can no longer be found on the ground. The end of your journey is beside an old farmhouse at the junction with Forest Road 1209. There's a big green Forest Service sign at the junction which announces that you are within the boundaries of the Piney Creek Wildlife Unit.

It is possible to reach this end of the trail from Arkansas Route 7. The road is much rougher, but the distance is actually shorter than the drive to Fort Douglas.

Take Arkansas Route 16 west from Route 7 at Lurton about two miles to Sain's Grocery and junction with Forest Road 1208. A Forest Service sign here tells you it is four miles west to Hurricane Creek. When you reach the junction of 1208 with 1209, turn left and you will see the Piney Creek Wildlife Unit sign and trailhead almost immediately.

Richland Creek Hikes

Location: Take Arkansas Route 16 east from Sand Gap (known as Pelsor on some maps) about eight miles to Ben Hur. Continue east another 2½ miles to Upper Falling Water Creek Road (Forest Road 1205). Turn north on 1205 for eight miles to a small Forest Service campground near the confluence of Richland and Falling Water creeks. This campground makes an ideal base for several hikes. We will describe two: (1) a single-day trip upstream to land Falls and to Twin Falls at the confluence of Big Devils Fork and Long Devils Fork, and (2) an overnight hike downstream past the Wasson School to the south end of Forest Road 1220 near Stack Rock Mountain.

Length: Upstream trip about 3 miles (but plan 5 or 6 hours to do it). Downstream trip about 9 miles with Wasson School roughly marking the halfway point.

USGS Quad: Snowball, Arkansas.

Description: Richland Creek, longest of the scenic Buffalo River's tributaries, winds for 32 miles from its beginning deep in the mountains of southern Newton County north to the junction with the Buffalo. Some 2,100 acres of the lands surrounding it have been designated as a study area to determine their wilderness potential.

The rich bottomland of lower Richland Creek offered one of the few areas in this part of the Ozarks suitable to the pioneers for farming. Cotton was grown there as early as the 1820s.

The hike upstream from Richland Creek campground is more heavily traveled because of the waterfalls; we will describe that one first.

Upstream Trip

Walk east from the campground along wide, flat banks of the creek for about ¼ mile to the point where Falling Water Creek flows in from the south. Continue west along Richland Creek at an elevation of about 1,000 feet.

Cliffs, towering two or three hundred feet above you, begin to edge closer to the stream, and soon you are proceeding through a deep, narrow gorge.

At the end of the first mile, you will notice a small stream, full in wet weather, coming downhill from the north.

In another mile and a half you will come upon Richland Falls, only about six feet high but an impressive 100 feet wide. This is one of three waterfalls in store on this day's trip.

There's a fork in the river nearby and if you bear right (north), you will soon come to the confluence of Big Devils Fork (the stream on the north side) and Long Devils Fork. Both of these empty into Richland Creek with major waterfalls situated within a few yards of each other.

Long Devils Fall is about 16 feet high and Big Devils Fall is about 18 feet high. Both are deeply undercut. The cliff walls are dark shale with layers of fossil-laden limestone near the top.

One could probably wander endlessly with pure delight up either of these tributaries or farther south along Richland Creek. There may well be other waterfalls that no one has yet bothered to describe. There certainly are abandoned homesteads and endless vistas of wooded hilltop and grassy stream bank. For now, however, we return to the Forest Service campground and description of a different hike north to Wasson School and Stack Rock Mountain.

Downstream Trip

We haven't hiked this part of Richland Creek ourselves, but we have a very detailed description from Mr. Richard Murray, a retired Corps of Engineers employee who may have explored more miles of Ozark hillside on foot than any other living human being.

If you are hiking with a group as he did and have access to extra cars, he suggests shuttling some of those cars to the trail's other end. Here's how. Drive north from the campground on Forest Road 1208 about five miles to Dickey Junction, then east on Forest Road 1201 about six miles to Forest Road 1220, then sharply right on 1220 across a ford of Richland Creek and the planned end of the hike.

For the first part of your trip north from the campground, you can walk along Drury Road on the creek's west bank or along an old logging road that follows the east bank. Mr. Murray's group chose the east bank. Large red oaks and sweet gum grew there along the creek, he reported. There was no evidence of very recent logging.

Bobtail Creek flows into Richland Creek in a small flat area about a mile north of the campground. An old homesite being used as a feed lot can be seen on the west side of the creek.

After passing through an old field, the logging road leads across the creek to the east side, traveling through woods for half a mile to within sight of an old tin-roofed house on the creek's west side. If you cross the creek and explore, you'll find a curbed spring under the bluff downstream from the house about halfway to the horselot. The water in Ozark springs is almost *always* safe to drink; the water in Ozark creeks almost *never* is, unfortunately, because of the cow pastures located along the banks of those creeks and on mountaintops near their sources.

From this old house, the road leads through bottomland woods on the east side of the creek for about a mile to another field. Rock formations on the creek at this point are smooth and almost level, and the creek is only a small trickle in all but the wettest seasons. You may decide, therefore, to walk downstream in the creekbed for awhile. You will notice some limestone mixed in with the sandstone boulders.

If you return to the road at the southern end of the field, it will take you up over a hill through a woods to intersect another road descending the hill from the east and leading to the hamlet of Magic Springs.

The road along the creek continues north past a cow pasture where Sulphur Creek pours into Richland Creek from the east. Just past this is another old homestead in a clearing. There's a spring flowing out of a rusty old pipe about 75 yards uphill behind the house.

The road branches past the homestead with the east fork continuing along Richland and the other heading northward up the mountain. Take the hilltop route; the other comes to an end rather soon at a sawdust pile. In another quarter mile, you will reach the Wasson School, where a broad grassy yard makes an ideal place to set up camp for the night.

The school is a single-room frame building, no longer in use, with rock veneer facing, about 30 feet wide and 60 feet long, with a small bell steeple on the gable facing the road. The place is fast falling into disrepair. When Mr. Murray was there, some of the tongue-in-groove flooring had been torn out, exposing the floor joists, apparently by hunters seeking kindling.

Your path downstream next morning will take you through woods to an old field dotted with persimmon trees, then through a gap in a rock fence at the north end of the field. There's a small stream, sometimes dry, to cross, then another wooded area and yet another old homestead, this one fairly large with the traditional dogtrot in the middle.

Mr. Murray found an old cemetery at the edge of the woods north of this old ruined homestead.

He said it was grown up in grass and encircled by a wire rectangular fence about 50 by 100 feet. All but one of the 20 or so gravestones were marked with the names of various Wassons, apparently the same ones for whom the school was named. The oldest stone he found was that of Jackson Wasson, 1814-1868.

In the second field past this old house is another house and, according to Mr. Murray, a large pear tree bulging with delicious fruit in season.

The road past this homestead climbs a hill and overlooks the creek from 100 to 200 feet. In the next open field, there's yet another old homestead, but there's also a modern house nearby complete with TV antenna and the most modern farm equipment. You are approaching civilization. Within the next half mile you will reach Forest Road 1220 and the automobile ford across Richland Creek. In the distance to your west you will be able to see the peak of Stack Rock Mountain, rising some 1800 feet above sea level.

Whitaker Creek

Location: About a mile south of Boxley on Arkansas Route 43 and just north of a bridge across the Buffalo River, take Cave Mountain Road west and uphill at a sharp grade for 5½ miles. You will pass Cave Mountain Church on your right, and if you have time a short visit to the church graveyard can be fascinating. Among early settlers buried there are the family of Whitakers for whom Whitaker Creek was named. There are also names of people on the tombstones that you will find carved on ancient beech trees along the creek bank.

Half a mile past the church, you will see on your right a rather large abandoned Ozark house, complete with dogtrot (breezeway) through the center. You can still see remains of the kitchen garden on the right side of the house as you face it from the road.

Take the first road on the left past this house to road's end at the old Faddis homestead (the name Faddis is written on the side of the house). The trail begins just behind this second abandoned home.

Length: 5 miles (but plan six hours for walking it)

USGS Quad: Boxley, Arkansas.

Description: Whitaker Creek is part of a 10,500-acre segment of Buffalo River headwaters country that has been designated a National Wilderness Area. Its steep hillsides have protected virgin timber from lumbermen. There are groves of giant beeches and sycamores, white oaks, and even a few black walnuts with a girth of more than six feet and a height of more than 40 feet before the first branch. Rare species of ferns, wildflowers, and fungi also find a home in this moist woods, according to Maxine Clark, a respected area botanist and co-editor of the Ozark Society Bulletin.

There is no formal trail once one has scrambled down the hillside; you simply follow the creek bank.

The hardest part is finding the easiest way down the mountain (a drop of some 800 feet in less than a quarter of a mile); fortunately, we had an excellent guide in Dick Murray, a member of the Ozark Society, avid hiker and explorer.

Mr. Murray led us through patches of poison ivy (fortunately it was autumn) along a narrow indentation in the ground which looked like a watercourse. He said it was a path schoolchildren used to take. At one point there was a sheer drop (with footholds) of about 20 feet. He had brought a stout rope which we used to negotiate the cliff.

We reached the creek in a narrow valley where it flows into the Buffalo River at an elevation of about 1300 feet. Along the banks in this valley were remnants of an old road and several crumbling chimneys and rotting cisterns from old homesteads.

We crossed the creek and headed west (to our right as we came down the mountain) upstream. The wooded slopes were gentle for the first half mile, and we scrambled around on them looking for stands of large timber and autographed beech trees. Some of the smooth-barked beeches contained carved messages; others had only names and dates. There were several from the 1930s.

The white oak trees were probably older than the beeches and sycamores but because the former grow so slowly they were less impressive. Some of the biggest sycamores straddled boulders in the very middle of the stream.

Mr. Murray (a spiritual cousin of Natty Bumpo) kept us busy looking for remnants of old pioneer trails and wagon roads. He dreams someday of building a trans-Ozark foot trail, using these old paths in many places and passing by the most scenic spots in the mountains. He already has much of the route figured out; the

Forest Service approves of his idea but has no funds to carry out the project.

The season was too far advanced for wildflowers when we walked Whitaker Creek, but we found a bright yellow fungus that looked like a piece of ocean coral and another one in a paler shade that held water in its upturned cup and looked like the most delicate species of buttercup.

Our gentle slopes disappeared and steep bluffs took their place about half a mile from the stream's mouth. Springs dripped down and mosses and ferns grew lush on the north-facing slopes. The rocks in the creek bed grew larger and larger, until finally they towered over our heads and we had to crawl around them.

Several smaller streams poured down the mountainsides, mostly from the north, to join Whitaker Creek. The water tumbled over dozens of tiny, jewel-like falls into quiet pools and we dutifully took pictures.

As a result we had almost run out of film by the time we reached the first of the two big falls Mr. Murray had mentioned only casually. We were completely unprepared as we entered a deep, round box canyon and saw a cascade of water dropping down from at least 40 feet above us. The pool beneath the fall was deep and wide enough for swimming and its banks were surrounded by wildflowers and ferns. The place was a type specimen for paradise.

We took a quick dip, then retraced our steps to go up and around the canyon and continue our trek west.

Less than half a mile farther along, we came upon the second waterfall. This one was almost as high and the box canyon was just as big, but we were prepared this time and so not quite as thrilled.

We were gradually making our way back up that 800 feet we had descended so precipitously at the mouth of Whitaker Creek. The creekbed itself grew steeper and the slopes at the side grew correspondingly gentler again. The stream flow was much diminished. Whitaker Creek is one of those Ozark streams that occasionally disappears under the rocks of its bed, only to reappear a few yards downstream. One of the effects of this is that fish are pretty well kept out of the upper reaches of many creeks.

We began to look for a fence corner with one side heading uphill toward the road. The creek curved southwest soon after we found it and we headed north up a ravine to rejoin Cave Mountain Road across from an old tar paper shack about three miles west of where we had left our car.

Leatherwood Creek

Location: On Arkansas Route 74 at a bridge at the bottom of a hill just east of the junction with Arkansas Route 43 at Ponca.
Length: 2¾ miles
USGS Quad: Ponca, and Murray, Arkansas.
Description: The bridge on Route 74 marks the mouth of Leatherwood Creek where it flows into the Buffalo River. An easy day trip south and east up the creek will give you a good look at the wide variety of Ozark vegetation and animal life. The micro-climate along the creek is said to be so mild that wood frogs stay active all year.

The stream gets its name from the leatherwood tree (actually a shrub), so tough and yet so flexible that its bark and twigs can easily be tied in knots. Indians used the limbs to weave water-proof baskets and early settlers used them to make minnow seines, according to University of Arkansas zoologist Dr. Douglas James. In an Ozark Society Bulletin article about hiking up the creek, Dr. James noted also that it takes a century for leather-wood to produce a two-inch diameter trunk.

The streambed of Leatherwood Creek near its mouth is made up of layers of smooth limestone, and the foliage in spring and summer forms a shady arch over the creek.

For the first mile of your trip, the water flows between steep narrow walls that rise quickly from the streambank elevation of about 1100 feet to a clifftop elevation of 1500 feet.

Farther upstream, the limestone plates give way to gravel, with occasional punctuation by those massive boulders which seem characteristic of so many mountain streams and hillsides in the Ozarks. The flat tops of these boulders, according to Dr. James, "wear caps of foliage comprising isolated plant communities rich in ferns, mosses, and forbs and even small trees."

Tributaries of the Leatherwood tumble into it at frequent inter-vals over cliffs that form box canyons and an even more favor-able climate than the streambed in general for moist weather plants like ferns and liverworts.

After a mile and a half the creek forks. If you take the left fork you will climb gradually for half a mile to the stream's beginnings at an elevation of 2100 feet.

The right fork is more rugged, with steep-sided walls enclosing you in a dark, verdant jungle. This fork takes ¾ mile to reach the creek's beginnings and an elevation of 2100 feet.

Lost Valley [Clark Creek] Hike

Location: Three miles south of the junction of Arkansas Route 43 with Arkansas Route 74 at Ponca, Route 43 fords a small stream (Clark Creek) coming down from a minor side valley of the Buffalo River. There's a sign here that directs you west on a gravel road up the creek for about a mile to Lost Valley State Park. A good day hike leads upstream from the campground in this park.

Length: 3½ miles (roughly)

USGS Quads: Ponca and Osage SW, Arkansas.

Description: The focal point of this hike is Cob Cave, spectacular for the scenery around it and interesting for the ancient Indian artifacts that have been found there. Its archeological significance was not realized, until Professor S. C. Dellinger of the University of Arkansas explored it in 1931. He determined from corncobs, pieces of gourds, and woven baskets that the site was between 1,000 and 2,000 years old.

The bluff that shelters Cob Cave is more than 200 feet high. The cave opening at the base of the bluff forms a kind of natural bandshell, 150 feet deep, 50 feet high, and 260 feet from end to end.

Clark Creek sweeps 50 feet back under the roof, but at one end the shelter has a high dry shelf that is protected even from windblown rain.

The scenic advantages of the area around the cave weren't recognized widely until a state publicity director and a National Geographic photographer wandered in there in 1945 with a group of high school students from Harrison. It was the state official, whose name was Bud Green, who gave the name "Lost Valley" to the place even though it is neither a valley nor, strictly speaking, lost.

Elevation on the creek at the state park campground is 1100 feet. As you proceed upstream, you will climb gradually to an elevation of 1600 feet near the creek's source about 3½ miles west and north.

Very near the campground you will encounter a natural bridge with water coming through a tunnel about 10 feet wide in the middle of the rock.

Less than 150 feet farther along, you will stumble upon a shallow cave that isn't as big and impressive a shelter as Cob Cave, but it is still interesting.

Cob Cave is near the northwest boundaries of the park, close to where the creek forks about three miles from the campground. (Each of these forks leads about half a mile north to its beginning in mountainside springs).

Past Cob Cave there is a series of four waterfalls, descending in orderly steps down a 200-foot gorge. Yet another waterfall comes into this gorge from the left. If you follow the stream behind that one, you will encounter a third cave.

This latter cave, we are told, has an entrance room that is 10 or 12 feet wide and a ceiling tall enough to allow plenty of standing room for adults. In a second room reached by a narrow passageway there's a fourth waterfall, cascading some 35 feet over a ledge.

Caves are among the Ozarks' most impressive features. They are also extremely dangerous to explore if you don't know what you're doing. Unless you're equipped with a hardhat, carbide lamp, stout rope, and a good cave guide, we recommend that you stay out of all non-commercial caverns.

Other Boston Mountain Attractions

There are a number of scenic areas in the Boston Mountains that are worth visiting even though they don't involve long hikes. Some of these are pinpointed on the national forest map; others are known only to local residents. We would feel remiss if we didn't mention a few of these to you in passing:

Pedestal Rocks and King's Bluff: Take Arkansas Route 16 east six miles from Pelsor (Sand Gap) to a Forest Service sign that says Pedestal Rocks. Turn south on the gravel road and continue by car until the road grade becomes extremely steep. Park there and walk up to the bluffs on foot.

King's Bluff is about a mile north of Pedestal Rocks along the North Fork of Illinois Bayou and has not been publicized. The formations in both areas are of sandstone.

The Pedestals are stacks of rectangular rocks and are said to be formed when a capping stratum of hard rock is underlain by a softer, more crumbly foundation and a favorable system of "joints." Joe Clark, a geologist and one of the *Ozark Society Bulletin's* editors, has explained that the geological term "joint" refers to a fracture or parting which interrupts the continuity of a rock mass.

At King's Bluff there is a hundred foot "pour-off" of wet weather waterfall. The elevation is between 1500 and 1750 feet above sea level and the cliffs rise some 250 feet from their base to the tops.

Sam's Throne: Take Arkansas Route 123 north from Lurton about eight miles. There should be a Forest Service sign there to direct you. The throne is a remnant of the bluff line which has eroded away to make a giant stool-like formation. The high bluffs in the area provide a long scenic overlook of the Big Creek Valley.

A rather eccentric preacher named Sam used to climb out on a log from the bluffs to his 'throne'. He pulled the log in after himself, and then preached sermons to the rocks.

Alum Cove Natural Bridge: From Arkansas Route 7 and 16 about eight miles northwest of Lurton, turn south on Forest Road 1202, then almost immediately turn west on Forest Road 1206 about two miles to a Forest Service picnic area. This bridge is typical of many such rock formations that occur in the Ozarks where water has worn through limestone to leave harder surface rock strata intact. This natural bridge is more easily accessible than most, however.

Hemmed-In Hollow: Half a mile south of Compton on Arkansas Route 43, a small stream that is a northside tributary of the Buffalo River, crosses the road. Walk southeast along the creek about half a mile to this huge box canyon with a spectacular 200-foot waterfall.

Indian hieroglyphs: At a mailbox ¾ miles east of Nail on Arkansas Route 16, there's an old logging road. Follow it to the end of the bluff where there's a kind of half moon formation. Walk west under the bluff on the talus slopes until you see the hieroglyphs.

SYLAMORE FOREST

The Sylamore District is separated from the rest of the Ozark National Forest by distance — it's about 25 miles east — and by geology. It's in the Salem Plateau, lowest in elevation and least rugged of the three subdivisions of the Ozark Plateau. Lumbering has taken a much bigger toll here than it has in the Boston Mountains, mainly because the timber has been much more accessible. There are still a surprising number of untouched areas, though.

There are no formal hiking trails (except for a short horse trail in the Blanchard Springs Recreation Area), but some excellent day or overnight trips can be made by hiking up any of the several hundred small creeks in the district. North Sylamore Creek, the main stream that flows through the area, is often so full that wading across it can be extremely inconvenient. Its tributaries usually provide great walking terrain, however.

We will describe one sample hike up one of those tributaries. You may wish to try that one or to buy some geological survey maps and a compass and design your own cross-country trip.

The main tourist attraction in this district, by the way, is Blanchard Springs Caverns. When Glenda was a child and lived nearby, she used to hike in to see this cave and the spectacular

Blanchard Springs themselves, before the area was commercial-
ized. The place is much easier to reach these days. Drive north
from Mountain View on Arkansas Route 14 and turn right (there
will be a Forest Service sign that says Blanchard Springs) on Forest Road 1107. It's about two miles to the spring and caverns.

Sandstone Creek Canyon

Location: This back country area in the Sylamore District of the
Ozark National Forest includes approximately 305 acres of wild
land that includes virgin timber stands and a number of interesting rock formations. A good day hike that will take you up the
creek from its mouth at North Sylamore Creek to its headwaters
just south of Forest Road 1113 near Green Tower begins at Gunner Pool Recreation Area on Forest Road 1102.

Length: 3 miles

USGS Quads: Fifty-six and Calico Rock, Arkansas.

Description: North Sylamore Creek flows northwest to southeast
through Gunner Pool Recreation Area and Sandstone Creek flows
into it from the north.

This part of the Ozark Plateau is much less rugged than the
Boston Mountains to the west and the elevations seldom get
more than 1100 feet above sea level. The elevation at Gunner
Pool is less than 500 feet above sea level, and the elevation of the
creek bed at its headwaters is only about 900 feet. The steep-
sided cliffs that border the creek to form the canyon rise about
200 feet above the streambed.

One of the most interesting features of this hike is the bluff
overhangs that are to be found up every side canyon along the
tributaries that flow into Sandstone Creek.

Few people have explored here and you are not likely to find
gum wrappers and beer cans. You can still find Indian arrowheads,
and you may see some fading yellow signs which marked the
boundaries of the old Livingston Creek Game Refuge. This refuge,
according to John Heuston, an Ozark Society member who has
explored Sandstone Creek, was one of those instrumental in the
successful program to restore deer to Arkansas in huntable numbers.

There are some excellent specimens of virgin shortleaf pine,
white oak and black jack along the creek but if you continue to
follow it to its headwaters (when you come to a major fork in the
stream, stay on the left or westernmost fork) you will see evidence of aerial spraying to deaden timber. This practice has mar-
red the beauty of the entrance to the canyon.

If you prefer not to retrace your steps back down the creek,
you can climb straight north up the mountain from the stream's

beginning a few hundred yards (partly on a logging road) to Forest Road 1113. Turn left (west) on this road a few hundred yards to Forest Road 1102. Walk south on 1102 about 2¼ miles to Gunner Pool.

Our thanks for help on the Ozark research go to members of the Ozark Society in general and particularly to Glenn and Helen Parker of Dutton, John Heuston of Little Rock, and Dick Murray of Fayetteville. Mr. Murray not only accompanied us on the Whitaker Creek hike but presented us with two beautiful walking sticks of his own design and construction.

The Ozark Society is an environmental group formed in the early 1960s primarily to save the spectacularly scenic Buffalo River from impoundment by the Army Corps of Engineers. If you live in the Ozarks or nearby, this organization is worth joining for the good causes it espouses and for the canoe trips, hikes, and other outings it sponsors. Whether you live nearby or not, membership is worthwhile just for the accompanying subscription to the *Ozark Society Bulletin* edited by Joe and Maxine Clark. The *Bulletin* is both visually and verbally a delight, and its issues are filled with accurate descriptions of area geology and plant and animal life.

For complete information on how to become a member, write The Ozark Society, Box 38, Fayetteville, Ark. 72701.

Hot Springs National Park Trails

Location: About 46 miles southwest of Little Rock via Interstate Route 30 and U.S. 70.

Length: There are networks of trails on West Mountain, Hot Springs Mountain, North Mountain, and Indian Mountain that total about 18 miles. The longest single continuous circle trail one can take without exploring side paths is about four miles.

USGS Quad: Hot Springs North, Arkansas.

Description: Hot Springs is unusual among national parks in that it is located in the middle of a city (population 35,631). The inhabited parts are almost all on the relatively flat land, however, and the range of mountains that runs southwest to northeast through the town's center are completely wooded and contain hardly any buildings at all. The hiking trails are located on four of these mountains.

The park is known, mainly, of course, for its springs rather than for its mountain trails. There are 47 of these springs and they produce almost a million gallons of water per day with an average temperature of more than 143 degrees Fahrenheit.

Healing powers, especially for people with arthritis and related ills, have been ascribed to the waters since Indians camped there long before Hernando de Soto visited the place in 1541. A town had begun to grow up around the springs as early as 1810, and in 1832 the U.S. Congress felt it necessary to protect this natural resource from destruction and undue exploitation by declaring the springs and four square miles of adjacent land a Federal Reservation. In 1921 the name was changed to Hot Springs National Park.

Nobody knows for sure why the water is hot, but it is known that all the springs are located in a 20-acre area along a fault line located in the valley between West and Hot Springs Mountains (where Central Avenue runs through the city). The sandstone from which the springs come is about 200 feet thick and was formed during the Mississipian Era of geologic history. The rock was subjected to lateral compression during the Pleistocene which lifted the Park area and produced severe folding and fracturing in the rocks.

A good place to begin your hike in this national park is on the mile-long Promenade Nature Trail on the hill above Bathhouse Row. It begins at the visitor center on the corner of Reserve and Central Avenues and proceeds north to Fountain Street. Numbered markers and a brochure available from the Visitor Center provide a good introduction to geological features and vegetation.

Most of the springs are sealed off now and run by pipes to the concessionary bathhouses and to hotels. On the Promenade, however, you will pass by the two Display Springs which are kept in their natural state. Pay special attention to the blue-green algae which grow in these springs. This sort of primitive plant is common in cooler lakes and streams, but it takes a remarkable adaptation for it to survive in temperatures of 143°. This species is extremely rare. It helps convert calcium and silica salts in the water into rock deposits called tufa.

If you walk east from the Promenade near the Display Hot Springs on the southern slopes of Hot Springs Mountain along Dead Chief Trail you will reach the park's only campground at Gulpha Gorge in about 1⅓ miles. The gorge is situated at the east end of Hot Springs Mountain and between North Mountain and Indian Mountain.

If you take the widest possible circle around Hot Springs and North Mountains, you will proceed (at an elevation of about 800 feet) via Dead Chief Trail, Gulpha Gorge Trail, Goat Rock Trail, Dogwood and Arlington Trails back to Bathhouse Row in about four miles. An endless variety of side trails crisscrosses this wide circle.

You should certainly take one of these which leads to the top of Hot Springs Mountain (elevation 1040 feet) for a beautiful view of the city and Ouachita Mountains to the west. There's a park building containing craft exhibits on top of this mountain, too. Another side trail takes you to the top of North Mountain (elevation 1120).

From the campground at Gulpha Gorge, a separate trail (not connected to any of the others) leads east about half a mile up Indian Mountain to some old Novaculite quarries excavated by the area's former Indian inhabitants. Novaculite is more commonly known as Arkansas whetstone and has been compared for its whiteness, closeness of texture, and subdued waxy luster to varieties of Carrara marble. The Indians used it for arrowheads and other tools.

On the west side of Central Avenue between Whittington Avenue and Prospect Avenue is another network of trails, up and around West Mountain. A circle completely around the mountain takes you only about 2¾ miles; once again, however, there are a number of side trails to explore. When you reach the junction with Sunset Trail at the far west end of the mountain, be sure to take it east to the summit of West Mountain (elevation 1200).

All these trails are well-marked, labeled and blazed. Oaks, pines and hickories dominate the forest, and blooming shrubs like huckleberry, spicebush, serviceberry, dogwood and redbud form a thick understory.

You will notice white streaks in the sandstone along the trail. These streaks are quartz veins. There are also good exposures of conglomerate or "pudding stone," fragments of different kinds of sedimentary rock held together by a natural cementing agent. The cement in these rocks probably comes from minerals deposited by the hot springs water.

OUACHITA NATIONAL FOREST

The Ouachita (pronounced Wash-i-Taw) Mountains lie south of the Kerr-McClellan Navigation System (known to the Indians as the Arkansas River) in western Arkansas and eastern Oklahoma. Unlike the major mountain ranges of North America, the Ouachitas are an east-west range, a fact that has significant ecological consequences.

More than 1,500,000 acres of these mountains lie within the boundaries of the Ouachita National Forest. The U.S. Forest

Service is in the process of creating a major scenic trail on the forest. It will eventually be about 300 miles long, running from Lake Sylvia campground about an hour's drive west of Little Rock westward as far as Talihena, Oklahoma.

Most people think of the Ozarks when they think of mountains in Arkansas, but the Ouachitas are geologically quite a separate group. Pinnacle Mountain in Little Rock is the easternmost extension of the range. In the north, the mountains of the Arkansas River valley such as Magazine Mountain, Petit Jean, and Nebo are a part of the Ouachitas. The major ranges in the Ouachitas include the Fourche, Cossatot, Black Fork, Jackfork, and Potato Hills.

Elevations range from 500 feet along the banks of the Ouachita River, to near 3000 feet on the peaks. The highest peaks are in the western portion of the range, particularly Rich Mountain and Winding Stair Mountain — both of which lie on the Ouachita Trail route.

The ridges of the Ouachitas are generally of a rounded contour, and the landscape lacks the sheer cliffs and spectacular bluffs of the Ozarks. One of the notable features of the area is the rock glaciers. These are great fields of boulders spread out across the mountain sides, moving slowly downslope in response to gravity. The rocks move as a mass, just as an ice glacier does, rather than tumbling over each other. Local names for them are rock rivers or rock flows.

The downhill movement of these rocks prevents the growth of vegetation except at the lower end of the mass, leaving the slides as vast bare patches on the otherwise tree covered slopes.

The rocks of these mountains — sandstones and shales — were created from sediments laid down during the Paleozoic area. When the mountains were created, these rocks were thrust upward by great lateral pressure that produced extensive folding and faulting.

The forests that cover these slopes are basically oak-hickory, with black walnut and locust, basswood, maples, and beeches, some of impressive size, along the creek banks. Short leaf pines are also quite numerous, sometimes occurring in pure stands on south slopes. Dogwood, pawpaw, umbrella magnolia, buckeye and redbud are dominant plants of the forest understory.

Near the ridge crest, the forests — here mostly oak — are dwarfed, a consequence of the east-west orientation of the range. During the winter, prevailing winds are from the south, bringing moist air from the Gulf of Mexico. As the air moves north and rises up the slopes of the mountains, it produces ice storms, freezing fog, mist, and rain, an environment that is demonstrably hard on trees.

The soil on the north slopes tends to be extremely rich (hence the name of Rich Mountain) largely as a result of the heavy plant growth in these favored spots. The slopes are too steep for farming, but they produce a great crop of wild flowers.

The fauna is basically eastern, but in recent years some western species have moved in. The red wolf was native to this area, but it has been extirpated. Indeed, it may be extinct. Its place in the Ouachitas has been taken by the coyote, which moved in from the west, along with the nine-banded armadillo.

White-tail deer are common, and there is a small population of black bears — somewhere around 50 to 60 individuals. A few elk, perhaps 15, still remain in the forest. Bobcats are around for sure, and every once in awhile somebody comes across a mountain lion track. We talked to a ranger who had seen one a few years ago, but no one has actually seen an animal for a long time.

The birds, too, are generally eastern. In recent years, a few western species such as the scissor-tailed fly catcher and the road runner have moved in. Golden eagles are also found in the area, particularly in winter.

One eastern bird that thrives in the Ouachitas is the wild turkey. Population estimates say that as many as 20,000 turkeys live in the mountains.

Among herps, reptiles and amphibians, this area is also a meeting place of east and west. Thirty species of snakes live here, including some you will want to avoid. These include the timber rattler, the northern copperhead, and the western cottonmouth, among eastern snakes, and the western diamondback from the other direction.

For amphibian fanciers, the area offers eight species of salamanders, including two endemic species, the Rich Mountain salamander and the Ouachita Mountain redback salamander.

The name of these mountains is said to originate in a Choctaw Indian word meaning "hunting trip." The Choctaws lived in Mississippi, but they ranged as far west as the Ouachitas on hunting expeditions.

In the 1830s, they were moved to eastern Oklahoma, including the Ouachitas, and they are still a large part of the population in the area. White settlement on the Arkansas side began with homesteaders moving in during the 1860s. They are gone now from the ruggeder parts of the range, but the remains of their work are still visible in many areas. Foundations and chimneys can be found here and there on the forest, and apple and peach trees sometimes grow amidst the wild trees.

The Oklahoma side was closed to white settlers until the 1890s. About that time, the lumber industry moved into the Ouachitas on both sides of the state line. The fact that the Ouachitas were settled much later and much more thinly than the Ozarks may account for the survival here of the black bear and elk which were hunted out to the north.

Ouachita Trail

The trail description that follows is based on information current in September, 1974. Construction crews were out on the forest extending the trails at that time, so that by the time you read this, more sections will be finished. For current information on the state of trail construction, contact: Forest Supervisor, Ouachita National Forest, Federal Building, P.O. Box 1270, Hot Springs, Ark. 71901.

We will describe the trail from east to west, since the completed sections in the east are longer. For areas where the trail has not been completed, we will give brief descriptions of planned routes.

Ouachita Trail — Easternmost Section [Lake Sylvia to Ark. Route 298]

Location: The eastern terminus of the trail is at the Forest Service's Lake Sylvia Recreation Area. This is a campground which you can reach by taking Arkansas Route 10 west from Little Rock as far as Arkansas Route 9. Turn north for a few miles to Forest Road 152. The campground is about two miles west of the highway. The trail goes southwest, hitting the North Fork of the Ouachita River at Arkansas Route 298 between the hamlets of Lena and Fannie.

Length: Approximately 42 miles

USGS Quads: From east to west: Paron, Ark.; Paron S.W., Ark.; Nimrod S.E., Ark.; Hamilton, Ark.; and Avant, Ark. The trail crosses very briefly into the Thornburg, Ark., and Arlin, Ark., quads, but these two maps are not required.

Description: The trail begins at the north edge of the Lake Sylvia campground. A large sign tells about the trail, and a small sign gives distances to significant places: Brown's Creek, 4½ miles; Flatside Pinnacle, 8 miles; and West Crystal, 12½ miles. The main trail is well marked with white paint blazes on trees and rocks, and with the trail symbol, an "O" superimposed on a "T." Side trails are blazed in blue.

The trail heads southwestward from the campground, climbing first slowly and then more steeply, going from 632 feet at the trail head to 1512 feet at North Fork Pinnacle. There is an old fire tower on top of this peak, but the main trail does not climb all the way to the top. A ¼ mile spur trail does.

The trail then heads northwest rather steeply down hill to the South Fork of Brown's Creek at 650 feet. The trail crosses the creek and a dirt road that runs along it and then climbs northwest up to 900 feet. It then angles west and southwest passing on the south slope of Flatside Pinnacle. A ¼ mile spur trail leads to the top of the Pinnacle at 1560 feet.

The Pinnacle offers some excellent views to the west, especially of Forked Mountain with its side by side peaks.

The trail heads downslope from Flatside to Crystal Prong (1.7 miles), and then angles southeast on the hillside above the creek. It passes around the headwaters of the creek and then turns west along Crystal Mountain ridge, paralleling Forest Road 132 to the south. The trail stays between 1200 and 1400 feet along the north slope of the ridge.

The trail turns south and crosses Forest Road 132 just east of the road junction with Forest Roads 114 and 124. The elevation at the road crossing is about 1500 feet, and from there the trail goes downhill to cross North Alum Creek at about 1000 feet. It follows the creek bottom upstream to the west to a junction with Forest Road 124. For the next three to four miles, the trail climbs up to over 1400 feet and then downslope again to strike Arkansas Route 7 at 1000 feet about one mile north of the Iron Springs Recreation Area.

The trail crosses the highway and the Middle Fork of the Saline River, and then climbs slightly, rising about 300 feet in ½ mile. It heads downhill into a draw which is the source of Merriott Creek, which is an intermittent stream at this point.

Three miles from the highway, the main trail meets a three-mile spur trail that runs southwest along Short Mountain from the Iron Springs Recreation Area. This spur trail and the main trail can be combined with a one-mile walk along the highway to produce a seven-mile loop.

Just south of the junction, the trail crosses into the Hamilton Quadrangle. It is 19.5 miles from Arkansas Route 7 to Arkansas Route 298, and for most of this distance, the trail runs along the top of the ridge of Blue Ouachita Mountain. It is 12 miles from Route 7 to the Ouachita Pinnacle Lookout Tower, also known as the Blue Mountain Lookout Tower. Climbing up from Route 7, the trail reaches 1500 feet on the ridge, and then climbs slowly to its high point at the tower: 1961 feet. For four and a half miles of the hike along the ridge, the trail follows Forest Road 107. Since this road dead ends at the tower, it is not likely to be heavily traveled.

A sign along the road less than a mile east of the tower points downhill to a stream which is one of the few water sources along the ridge. At the tower itself, a rather large area has been cleared and planted in grass. This could make a good campsite.

West of the tower, the trail continues on the ridge, heading out to Pilot Knob, 2½ miles away. The elevation here is 1680. From there, the ridge begins to lose altitude, and the trail follows it down, hitting Route 298 5½ miles away at an altitude of 650 feet. The trail crosses a dirt road just before reaching the state highway, which is itself not paved. There should be no problem in recognizing the state highway, however. Here the trail forms a V, coming down off the ridge to touch the highway and then turning north immediately to cross the North Fork of the Ouachita.

About one mile west of the trail's junction with 298 is the C.V. Meredith Grocery store, an excellent country store complete with a sleepy old front porch hound dog.

The section of the trail leading northwest from Route 298 was under construction in September, 1974. The trail route had been cut and was marked with red plastic streamers tied to tree limbs. However, no signs were yet in place.

The planned route will take this section north across the North Fork of the Ouachita and then northwest across rolling land between Big Branch and Muse Creek. It will cross Muse Creek, climb over a ridge and cross Redbank Creek. After fording the Irons Fork River, it will climb over Sandlick Mountain and then go downhill to Arkansas Route 27.

West of Route 27, the trail exists only as a tentative planned route as far as Ouachita Lake. The trail will probably go west from 27 up the north bank of Muddy Creek to the first road bridge. It will cross the creek on the bridge, take a sharp climb up to Chalybeate Mountain, also known as Big Round Top, and then head south along the ridge, going downhill to cross Lake Ouachita on the Route 27 bridge at Buddy's Landing. This section will probably not be completed for some time in part because substantial parts of the projected route are on private land.

Ouachita Trail — Route 27 to Rocky Shoals Float Camp

Location: The east end of this section is at Buddy's Landing on Arkansas Highway 27 at Lake Ouachita. The western end is on the Ouachita River at U.S. Route 270 about seven miles west of Mount Ida, Ark.

Length: 10 miles
USGS Quad: Mount Ida, Ark. (15 minute, 1:62,500)
Description: This section of the trail traverses low rolling country along the south bank of the Ouachita. Don't expect any vistas. Crews were working on the trail in this section during our visit. Only the middle sections were completed, while at either end, the route had been planned but not cut.

When the whole section is finished, the trail will head west from Buddy's Landing over a low divide. It will then go along a stream up the hollow between Wolf Mountain and Reed Mountain. From there it will go straight west to the Rocky Shoals Float Camp. Two side trails marked with blue blazes will go north from the trail to the River Bluff and Fulton Branch campgrounds along the Ouachita River. River Bluff is east of Fulton Branch.

If you wish to hike in this area, we strongly suggest checking with the Forest Supervisor in Hot Springs or with the Womble Ranger District office in Mount Ida to learn the current status of trail construction.

West of the Ouachita River and the Rocky Shoals Float Camp, the route of the trail is quite tentative. Current plans are to follow the ridge line of Gaston Mountain across Sulphur Creek into the town of Big Fork. From there, the trail will go south across several sharp ridges to the headwaters of the Little Missouri River. It will then cross Forest Road 38, go over a divide, and then go downhill into the valley of Caney Creek.

Caney Creek Trail
Location: To reach Caney Creek take Arkansas Route 84 west from the town of Salem which is about 40 miles west of Hot Springs. Follow 84 to Athens, Ark., and then take Arkansas Route 246 about two miles west. A road going north from here to Shady Lake and Bard Springs Recreation Areas becomes Forest Road 38 at the forest boundary. Follow this road north to its junction with Forest Road 106. Just north of the junction is a sign identifying the Caney Creek Trail and a parking area at the trailhead.

To get to the western end of the trail, follow Arkansas 246 until it crosses the forest boundary. Just west of that point, Forest Road 31 goes north. Follow this road to its junction with Forest Road 30. Turn right at the junction and go three miles. A short side road (less than ¼ mile long) branches off to the right. It leads to the Cossatot River. The trail starts just across the river from the end of the road.

Length: 9 miles
USGS Quad: Umpire, Ark. (15 minute, 1:62,500)

Description: Caney Creek lies in a 14,433-acre area that has been designated a wilderness.

The Caney Creek Trail is largely the creation of hikers' feet. The Forest Service has put up a few signs, but has otherwise left things pretty much alone. Caney Creek was at least partially logged over at some point in the past, and for a part of the way, the trail follows the old roads, making it extremely easy to follow.

We took an overnight trip on the Caney Creek Trail, covering its whole length. We started from Forest Road 38 at the east end of the trail in the early afternoon. The trail heads uphill from the road, climbing about 200 feet on a moderate grade to go over the divide and meet Caney Creek near its head. From road to creek, the trail is on the old logging road.

Once you reach the creek, perhaps a mile from the road, the route of the trail is sometimes a bit obscure. Both banks are often nothing but rocks, and it is hard to wear a footpath into that kind of material.

You can't get too seriously lost if you stick to the creek. We counted 29 crossings of the creek along the trail, so if you lose thr trail on either bank, you are bound to hit it again if you just keep going downstream. White blazes on trees offer occasional guidance, but they are not very prominent.

The strategy for dealing with this kind of situation is just to take it slow. Pay attention to the route in front of you. When the trail takes you down to the creek bank, take a good look at the opposite side. Usually you can pick out the trail route ahead. If you can't, check behind you to be sure you haven't strayed from the path.

Along the upper creek, the banks tend to be fairly high. There are several flat areas of sufficient height to make them good campsites. The signs of other campers are a bit too prominent, but it is probably best to use the same sites in order to keep the damage from spreading. We camped in a large oak grove at the base of Katy Mountain, the ridge that flanks the creek to the north.

The next morning, we left our packs in the grove and headed downstream for the western end of the trail. A few hundred yards from our campsite, we crossed Katy Creek which flows into Caney Creek from the north. A sign there says that it is four miles back to Forest Road 38, our starting point, and five miles to the other end of the trail.

The banks got lower and wider as we went down the creek. The trees in this area were oaks and hickories with a considerable admixture of big short leaf pine. Beeches, some of impressive size, clung to the banks. Often erosion had left their upper roots exposed, but they still hung onto the rocky ground. Under the canopy of the big trees, the very tropical looking umbrella magnolia was a common sight.

Along the lower creek, great stands of cane grew on the low lying banks. It was obvious from debris clinging to tree trunks and cane stems that Caney Creek had flooded during the spring. It does that regularly. We talked to one hiker who told us he had had to wade through waist deep water along the trail after a heavy springtime rain. Fall may be the time to take this trip.

We were accompanied that day by the maniacal laughter of a pair of pileated woodpeckers who were messing around in the tree tops. These crow-sized birds favor mature stands of hardwood along creek banks. During the heyday of cut-every-stick-and-get-out lumbering in the south, they were becoming quite rare. Mature stands of hardwood were getting scarce. Fortunately, both the birds and the trees have made an impressive comeback in recent years.

The only other notable animals we saw that day were two cottonmouths, a sight we could have done without.

About two miles downstream from Katy Creek, we passed a sure sign that this area was once logged. A huge pile of sawdust lay beside the trail. These things endure for a long time.

About a mile and a half beyond the sawdust pile, the trail leaves the creek, turning north alongside a small tributary to Caney Creek. The turn is easy to see, and the trail up the hill is again apparently the remains of a logging road. The trail soon climbs above the little stream, continuing north briefly and then turning west again to the Cossatot River.

The Cossatot is a considerable stream, perhaps 25 yards wide. In mid-September, the water was about half way up our calves. The current is quite fast, and at high water wading the Cossatot might be inadvisable.

Just across the river is the road that leads out to Forest Road 31. We crossed the river for research purposes, and then headed back up Caney Creek to our car.

According to current plans, the route of the Ouachita Trail from Caney Creek will be west over West Hanna Mountain, then downhill along the slopes of Dog Mountain Ridge, across two forks of Brushy Creek, up again across Bee Mountain, down across Two-Mile Creek, and then over a low ridge into Mena.

The Kansas City Southern Railroad reached the site of Mena,

Ark., on August 19, 1896. On that day, a tent city of 5,000 people rose on the spot. The population of the town remains at around that level.

Mena is the eastern end of the Talimena Scenic Drive, a 54-mile road whose western end is at Talihina, Okla. The road follows the long ridges of the Ouachitas westward. There has been a road up on the mountaintops for some time, but the scenic drive itself was just completed in 1970.

For hikers, the road is an unfortunate thing. It preempts the ridge top, a natural route for a hiking trail. Only short sections of the Ouachita Trail have been completed west of Mena, and some of these are within earshot of the highway.

However, the road isn't all bad. It has led to the creation of the Talimena Scenic Drive Interpretive Association, which has published a detailed guide to the highway. Written by local people who have a deep interest and long familiarity with the area, it contains much information about the geology and natural history of the Ouachitas which is of interest to hikers. The Chamber of Commerce (Mena, Ark. 71953) sells the book for $1.50 a copy, including postage.

The scenic drive is Arkansas Route 88 going north out of Mena. A visitor's information center is located along the highway just outside of town. The trail will eventually run from there up to the Rich Mountain tower. An old trail covers this route today, and local people sometimes hike it. However, we don't recommend it unless you are willing to do some exploring, as the trail is not well marked.

Rich Mountain Tower to Winding Stair Mountain

Location: The Rich Mountain tower is 9½ miles west of Mena on Arkansas 88, the Scenic Drive. A dirt road leads from the highway up to the tower, a distance of perhaps 200 yards. The Winding Stair Mountain Recreation Area, a Forest Service Campground, is also on the Scenic Drive, 35 miles west of Mena.

Length: 22 miles

USGS Quads: Rich Mountain, Ark., and Mountain Fork, Ark.

Description: There is a large grassy area around the Rich Mountain tower and an operating well for campers. The elevation here is 2681. The trail actually branches off from the gravel road up to the tower within 20 yards of the Scenic Drive. The trail follows the rocky, wooded slope of the mountain westward for three miles to Queen Wilhelmina State Park. Just east of the park, a sign points to a short side trail to Lover's Leap, a spot that provides an excellent view.

Queen Wilhelmina State Park is a sort of roadside attraction. It was once the site of an elaborate inn built by railroad magnates to lure turn-of-the-century fashionables from Kansas City. The inn recently burned down, and when we were there, it was being rebuilt. Other features of the park include a tiny railroad with a loud whistle for your family fun, and a cutsey zoolet with storybook animals and such. There are campsites and picnic areas, but little incentive to linger in them.

The trail continues west from the park, still paralleling the road. Five miles along, it crosses into Oklahoma. Between the park and the state line are several reminders of the settlement of the area. An old cemetery near the state line contains several unmarked old headstones as well as a very modern stone marking the grave of Bill Hefley, the last settler to live on Rich Mountain. He left the mountain in 1949 and died in 1952.

From the State Line Historical Marker, the trail heads southwest into the valley of the Kiamichi River, heading down into the valley for about one mile, and then crossing the river and following along the bank for about 3½ miles. It then crosses the river again and climbs over Wilton Mountain, ascending from 1000 feet to 1500 feet before dropping about 500 feet to cross Pashubbe Creek.

Just east of Wilton Mountain, a spur trail (*Pashubbe Hiking Trail*) leads north up hill to the scenic drive. This trail is four miles long. A sign along the scenic drive 24 miles from Mena identifies the trail.

After crossing Pashubbe Creek, the trail meets the dead end of Forest Road 32. This road provides quick access to this portion of the trail. To get to it, take Oklahoma Route 259 south from the Scenic Drive or north from Oklahoma Route 63. Forest Road 32 is about ½ mile north of 63. It is 2½ miles from the highway to the dead end.

The Ouachita Trail comes into the dead end from the southeast, touches the end of the road, and then continues northwest. Another trail, the *Rich Mountain Trail*, heads northeast from the dead end, climbing up two miles to the scenic drive. A sign along the drive 26 miles from Mena marks the other end of this trail.

Another trail, the appealingly named *Rattlesnake Ridge Trail*, goes north from Forest Road 32 about one mile from the highway. This trail crosses the Ouachita Trail north of the road, and after about one mile, meets a dirt road (Forest Road 68) called Radar Road locally. It follows this road uphill to the scenic drive, a distance of about two miles. No sign identifies Radar Road on the

Scenic Drive, but it branches off to the south about two miles west of the Rich Mountain Trail.

The Ouachita Trail, heading northwest from its junction with Forest Road 32, crosses some rolling country and then Oklahoma Route 259. The crossing is about 1½ miles south of Pipe Springs, a Forest Service roadside picnic area. It is about 1½ miles north of Big Cedar. Big Cedar is two gas stations at the junction of Oklahoma 259 and 63. One station has chickens scratching around the gas pumps, the other doesn't. You can also get cold meat, bread, chips, soft drinks, and beer at the stations.

The Ouachita Trail continues west from 259, crossing Cedar Creek and then climbing up to over 2600 feet at the Winding Stair fire tower. The tower itself has been torn down, but a large grassy area remains. You can get some excellent views from here, as well as a close look at the stunted oak forest characteristic of the Ouachita ridge tops.

The trail follows the old road downhill to the north from the tower site. It is perhaps ½ to ¾ mile downhill to the Scenic Drive. For the last few hundred yards of this distance, the trail cuts through the woods, leaving the old road to the left next to a large black gum tree whose leaves were in fiery red fall display when we were there.

Across the Scenic Drive, the trail goes briefly through the woods and across a stile into the Winding Stair campground. There are some great views of the Ouachitas from the north edge of the campground.

From Winding Stair west, the Ouachita Trail has not been completed, but there are some trails in this section that are worth mentioning.

According to a number of sources, there is a trail running from the Scenic Drive south to the Billy Creek Recreation Area. We hunted for this trail at both its ends, but we couldn't find it.

Horse Thief Springs Trail

Location: Thirty-eight miles west of Mena on the Scenic Drive is the Horse Thief Springs Historical Site and Picnic Area. The trail starts here and ends at the Cedar Lake Recreation Area just north of Forest Road 5 west of Zoe, Oklahoma.

Length: 4 miles

USGS Quads: Blackjack, Okla., and Heavener, Okla.

Description: Horse thievery was once a big business in these parts, and the springs were a regular stopping place. The CCC built a fancy stone shelter over the spring. The water today sports a mantle of algae.

The thieves are gone now, thanks in large part to the activities of the Anti-Horse Thief Association, a group that operated until World War I, but the trail remains. It's downhill from the spring to Cedar Lake.

A two-mile trail circles Cedar Lake, an artificial impoundment that was nearly empty when we visited it. What had been a lake was a small pond surrounded by broad mud flats. A large flock of sanderlings — probably not common birds in the area — fed on the mud. We did see two flocks of turkeys between the Scenic Drive and Cedar Lake.

Wild Horse Hiking Trail

Location: From the Scenic Drive 41 miles west of Mena.

Length: About 2 miles

USGS Quads: Heavener and Blackjack, Okla.

Description: This is a short trail used mainly by hunters. It goes from the ridge top down into the Holson Valley Game Management Area.

Old Military Road Trail

Location: One mile from the western end of the Scenic Drive. It leads north to the Holson Valley Road, Forest Road 5.

Length: 3 miles

USGS Quads: Blackjack and Heavener, Okla.

Description: The trail starts at a picnic area on the Scenic Drive. It follows the route of a road built in 1832 over a route marked by woodsmen Robert Bean and Jesse Chisholm.

SUGGESTIONS FOR FURTHER READING

Buffalo River Country by Kenneth L. Smith. Copyright 1967, 1970 by The Ozark Society, Fayetteville, Arkansas.

Buffalo National River: A Field Investigation Report by the U.S. Department of Interior, National Park Service, Southeast Region, Richmond, Va. April 1963.

The Ozark Society Bulletin, a quarterly publication produced by The Ozark Society, Fayetteville, Arkansas.

Journal of a Tour into the Interior of Missouri and Arkansas in the Years 1818 and 1819, by Henry Rowe Schoolcraft.

Ozark Country, by Otto Ernest Rayburn. Little, Brown & Co., N.Y., N.Y., in association with Buell, Sloan and Pearce Inc., 1941.

Arkansas, A Guide to the State. Compiled by workers of the Writers' Program, Works Project Administration. Copyright 1941 by C.G. Hall, Secretary of State, Arkansas.

A Guide to the National Parks by William H. Matthews III. Doubleday/Natural History Press, Garden City, New York 1973.

Talimena Scenic Drive Guide — Arkansas, Oklahoma, by Aileen McWilliam, Lloyd Lane and Homer L. Johnston. Published by the Talimena Scenic Drive Interpretive Association in co-operation with the Forest Service, U.S.D.A. 1974.

Trees of Arkansas, by Dwight M. Moore. Published by the Arkansas Forestry Commission, Little Rock, Ark., 1972.

INDEX

VIRGINIA

Shenandoah National Park 38

Trails in the George Washington National Forest 43
  Lee Ranger District 43
    Massanutten Mountain 44
    Duncan Hollow 44
    Signal Knob 44
    Bear Wallow 45
    Massanutten Mountain North 45
  Pedlar Ranger District 45
    Cold Springs 45
    St. Mary's River 46
    Stony Run 46
    Kennedy Ridge 46
    Sherando Lake to Bald Mountain 46
  Dry River Ranger District 47
    Shenandoah Mountain 47
    Slate Springs Mountain 47
    Slate Springs—A 48
    Slate Springs—AA 48
    Hone Quarry Mountain 48
    Big Hollow 49
    Mines Run 49
    Timber Ridge 49
    Sand Spring Mountain 49
    Chestnut Ridge 50
    Grooms Ridge 50
    North River 50
    Dull Hunt 50
    Shenandoah Mountain 51
  Deerfield Ranger District 51
    Shenandoah Mountain 51
    Jerkemtight 53
    Jerrys Run 53
    Ramseys Draft 53
    Dividing Ridge 53
    Walker Mountain 54
    North Mountain 55
    Elliott Knob 55

Crawford Mountain 56
Chimney Hollow 56
Trails in the Thomas Jefferson National Forest 57
  Marion Ranger District
    Iron Mountain — western section 58
    Little Laurel Creek 58
    Mount Rogers 59
    Iron Mountain — eastern section 59
    Henley Hollow 59
    Horse Heaven 59
    Rocky Hollow 60
    Bournes Branch 60
    Yellow Branch 60
  Blacksburg Ranger District............................ 60
    Potts Mountain 61
  New Castle Ranger District 61
    Potts Mountain 61
    Potts Arm 61
    Price Broad Mountain 62
    Sulphur Ridge 62
    Lick Branch 62
    North Mountain 63
  Glenwood Ranger District 63
    Wildcat 63
    Pine Mountain 63
    Cornelius Creek 63
    Apple Orchard Falls 64
    Piney Ridge 64
    Hunting Creek 64
    Balcony Falls 64
    Gunter Ridge 65
    Big Belfast 65

WEST VIRGINIA

Monongahela National Forest 67
    Trails in the Dolly Sods Area 69
    Trails in the Otter Creek Area 72
    Trails in the Cranberry Back Country.................. 75
    Spruce Knob—Seneca Rocks National Recreation Area ... 81
    Trails in the Greenbrier District 84

NORTH CAROLINA
Nantahala National Forest 89
  Trails in the Cheoh District 89
    Trails Around Snowbird Creek 89
      Hooper Bald Trail 89
      Laurel Top Trail 90
      King Meadows Junction Trail 90
      Big Snowbird Trail 90
      Sassafras Creek Trail 90
      Middle Falls Trail 90
    Trails Around Slickrock Creek 90
      Ike Branch Trail 91
      Slickrock Creek Trail 91
      Hangover Lead Trail 91
      Nichols Cove Branch Trail 91
      Big Fat Branch Trail 92
      Deep Creek Trail 92
    Trails in Joyce Kilmer Memorial Forest 92
      Naked Ground Trail 92
      Haoe Trail 93
      Stratton Bald Trail 93
      Yellow Creek Mountain Trail 94
    Trails in the Tusquitee District 94
      Snowbird Mountain Trail 94
      Rim Trail 94
      Big Stamp Trail 95
    Trails in the Wayah District 95
      Trimont Trail 95
      Holloway Branch Trail 96
    Trails in the Upper Nantahala River Country 96
      Kimsey Creek Trail 97
      Lower Trail Ridge Trail 97
      Park Gap Trail 99
      Long Branch Trail 99
      Hurricane Creek Trail 99
      Big Indian Trail 99
      Bearpen Gap Trail 99
      Laurel Branch Trail 100
    Trails Around Appletree Group Camp 100
      Appletree Trail 100
      Nantahala Trail 101
      London Bald Trail 101
      Hickory Branch Trail 101

   Junaluska Trail 101
   Diamond Valley Trail 101
   Laurel Creek Trail 101
   Choga Trail 101
   Tusquitee Loop Trail 102
  Trails in the Highlands District 102
   Ellicotts Rock Trail 102

Pisgah National Forest 103
  Trails in the Pisgah District 103
   Shining Rock Wilderness 103
    Sorrell Creek Trail 104
    Art Loeb Trail 104
    Old Butt Knob Trail 105
    Little East Fork Trail .105
    Graveyard Fields Trail 106
    Big East Fork of Pigeon River Trail 106
    Fork Mountain Trail 106
   Bear Trail Ridge Trail 106
   Haywood Gap Trail 107
   Green Mountain Trail 107
   Courthouse Trail 107
   Summey Cove Trail 107
   Flat Laurel Trail 107
   Big Bear Trap Trail 108
   Coon Hollow Trail 108
   Buckeye Gap Trail 108
   Bearpen Gap Trail 108

   Art Loeb Trail [that part not in *Shining Rock Wilderness*] .108
   Farlow Gap Trail 109
   Cove Creek Trail 109
   Caney Bottom Trail 109
   Butter Gap Trail 109
   Cat Gap Trail 109
   Horse Cove Trail 109
   Kings Creek Trail 109
   Looking Glass Rock Trail 109

   Sharpy Mountain Trail 110
   Buckwheat Knob Trail 110
   Black Mountain Trai 111
   Buckhorn Trail 111
   Club Gap Trail 111

South Mills River Trail 111
Cantrell Creek Trail 111
Pounding Mill Trail 111
Mullinax Trail 111
Vineyard Gap Trail 112
Squirrel Gap Trail 112
Old Bradley Creek Gap Trail 112

Big Creek Trail 113
North Mills River Trail 113
Spencer Branch Trail 113
Trace Ridge Trail 113
Laurel Mountain Trail 114
Thompson Ridge Trail 114
Pilot Rock Trail 114

Trails in the Toecane District 114
Mount Mitchell Trail 115
Black Mountain Trail 116
Colberts Ridge Trail 116
Bald Knob Ridge Trail 117
Buncombe Horse Range Trail 117
Lost Cove Ridge Trail 117
Maple Camp Bald Trail 118
Big Butt Trail 118

Trails in the Grandfather District 119
Linville Gorge Wilderness 119
Pine Gap Trail 120
Bynum Bluff Trail 121
Cabin Trail 121
Babel Tower Trail 121
Linville Gorge Trail 121
Devils Hole Trail 121
Sandy Flats Trail 122
Spence Ridge Trail 122
Tablerock Trail 122
Shortoff Mountain Trail............................ 122
Conley Cove Trail 123
Pinch In Trail 123

Trails in the French Broad District 123
Pigeon River Trail 123

Great Smoky Mountains National Park Trails 124

SOUTH CAROLINA

Sumter National Forest 134
  Foothills Trail 135
Kings Mountain State Park Trails 137
Table Rock State Park Trails................... 139
Corbin Mountain 140
Sassafras Mountain to Hickory Nut Mountain 140

GEORGIA

Trails around Rabun Bald 143
  William Bartram Trail........................ 143
  Rabun Bald Trail 144
  Big Ridge Trail 145
Trails around Brasstown Bald 145
  Trail to Young Harris along Wolf Pen Ridge 146
  Arkaguah or Track Rock Trail 147
  Jack's Knob 147
Trails in the Cooper Creek Recreation Area 148
  Yellow Mountain Trail 148
  Mill Shoal Trail 148
Trails in the Cohutta Wildlife Management Area 149
  Jack's River Trail 149
  Rough Ridge Trail 150
  Tearbritches Trail 150
  Chestnut Creek Trail 150
  Conasauga River Trail 150

TENNESSEE

Tennessee — Introduction 155
Big Ridge State Park Trails 155
Frozen Head State Park Trails 156
Pickett State Park Trails 159
North Ridge Trail of Oak Ridge 161
Lookout Mountain Trails 164
Piney River Trail 165
Laurel-Snow Pocket Wilderness Trail 167
Honey Creek Pocket Wilderness Trail 168
Virgin Falls Pocket Wilderness Trail 169
Cherokee National Forest 170
  Tellico Ranger District Trails 171

Hiwassee Ranger District Trails 183
Ocoee Ranger District Trails 185
Nolichucky Ranger District Trails. 190
Unaka Ranger District Trails 192
Watauga Ranger District Trails 193
Proposed Scenic Trails for Tennessee 195

KENTUCKY
Daniel Boone National Forest Trails 199
Trails in the Pioneer Weapons Hunting Area 199
Big Limestone Trail 201
Trails in the Red River Gorge Area 202
[including Natural Bridge State Park]
Moonbow Trail 205
Trails in Cumberland Falls State Park 206
Cumberland Gap National Historical Park Trails 207

ARKANSAS and a piece of Oklahoma
The Ozarks 213
Ozark Hikes 216
Hurricane Creek Trail 217
Richland Creek Hikes 219
Whitaker Creek 222
Leatherwood Creek 225
Lost Valley [Clark Creek] Hike 226
Other Boston Mountain Attractions 227
Sylamore Forest — Sandstone Creek Canyon 228

Hot Springs National Park Trails 230

Ouachita National Forest 232

Ouachita Trail 235
Lake Sylvia to Arkansas Route 298 235
Route 27 to Rocky Shoals Float Camp 237
Caney Creek Trail 238
Rich Mountain Tower to Winding Stair Mountain
[with side trails: Pashubbe Hiking Trail, Rich
Mountain Trail, and Rattlesnake Ridge Trail] 241
Horse Thief Springs Trail 243
Wild Horse Hiking Trail 244
Old Military Road Trail 245